PAYING FOR COLLEGE

RELATED TITLES FOR COLLEGE-BOUND STUDENTS

College Admissions and Financial Aid

Kaplan Scholarships: Billions of Dollars in Free Money for College
Get Paid to Play: Every Athlete's Guide to Over $1 Million in College Scholarships
You're Accepted: Lose the Stress. Discover Yourself. Get into the College that's Right for You.

Test Preparation

ACT Premier Live
ACT: Strategies, Practice, and Review
ACT Strategies for Super Busy Students

SAT Premier Live
SAT: Strategies, Practice, and Review
12 Practice Tests for the SAT
SAT Strategies for Super Busy Students
Inside the SAT: 10 Strategies to Help You Score Higher
SAT Critical Reading Workbook
SAT Math Workbook
SAT Writing Workbook
SAT Subject Test: Biology E/M
SAT Subject Test: Literature
SAT Subject Test: Mathematics Level 1
SAT Subject Test: Mathematics Level 2
SAT Subject Test: Physics
SAT Subject Test: Spanish
SAT Subject Test: U.S. History
SAT Subject Test: World History

AP Biology
AP Calculus AB/BC
AP Chemistry
AP English Language and Composition
AP Environmental Science
AP European History
AP Macroeconomics/Microeconomics
AP Physics B & C
AP Psychology
AP Statistics
AP U.S. Government & Politics
AP U.S. History
AP World History

PAYING FOR COLLEGE

Gail A. Schlachter

New York

This publication is designed to provide accurate and authoritative information in regard to the subject matter covered. It is sold with the understanding that the publisher is not engaged in rendering legal, accounting, or other professional service. If legal advice or other expert assistance is required, the services of a competent professional should be sought.

© 2009 by Kaplan, Inc.

Published by Kaplan Publishing, a division of Kaplan, Inc.
1 Liberty Plaza, 24th Floor
New York, NY 10006

Printed in the United States of America

10 9 8 7 6 5 4 3 2 1

ISBN-13: 978-1-60714-483-0

Kaplan Publishing books are available at special quantity discounts to use for sales promotions, employee premiums, or educational purposes. Please email our Special Sales Department to order or for more information at kaplanpublishing@kaplan.com, or write to Kaplan Publishing, 1 Liberty Plaza, 24th Floor New York, NY 10006.

TABLE OF CONTENTS

CHAPTER ONE

Getting Started

"In a paradox of American life, at the very moment it's never been more important to have a quality higher education, the cost of that kind of education has never been higher."
—*President Barack Obama, April 2009*

Congratulations! If you've picked up this book, chances are either you or a child of yours will be starting college soon. You've probably looked at some schools, flipped through a few college catalogs and directories, and tried to get a sense of what this grand, life-changing experience is going to cost.

Then again, maybe you've been afraid to find out. The truth is, there's good news and bad news. Because most people prefer to deal with the bad news first, we might as well get that out of the way.

It will come as no surprise to you that a college education carries a hefty price tag. But did you know that it has never been more difficult for families to afford the cost? During the past 25 years, according to the National Center for Public Policy and Higher Education, college tuition and fees increased by an astonishing 439 percent. During that same period, however, the median family income rose only one-quarter that amount (147 percent). In fact, as the Bureau of Labor Statistics calculates it, college tuition and fees have increased three times faster than the growth of inflation during this decade. All of this has, as Vice President Biden points out, created a "challenge" for Americans wanting to attend college, because "the growth of college tuition is far outpacing that of family income."

> **Starting Early**
>
> "I suggest students and families visit a financial aid office as early as eighth grade, or when the student is a freshman in high school," offers Jack Toney, director of financial aid at Marshall University. "It gives families a chance to get an overview of what to expect to pay for college, and they'll have a few years to prepare."

And the current economy isn't helping, either. Unemployment is up, costs are increasing, debt is rising, average salaries are down, and investments have taken a beating. That means that families today will have to be more creative and informed than ever before, if they are going to be able to find ways to pay for college.

THERE IS HELP

With all this negative news, you might be tempted to be discouraged. But don't despair. There is good news, too. While there's no denying that times are tough and college costs are up, it's good to know that there is more financial aid available than ever before. According to a survey done by the National Association of Independent Colleges and Universities, 92 percent of its member colleges increased student aid budgets in 2009–2010 by an average of 10 percent. That's nearly twice the amount of average tuition increases! And, here's more good news, The College Board reports there is a record $143 billion in financial aid available.

Financial Help for Higher Education

Approximately three-quarters (73 percent) of undergraduates receive some type of financial aid, according to a 2009 report issued by the National Center for Education Statistics. Of these, 75 percent were attending public four-year institutions, 85 percent were attending private not-for-profit institutions, and 55 percent were attending private for-profit schools.

How can you find out about ways to reduce you cost of going to college and increase your chances of getting student aid? There's help all over the place if you know where to look. The government, businesses, foundations, and even universities provide information on how to manage and reduce the cost of getting a higher education.

Lucky you—you've already found a one-stop source of help. Kaplan's *Paying for College* was written specifically to help you understand and get through the process of finding and applying for financial aid. We've figured out a game plan for you and then organized the book around those action steps. While *Paying for College* is written with the parent of a college-bound student in mind, anyone at any age who's planning to go to college will find the information presented here helpful as well.

GETTING A GAME PLAN

Developing and implementing a plan to pay for college isn't a weekend project. Like other major purchases (buying a home or car), sorting out the process of paying for college takes time, effort, and planning. Most people wouldn't buy a car without some shopping around and number crunching, and you certainly wouldn't buy a house without doing research. The same should be true for college. Your student's education will likely cost more than a car (and, perhaps, as much as some condos or houses!); doesn't it make sense to put as much time and energy into the process as you would for those decisions?

You can't, and shouldn't, do this alone. Your student will need to become part of the process as well. Affording college is about things like budgets, living expenses, and spending money. Getting your student involved will emphasize the financial burden of college and the need for financial responsibility. If you're lucky, your son or daughter will take their education even more seriously as a result.

The game plan we've developed for you consists of 14 action-based steps. We'll identify each of them here and let you know what chapters will give you the information you need to act on them:

1. **Getting Started.** First things first. To move forward, you obviously need to get started. We hope we've motivated you to do that in this chapter.

2. **Learning the Basics.** Next, you'll need to begin at the beginning: learning the basics. In chapter 2, we describe the factors that contribute to your student's high college costs, examine common assumptions about financial aid, and set up a calendar for you to follow, to be sure you don't miss any crucial deadlines. You should also check out the "Financial Aid Dictionary" starting on page 193, to make sure you become proficient at speaking the financial aid language.

3. **Choosing a College.** In order to do this task, you need to know what colleges cost, the different types of colleges, the difference between a "dream" and a "safety" college, and the college-related issues you should discuss with your student. We cover those topics in chapter 3.

4. **Identifying College Costs.** Your next action step is to identify and understand what your student's potential colleges will cost. In chapter 4, we explain the difference between direct and indirect college costs and list the expenses that fall into these two categories. We provide worksheets there to help you keep track of those expenses and show you how to factor inflation into your estimates.

5. **Making the Most of Your Money.** Of course, you'll need to think about just where the money is going to come from to pay for these costs. Chapter 5 examines various sources of income and how each might be used to pay for your student's education.

6. **Getting Your Share of Financial Aid.** Once you've reviewed your income and know how much you have available to contribute to your student's education, you're ready to begin looking at your financial aid options. We explain these to you in chapter 6.

7. **Navigating the Process.** Millions of students get billions of dollars in federal and college aid each year. For your student to be one of them, you need to become familiar with the applications, forms, and documents involved in applying for financial aid, as well as what you can expect once the paperwork is completed. You'll find that information in chapter 7.

8. **Filing out the FAFSA.** If you fill out only one financial aid form, make it the FAFSA. We tell you why and teach you, line by line, how to complete that form in chapter 8.

9. **Calculating Your Need.** Now that you've completed the financial aid forms, your next concern, obviously, is about how much money you will be expected to contribute to your student's education. In chapter 9, we show you how calculate your Expected Family Contribution (EFC) and illustrate the process by taking you step by step through a sample case. After you finish reading this chapter, you should have all the tools you need to run EFC calculations.

10. **Evaluating Aid Packages.** When the financial aid packages start arriving from your student's colleges, you'll need to know how to read the offer letters, how to compare each packages, and how—if necessary—to negotiate for more money. Chapter 10 goes over all of that with you.

11. **Checking with Your State.** Did you know that your state awards billions of dollars each year to residents who want to go to college? As part of your game plan, you need to explore the state-based resources that might be available to your student. Chapter 11 focuses on the ways your state can help you pay for college and lets you know how to write, call, email, or go online to get this information.

12. **Searching for Private Scholarships.** Don't overlook the billions of dollars available in private scholarships offered by clubs, organizations, companies, foundations, and even individuals. Chapter 12 examines common scholarship myths, describes where to search for funding, lists the best strategies to use in your search, and alerts you to possible scholarship scams.

13. **Finding Alternatives to Financial Aid.** Now that you've searched and applied for all the traditional forms of financial aid, your next step should be to consider some creative school-based and work-based alternatives to financial aid that you might be able to use to help you pay for college. We detail those in chapter 13.

14. **Making It Work.** This is the last step in the game plan. In all likelihood, you're going to have to tap your own resources to pay part of your student's college costs. So, now you're going to have to make some choices about which family resources to use to pay the remaining amount. We make some suggestions in chapter 14.

We've written this book with the idea that after you've read through the chapters and absorbed the information, you'll feel both empowered and proactive when it comes to figuring out how to pay for your student's education. That's why we've not only developed the 14-step game plan for you, but we've used the real-life experiences of other parents and financial aid officers to help you understand how to proceed. And in each chapter, as well as in the "Going Online" section starting on page 219, we've identified other resources you can use as you work through the process. We've provided worksheets, tables, and forms throughout, so you won't have to guess or run calculations in your head. At the end of each chapter you'll find checklists to suggest things you and your student should be doing along the way; while these are by no means comprehensive, they are a good place to start. All of these features have been included to save you time, simplify the process, and help you succeed at your game plan to lower the cost of higher education.

Degrees in Demand

These majors are the top ten degrees in demand at the bachelor's degree level, as noted by employers (listed in descending order):

1. Accounting
2. Business administration/ management
3. Computer science
4. Electrical engineering
5. Mechanical engineering
6. Information sciences and systems
7. Marketing/marketing management
8. Computer engineering
9. Civil engineering
10. Economics/finance

Source: National Association of Colleges and Employers Job Outlook Report 2007.

Even though there are no liberal arts majors on this list, it doesn't mean students should be dissuaded from pursuing such a degree. As the job market changes and employers' needs evolve, different majors will rotate on and off the list. In fact, the job that your student may have as a 30-year-old might not even be invented yet!

School-Sponsored Financial Aid Workshops

Admissions and financial aid counselors recommend that you take advantage of any financial aid seminars offered at your student's high school, starting in ninth grade—or even earlier. If your student's school does not offer financial aid seminars, look for them at your local community college or other high schools in your area.

YOU ARE NOT ALONE

Remember, you're not alone in this process. Millions of other American families are going through the same steps and facing the same problems. Even financial aid officers send their children to college. "There's a lot of confusion and incorrect assumptions out there," says Connie Gores, a vice president at Winona State University and a parent of a college student. "A lot of parents also don't understand the differences between a public and private school. Also, I'm learning that a lot of families don't understand the financial aid process, so there really are a lot of people out there that need help and guidance." She adds, "The one thing that surprised me, even being in this field, is the anxiety this process can create. There's an immense amount of pressure on students and families during the whole process, and I never realized it until I went through it myself."

There may be times when dealing with financial aid feels like balancing your checkbook, doing your taxes, and taking a test all at once. Understanding the process is half the battle. When it comes to financial aid, knowledge is power, and this book will give you the information and guidance you need to make the best decisions to help you pay for the best possible education your son or daughter can have—without going to the poorhouse.

KAPLAN

MOVING ON

The next chapter describes the second step in your action plan: learning the basics of financial aid and, in so doing, separating the myths from the facts (and it's not all bad news!). To keep you on track, we'll also provide you with a calendar, organized by month, so you won't miss any important deadlines.

✓ **CHECKLIST:**

1. Review the 14-step game plan. Then read through the book, chapter by chapter, to get the information you need to take the action steps required.

2. Attend "College Nights" and school-sponsored financial aid workshops. The majority of high schools hold these types of events, where representatives and alumni from various universities, as well as financial aid experts speak at your student's school. These events give you an opportunity not only to learn about the colleges, but also to get some useful financial aid information.

CHAPTER TWO

Learning the Basics

When was the last time you bought something at full price? If you're like most people, the answer may take a little bit of thought. As Americans, we are a nation of bargain seekers and coupon clippers, and as such, companies know that with all the options out there, they'd better give us a good reason to put down our hard-earned cash for their product.

It's not surprising, then, that we live in a society of discounts. Televisions and radios bombard us with ads proclaiming "no money down," "no payments for 12 months," or "get 50 percent off." To make things even more interesting, the Internet has become a great tool in increasing people's buying power. Comparison websites and online services mean that hardly anyone need pay full price these days. Although colleges don't advertise it, a similarity does exist.

Almost no one pays the full cost of a college education, which is a good thing because the skyrocketing cost of a higher education may exceed what you paid for your car and may approach the value of your home. Of course, if you've already seen the figures for your student's prospective colleges, you're well aware of this. Let's take a look at what drives these rising costs.

> **How Much Financial Aid Do Students Get?**
> Full-time students at private four-year colleges receive an average of $10,200 in aid per year. At public two-year colleges that figure is $3,700 and at public two-year colleges it is $2,300. Trends in College Pricing 2008, www.Collegeboard.com

WHY IS COLLEGE SO EXPENSIVE?

The cost of going to college continues to rise because of a number of factors:

- According to Sandy Baum, senior policy analyst for the College Board, the "most obvious reason why tuition levels at public colleges and universities are rising more rapidly is tight state budgets and declining appropriations." When state appropriations decline, tuition levels tend to increase rapidly.

- At the same time that funding is being cut, the costs faced by colleges are increasing. Just as higher energy prices mean a higher electric bill for you, colleges are also paying more for utilities. As campuses grow in size and student populations increase, more money is needed for maintenance, food, and housing. Another key factor is the increasing cost of health insurance for college employees.

- According to Ernie Shepelsky, vice president of enrollment management at Vaughn College of Aeronautics and Technology, colleges are forced to spend more and more on their recruitment efforts. "Students have easy access to so much information on colleges now," says Shepelsky. "This means that schools have to constantly spend money on websites, publicity, enrollment management tools, and other recruitment efforts in order to stand out and attract students."

- Hand-in-hand with the recruitment efforts are the near-constant improvements and updates to campus services that students have come to expect. Wireless Internet, laptops, luxurious residence halls, smart classrooms, and top-notch food service at the dining halls—these are all upgrades that cost colleges money and those costs get passed along to the students.

- Finally, there's the projected decline in alumni donations and private support. While donations to colleges peaked in 2008 (reaching a record $31 billion), the immediate future, unfortunately, looks anything but rosy. The number and size of gifts have already started to fall. In fact, the Council for Advancement and Support of Education (CASE) predicts that private giving will continue to decline. And, as John Lippincott, president of CASE, puts it, "I think the real question is not will there be a decline but how much of a decline."

Rising Costs

College tuition and fees at public universities increased more than 6 percent from 2007–08 to 2008–09. Trends in College Pricing 2008, www.collegeboard.com

Universities need to offer salaries that attract well-established researchers and professors with terminal degrees (Ph.D.'s, M.B.A.'s, and J.D.'s). They need a high-level technological staff to maintain and fix the incredibly sophisticated technology underlying campus operations. Administrative and legal needs continue to grow as colleges must comply with the ever-changing and complex state and federal regulatory requirements. Any addition, change, or improvement to a college results in some kind of increased expense.

Perhaps most importantly, the growing student expectations push colleges to continue spending. No longer is it acceptable for a college's library to be open until 10 or 11 P.M. Instead, libraries are often open 24 hours a day. Likewise, it's not enough to have each dorm room wired for telephones and dial-up Internet access; when it comes to a college's technology, things like Wi-Fi networks are rapidly becoming the norm.

"As a college, if you don't offer those things, then you're not able to compete with other schools," explains Karen Krause, director of financial aid at the University of Texas at Arlington. "The expectations are already there. Unfortunately, none of these costs are included in financial aid."

These expectations for improved libraries, athletic facilities worthy of a pro football team, cutting-edge technology, sophisticated laboratories, and top-notch student centers all are causing schools to spend more money each year. "Schools can't afford not to spend money on these things, however," states Ernie Shepelsky. "Students are at the heart of the technology revolution and if schools are seen as 'behind the times' then they will lose those students that they have tried so hard to recruit."

While all these factors aren't going to affect the process of applying for financial aid, it will be to your benefit to stay informed about them. State education appropriations, college budgets, teacher salaries, and other related educational developments will all affect how much you pay for your student's education. Moreover, as someone who pays for these things, your opinion matters.

> **Role of Financial Aid in College Selection**
>
> "I'm amazed how many students apply to certain colleges because of things they hear. Parents can often times be the same way, and it seems that many families apply to schools having done very little research. Then once they get accepted to these schools, financial aid becomes important. Really, it should be an important part of the selection process."
>
> *Connie Gores, vice president for student life and development, Winona State University*

FINANCIAL AID ASSUMPTIONS

Have you ever started your car and thought, "I've got plenty of gas," only to have the engine cut off minutes later? How about writing a check as you tell yourself, "There's probably enough in the account to cover it," only to have the check bounce days later?

At one time or another, we've all made assumptions that turn out be wrong, and although you may not realize it, people make assumptions about financial aid that are incorrect as well. Just as bouncing a check can cause frustration and headaches, so can believing these myths. To save trouble and worry down the road, let's examine the validity of some of these common assumptions.

Assumption #1: Financial Aid Will Pay for Everything

Financial aid is just what it claims to be—assistance. By assuming that government, state, and/or private financial aid programs will pay 100 percent of your son or daughter's education, you're making a dangerous error. The purpose of these programs is to help people afford college, which is completely different from saying, "I can't afford college, so the government will have to pay for it." Parents and students who think this way are in for a harsh wake-up call.

Even the well-to-do can miscalculate. "Financial aid really is not designed to cover discretionary costs," adds University of Texas at Arlington's financial aid director Karen Krause. "But some wealthy families have a tough time understanding this."

Assumption #2: I Can Depend on Financial Aid to Help Me Pay for Some of College

It is true that most families will qualify for some sort of financial aid. The problem is, right now you don't know how much financial aid you'll receive. If you're fortunate, your son or daughter may have a significant amount of their education paid for through scholarships, loans, and/or grants. Most families, though, find that financial aid covers only half or less of the cost of college. So while expecting financial aid is one thing, relying on it to cover the bulk of expenses associated with your student's college experience is risky.

"Many families I've talked to don't think about financial aid until after they receive their aid packages," explains Connie Gores, vice president for student life and development at Winona State University. "Once they get them, then they want to know how they can get additional assistance. They didn't consider aid as part of the application process."

Assumption #3: I Will Have to Make a Financial Sacrifice for My Student's Education

Financial aid is based upon your family's ability to pay for school, not how much you're willing to pay. As you'll soon find out, state and federal programs use a formula that looks at your income, assets, and even age to calculate how much your family can afford to pay (your family's contribution) and, based on that, how much financial aid you can qualify for. The expected family contribution (EFC) in these calculations represents the financial responsibility you will be expected to have for your student's education, and financial aid from the federal government, state government, and/or college attended is available to cover part, most, or all of the difference. So even though you may disagree with your EFC, it's non-negotiable. Just as you can't change your tax rate because you need the extra money, you can't change your EFC because you don't have the money handy.

Billions in Student Loans

In the decade between 1998 and 2008, student loans more than doubled, from $41 billion to $85 billion, and the number of students taking out those loans soared from 4.1 billion to 6.1 billion, according to *Measuring Up, 2008*.

"A big misconception is that your EFC is what you'll pay for college, and that's really not true," says Jade Kolb, manager of financial aid for New York University. "It's a government analysis, and it may be the same as the amount you'll pay, or it could be more or less depending on the school."

Assumption #4: My Financial Status Doesn't Matter to Colleges

Currently, federal and state financial aid programs, as extensive as they are, have barely been able to keep up with the rising cost of education. An increasing number of colleges recognize the impact this has on lower-income families and consider a family's financial status before awarding financial aid. This practice is called "need aware," while colleges that do not consider a family's financial status in awarding financial aid are called "need blind." In addition, many schools that are need blind offer merit-based aid as a way of providing financial aid to top students regardless of their families' income. Since merit-based aid is often determined by how well your student performs in high school, you should stress that what they do in the classroom everyday does matter.

The main reason for clarifying these myths is so you won't make any costly and frustrating decisions down the road. The bottom line is, instead of making assumptions about financial aid, you should prepare to contribute as much as you can to your student's education. (We'll help you figure out how to do this later on, so don't panic.)

Assumption #5: What Colleges Charge Is What I Pay

As we stated earlier, planning for college can be similar to shopping for a car. When you head out to look for a new car, you see something you like, look inside, kick the tires, and maybe take it for a test drive. But once you take a glance at the price sticker on the side window, your heart almost stops beating, you gasp, and you slowly begin to wonder just how long it would take to bicycle to work.

It's called sticker shock, and once you see the cost of tuition and board at your student's favorite university, you'll probably feel the same way. It used to be that the most expensive purchases a family could make would be a house and a car. Today, it's a house and college, with a car just behind them. In fact, according to The College Board, which administers the SAT exams, the average annual cost of attending a four-year public university in 2008–09 was $14,333 for a student who lived on campus. Students who lived on campus at a private college averaged $34,132. Multiply that times four years of school, and you could spend $136,528 or more on your student's education—and that doesn't even factor the annual cost increases into the equation!

Still, there's no need to panic. When sticker shock happens to car shoppers, they almost immediately remember their trade-in, which reduces the price of a new car significantly. They also begin deciding what options they can do without—leather interior, air-conditioning, that computer voice telling you that your car door is open. Factor in special rates, discounts, and dealer reductions and there can be quite a difference between a car's sticker price and what you'd actually end up paying.

Sticker vs. Actual Price

When a parent expresses "sticker shock" about the cost of college these days I say, get over it! Never be afraid of the sticker price of a college. Find the college that your student wants to attend and after they have been accepted talk to both the Office of Admissions and Financial Aid to discuss what options might be available. Tell them that this is your number one choice and you really want to attend.

—Carly T. Connors, director of admissions, Albany College of Pharmacy

The same is going to be true for college, without the salesmen, balloons, or haggling. Instead of having a trade-in, you and your son or daughter may well have financial aid to reduce the cost you're quoted. Just as you may do without leather seats, your son or daughter might be able to do without things like the most expensive meal plan. Also, discounts and reductions are available to some students in the form of grants or scholarships. So take a closer look at all your prospective colleges, and don't dismiss any one on the sticker price alone.

Assumption #6: Cost Should Be a Major Factor in Choosing a College

The unfortunate reality for most families is that cost is a very real factor in college decisions. "Wait a minute," you're probably thinking. "Didn't I just read that I shouldn't dismiss a college based on cost?" Yes, you did, but it's important to understand that these two statements don't contradict each other.

Samuel Ellison, a student work program coordinator at Morehouse College, notes that it's financial aid that plays a factor in affording college, not cost. If you decide not to apply to a college based on cost alone, you'll never find out if your student would have been offered scholarships or other types of financial aid. In other words, a college that's much more expensive than your other prospective schools may offer more financial aid to be competitive—but you'll never find out if your student doesn't apply there.

The bottom line is, don't let cost alone keep your student from applying to that expensive school. Once the acceptance letters arrive and you start getting financial aid offer then you'll have the information you need to look at the reality of what your family can afford. We'll go into more detail about this later, but for now, remember to keep your options open.

WHAT TO DO WHEN

Now that we have considered six common assumptions, we have one more task to address before we move on to the other steps in our game plan. We need to identify and organize all the deadlines you'll have to meet in the year before your student graduates from high school.

When it comes to college applications and financial aid, timing is everything. To keep you on track, we've listed all significant deadlines month by month. That way, you can see easily what you and your student must do when. Bookmark these pages, tear them out, photocopy them, or enter them into a computer. Keep them close at hand. Check off the tasks as you get them done. These deadlines are crucial and you don't want to limit your options because you didn't act on time.

Although we could have the calendar start back in your student's freshman or sophomore years, we know that most of you are reading this book when your student is at least part way through the junior year of high school, so we'll begin 14 months before most students start college and go from there.

Summer Months Before the Senior Year

- Become familiar with the special terms and phrases used by colleges starting on page 193 and in the financial aid process.
  For more information, see the "Financial Aid Dictionary" near the end of this book

- Begin looking and applying for state and private scholarships and grants (continue this throughout your student's senior year).
  For more information, see chapters 11 and 12.

- Have your student begin to prepare for AP exams.
  For more information, see chapter 13.

- Explore other ways, in addition to financial aid, that your student can use to cut the cost of college.
  For more information, see chapter 13.

- Begin talking about the types of colleges your student might be interested in.
  For more information, see chapter 3.

- Compare the costs of colleges in your state, as well as any other states your student is interested in.
  For more information, see chapter 4.

- Create or narrow your student's list of prospective schools, including dream and safety colleges.
  For more information, see chapter 3.

- Request applications and catalogs from prospective colleges; consider using the summer to visit colleges of interest.

- Create folders for prospective colleges.

- Develop a record-keeping system for requests and/or receipt of applications, forms, recommendations, verifications, and acceptances/rejections.

- Make sure your student's résumé is up to date, and set up a procedure to keep it that way.

- Have your student get to work on some core essays to use in college and financial aid applications.

September

- Review college selection plans with your student's high school counselor.

- Have your student begin to ask for letters of recommendation for college and state or private financial aid applications.

- Begin looking at your family's budget, and find ways to save money or cut expenses in light of upcoming college costs.
  For more information, see chapter 5.

- Find out which financial aid applications your student's prospective colleges require, and get copies of them.
  For more information, see chapter 6.
- Decide if your student is going to request Early Action/Early Decision. If that's the plan, be sure to consult with those colleges about when financial aid awards will be offered.

October

- Make sure you and/or your student attend College Night and any financial aid seminars at the high school. Be wary of financial aid seminars offered by for-profit sources.
  For more information, see chapter 12.
- Visit prospective colleges and financial aid offices, if possible.
- Complete a Cost of Attendance worksheet for each prospective school your student is considering.
  For more information, see chapter 4.
- Register for the CSS Profile (if necessary).
  For more information, see chapter 7.
- Request paperwork for any financial aid programs you are interested in.
- Take SATs, if appropriate.
- Send in Early Decision applications (generally due by November 1), if applicable.

November

- Contact your employer to determine if your student will continue to be covered under your insurance.
- Review your family's investments to find ways to help pay for college. If your family has a financial advisor, set up a meeting to begin planning for college costs.
  For more information, see chapter 5.

December

- If you haven't been doing so all year, now's the time to pull together your family's pay stubs and other financial documents.
  For more information, see chapters 7 and 8.
- Begin educating yourself and your student about various types of student loans.
  For more information, see chapter 6.
- Fill out and file CSS/Profile forms, if necessary.
  For more information, see chapter 7.
- If your student applied for Early Decision, watch for responses to arrive this month and next; if your student is going to accept one of these, pay particular attention to stated deadlines.

January

- Complete and file federal income tax forms.
- Submit the FAFSA as soon as possible after January 1 (but no later than June 30).
  For more information, see chapters 7 and 8.
- Complete admissions applications.

February

- Call each potential college to verify that your applications and financial aid information are complete.
- Begin contacting lenders about various types of student loans. Compare rates and terms for later use.
  For more information, see chapters 6 and 14.
- Watch for signs of "senioritis." Don't let your student slack off. Some admissions are conditional on maintaining a certain GPA, or class ranking.

March

- Review your student's SAR, and make corrections if necessary.
  For more information, see chapter 7.
- Provide verification information to colleges, if requested.
  For more information, see chapter 10.
- If your circumstances have changed in any substantive way since you submitted the financial aid forms, notify the appropriate colleges and financial aid sources.
- If you're interested, request and complete the necessary forms for calculating Federal Methodology and Institutional Methodology, either in paper or online.
  For more information, see chapter 9.

April

- Begin receiving acceptance and financial aid packages from colleges around mid-April. (Be sure to note deadlines for acceptance.)
  For more information, see chapter 10.
- Compare packages, and negotiate offers if necessary.
  For more information, see chapter 10.
- If your student has received any outside or private aid, be sure to notify your student's prospective colleges and find out if it will impact aid packages.
  For more information, see chapter 12.
- Accept award package from the college your student will be attending (generally, this should be done by May 1).

- Notify the other colleges your student will not be attending.
- Make sure your student writes thank-you notes to anyone who has helped in the application process.

May

- Watch for housing information from your student's college, as well as other financial aid paperwork.
- Contact your student's college to find out key dates in the payment cycle.
  For more information, see chapter 14.
- Request information about the tuition payment plan at your student's college.
  For more information, see chapter 14.
- Have your student start to look for a summer job or volunteer position.
- If appropriate, have your student take the AP exams.

June

- Make sure final high school transcripts are sent to your student's college (if necessary). They may be required for the disbursement of federal funds.
- Research various types of loans to determine which is best for you and your family.
  For more information, see chapters 6 and 14.
- Complete loan paperwork and prepare to pay your tuition bill in the near future.
  For more information, see chapter 14.
- Make sure your FAFSA has been filed (June 30 is the deadline).
  For more information, see chapters 7 and 8.

Summer Months before College

- Receive and pay the tuition bill from the college.
  For more information, see chapter 14.
- Make travel plans early, to get the best fares.
- Make sure your budget and your student's budget is in place for the Fall.
  For more information, see chapter 4.
- Have your student sign up for the first-year orientation, if offered.
- If your student received a Stafford Loan, make sure an "entrance interview" has been scheduled (funds won't be disbursed until this is done).
  For more information, see chapter 6.
- Make sure the promissory note has been signed if a Perkins Loan was awarded.
  For more information, see chapter 6.

- Set up a bank account and credit cards for your student.
  For more information, see chapter 14.

- Congratulate yourself on a job well done.
  For more information, see chapters 1 and 14.

- Don't stop now. You and your student should start looking for financial aid for next year!

MOVING ON

This chapter covered the second step in your action plan: learning the basics. We reviewed the current financial state of colleges, so you'd have a better understanding of why college seems to be so expensive, and why it may keep getting more costly. We examined six common assumptions about financial aid, including how almost no one pays the full price of college. To explain this, we compared colleges to cars, discussing the difference between a "sticker price" and what students and families actually pay. Although cost alone should not keep a student from applying to a school, we acknowledged that it's a very real and important factor for almost everyone when going through this process. We ended the chapter by setting up a calendar of important deadlines to keep in mind as you and your student apply for college and search for financial aid.

In the next chapter, we'll take a look at the various college options open to your son and daughter, and discuss the decisions involved and how to factor costs and aid into the equation. We'll look at the different types of schools, including "dream schools" and financial safety schools, and we'll discuss how to get your son or daughter involved in all aspects of the decision-making process, including the financial ones. Before you move on, however, take a look on the next page at the checklist for this chapter.

✔ **CHECKLIST:**

1. Begin educating yourself about the financial issues facing universities. For example:
   - Is your state planning on cutting back university funding?
   - Are tuitions expected to increase drastically in the next few years?
   - Since the cost of a college will most likely change during the years that your student is enrolled, you should look at the average increases per year for each potential college. Changes taking place now may affect your son or daughter's education as early as next year, and it helps to be informed.

2. Begin looking at your family's budget, and find ways to save money or cut expenses in light of upcoming college costs. For example:
   - Can you put money aside each month to help with college?
   - Are there expenses that can be reduced or cut to help out?

3. Contact all your potential colleges to determine if their financial aid is need aware or need blind. If they are need aware, ask for information or request any additional forms that might be necessary. Keep notes of your findings.

4. Refer to the deadline date calendar we included in this chapter, now and every month until your student starts college, to keep yourself on track.

CHAPTER THREE

Choosing a College

There are many different kinds of colleges, each creating a different financial picture for your family. The first decision your student has to make is what kind of college he or she wants to attend. In this chapter we look at the options, including the best values for your student's goals and your bank account.

TYPES OF COLLEGES

In the broadest sense, college is simply where your student will go after high school to continue his or her education. From this view, there are three basic kinds of schools your student could attend: a traditional four-year college or university, a career college (or trade school), or a community college.

Four-Year Schools

The traditional American college or university is a four-year institution accredited by a recognized accrediting agency (this means the school has passed a review and meets certain standards of educational quality). These schools offer a Bachelor of Arts (BA) or Bachelor of Science (BS) degree.

A college education can cost next to nothing (if you are accepted at a military academy or a tuition-free school like Berea College or Cooper Union) to $50,000 or more (at schools like Sarah Lawrence College) to anything in between. Every year, numerous online and print lists are issued of the best "bargain" colleges and the most expensive schools. To put the range of college costs in perspective, let's take a look at two of these.

Here are FindCollegeCard's online selections (*www.findcollegecards.com/blog*) for the four-year colleges in 2009 with the least tuition.

The Bargains
University of Nevada at Reno: $2,682
Florida State University: $2,890
San Diego State University: $2,936
University of Florida at Gainesville: $2,955
Florida Atlantic University: $3,092
Texas A&M University: $3,109
Florida International University: $3,156
University of South Florida: $3,167
University of Central Florida: $3,180
University of Nevada at Las Vegas: $3,210

And, here are the colleges selected by CampusGrotto (*www.campusgrotto.com*) whose total cost of education may make you gasp:

Yes, This is Only for One Year
Sarah Lawrence College: $53,166
George Washington University: $50,312
New York University: $50,182
Georgetown University: $49,689
Connecticut College: $49,385
Bates College: $49,350
Johns Hopkins University: $49,278
Skidmore College: $49,266
Scripps College: $49,236
Middlebury College: $49,210

Public versus Private

Four-year schools are either public or private. Public colleges and universities, which you may hear referred to as "state schools," receive substantial financial support from state and federal governments through tax dollars, while private colleges and universities may or may not; when they do, they usually receive less than public institutions.

A major difference between the two types of schools is cost. Private colleges are usually much more expensive than public ones, as you can see in the lists above; all of the colleges in the "bargain" list are state institutions and all of those in the high-price list are private schools. Another difference is that private colleges tend to have smaller enrollments and smaller class sizes. Lastly, public colleges tend to have a greater percentage of students from a particular area. As "state schools," public colleges will attract a large number of students who can benefit from the "in-state" tuition rate (more on "in-state" benefits later in this chapter).

Ellen Frishberg, director of student financial services at Johns Hopkins University, points out one of the biggest differences between public and private colleges. "I see a lot of people who don't understand the different costs of public and private schools, and explaining these differences is really necessary. As taxpayers, people pay subsidies to public schools through their taxes, which reduce their costs to students. So really, when you take those taxes into account, public colleges cost about the same as private schools. It's just that you've already paid some money through your taxes."

Public and Private College Tuitions—2009

- At four-year private institutions, tuition and fees averaged $25,143, a 5.9-percent increase over the prior year.

- At four-year public institutions, tuition and fees average $6,585, a 6.4-percent increase over the prior year.

- At two-year public institutions, tuition and fees average $2,400, a 4.7-percent increase over the prior year.

Source: Trends in College Pricing 2008. Collegeboard.com

Most of the time, private schools tend to be thought of as more prestigious than public colleges. After all, Harvard, Stanford, and Yale are all private universities, as are other Ivy League schools. However, it's important to note that not all private universities are the same. Research has suggested that mediocre private schools may not offer a better education than a good public college. Moreover, depending on your student's future plans, even a top-notch private school may not make a difference. Therefore while you shouldn't rule out private colleges because of their cost, you also shouldn't assume that private schools always provide a better education.

In addition—and this may surprise you—a private college, when aid and loans are factored in, may be less expensive than a state school, especially an out-of-state school. "A friend of my daughter lives in North Carolina," says Connie Gores, vice president for student life and development at Winona State University, "and she applied to both in-state and out-of-state schools. The out-of-state schools accepted her, while the in-states didn't. So now, she's having to choose between options that really may not be the best fit for her, and because the family assumed that private college would be too expensive, she didn't apply to any."

Room and Board—2009

- At four-year private colleges, room and board averaged $8,989, a 5.6-percent increase over the previous year.

- At four-year public colleges, room and board averaged $7,748, a 5.2-percent increase over the previous year.

Source: Trends in College Pricing 2008. Collegeboard.com

So despite that churning in your stomach, don't automatically assume a particular college shouldn't be considered because of cost. Regardless of sticker shock, you should compare state schools to private schools to see what you can afford. This early in the process, don't let price stand in your way. Several factors will influence your final decision, and cost is only one of them.

In-State versus Out-of-State

This may seem obvious, but an in-state school simply means it is in the same state as where you live. If your son or daughter leaves their home state to go to college, it is considered out-of-state. These terms are used to refer to both students and colleges. These terms exist because most colleges charge out-of-state students a higher tuition than in-state students. This is based on the idea that in-state students already give the college some money by paying state taxes that are passed on to the college. Some schools, however, offer a "good neighbor" tuition break to students from nearby states, sometimes charging only in-state tuition, especially for students with high grade point averages or SAT scores (more on this in chapter 13).

It's important to note that any combination of these four terms can be applied to a college. Your student could go to an in-state private school or an out-of-state public school. The important thing to realize is that while these words describe a college, no one type is better than another.

Community Colleges

For students who do not want to attend a four-year college for any number of reasons, community colleges provide an extremely affordable option. Designed for students living at home (thus saving fees for room and board), they offer a two-year degree (called an associate degree) that can mirror the first two years of education a student would get at a four-year college; alternatively, students can enroll in career-oriented programs, studying for professions that are in high demand in technology, allied health, and other fields. Community colleges also offer remedial study in preparation for college work.

Associate Degrees in Demand

The top degree areas in demand at the associate degree level are (in descending order):

1. Business
2. Engineering
3. Drafting
4. Design
5. Computer Science

Source: National Association of Colleges and Employers Job Outlook 2009.

Many students who finish a two-year community college program—usually in the lowest price range for any higher education—are able to move on and receive their bachelor's degree after two more years at a traditional college, saving thousands of dollars. To make this process as easy as possible, Bill Sliwa, vice president for enrollment management at Lees-McRae College, recommends that students "have a four-year college that they would like to transfer to in mind while enrolled at a community college. The student should look into articulation agreements (agreements that facilitate the transfer of students from a two-year to four-year college) between the schools and ensure that his or her course work will transfer toward a degree at that four-year college."

Career Colleges

Career colleges (also known as technical institutes) are postsecondary institutions that provide training for skill-based careers in law, business, information technology, health care, criminal justice, and more than 200 other fields. In contrast to community colleges, which are usually funded by state or local governments, career schools are independent, privately-owned institutions. Career schools account for 47 percent of all postsecondary educational institutions in the United States. At many career schools, the majority of programs are related to one career field, such as health care (Maric College in San Diego) or automotive (Wyoming Technical Institute in Laramie). Other career colleges offer training in multiple fields, with online study options. Programs in allied health, arts and sciences, criminal justice, design and graphic arts, information technology, paralegal studies, and travel and tourism are among those available.

Career colleges primarily offer occupational degrees, rather than the academic degrees conferred by colleges and universities. The training is much more focused on the practical skills and knowledge needed for a specific career. If what your student wants is practical training for a specific career, a program at a career school might save him or her time. Depending on the profession and college, a student may earn a degree in as little as 18 months. A student who attends a program on radiation therapy, for example, can earn as much as a graduate of a traditional college.

Tuition for career colleges can vary widely, so before you commit to a loan, find out how long the program takes to finish and how much it will cost. Look into whether the school offers scholarships, and what other types of financial assistance are available. Check the school's accreditation status. Accreditation by a reputable national or regional accrediting body means the school has passed a thorough examination of its educational quality. Besides ensuring quality, accreditation by one of the accrediting bodies recognized by the Department of Education means that students are eligible for federal financial grant and loan programs. Students attending a non-accredited school, or a school accredited by a nonrecognized agency, generally cannot qualify for federal aid.

Check Out the Financial Aid Office

"You really need to see how you're treated by the financial aid office before you apply, because that's a good indicator of how much help you'll receive," remarks vice president for student life and development Connie Gores, parent of a college-aged daughter. "If a financial aid office isn't helpful and treats you like just another number before your student even goes there, you can bet it'll be worse if your student attends."

OTHER OPTIONS

College Abroad

While study abroad doesn't describe a certain type of college, it does refer to an educational process, where students start or continue their education outside the United States. In fact, study abroad can take place in almost any type of college we've mentioned (except for community colleges). Adventurous future chefs may become an expert in creating pastries by studying in Paris, while a future translator for the United Nations may become fluent in German by attending a college in Berlin. In addition, many U.S. schools offer a semester or year of study abroad at a cooperating institution in the host country. This option can prove to be an added expense that will need to be factored into your college cost equation if your student has his or her heart set on it, but bargains are available for those who plan ahead. Check if the tuition you will pay for study abroad will be that of your son or daughter's primary school or the host school abroad. It's possible to save money if the foreign institution charges a lower tuition. Plus, there are a couple of ways to find funding to support your student's activities abroad. Look for this book in the library or bookstore: *Financial Aid for Study and Training Abroad* (described here are nearly 1,000 funding opportunities available to help you pay for studies outside the United States). Or, search for scholarships online at such sites as:

- Go Abroad.com
  scholarships.goabroad.com/index.cfm
- IIEPassport's Study Abroad Funding
  www.studyabroadfunding.org
- University Minnesota's Learning Abroad Center
  www.umabroad.umn.edu/financial/scholarships/index.html

Online Programs

Online and distance education programs have become increasingly popular in recent years (currently, more than three million students are enrolled), because they break many of the barriers people confront when trying to enroll in traditional college programs. Online students can study anytime, anywhere. Tuition for online schools is competitive when compared to traditional colleges and universities. Many online institutions also offer scholarships, payment plans, and other methods of making tuition payment more convenient. However, while online degrees are gaining in acceptability and even status, they may not be as attractive in the job market as a "regular" degree. One reason for this, according to Bill Sliwa at Lees-McRae College, is that "not everything one learns in college is learned in the classroom. There is significant value to the residential experience. Students learn to manage their independence and how to deal with other people."

If you're looking at an online school, investigate its accreditation. As we discussed earlier in this chapter, accreditation is important not only because it is an indication of quality but because only students in appropriately accredited institutions can take advantage of federal financial aid program. Always check with the institution you're considering to see if it is able to offer such aid.

Because the majority of students attend traditional four-year and community colleges each year, the government forms and requirements we will discuss later will be applicable to them. Nevertheless, if your son or daughter is attending one of these other types of colleges, this book will still be helpful. We're going to cover everything from private loans to grants and scholarships than can help you no matter where your student intends to go to school.

GETTING YOUR STUDENT INVOLVED

Very few students know for certain what they want to do with their lives after graduating from high school, and odds are yours may feel the same way. (If not, great! Your problems aren't completely solved, but you're off to a good start.) Therefore, before we even get into financial aid, budgets, and loans, it's essential to make sure you and your son or daughter are on the same page to avoid future headaches and wasted time.

As mentioned in the introduction, this book is based on the idea that affording college is both your and your student's responsibility. After all, the decisions you're making affect them as much as you. If you haven't already talked about college with your son and daughter, it's time to get started. Here are some basic issues you and your student should discuss.

What Does Your Student Want from College?

This doesn't mean they have to choose a major right now, of course, but do they have any idea of what they want to study? Is your daughter torn between acting and writing? Maybe your grandson wants to go into science, but loves both chemistry and math.

What about sports or activities? Does your student want to pole vault for a college team? Is your student thinking about moving on from playing with your home video camera into learning about filmmaking?

It's not uncommon for students to insist that they attend an out-of-state college because they want to become independent from their family. Still others may have a certain city or area of the country in mind where they want to go. An actor may want to attend college in New York or California, or a future politician may want to get an education near Washington, D.C.

The point is, most students probably have some idea of what they want from college, even if they haven't told their parents about it. A desire to go into a certain field or live in a certain place will impact not only the cost you two will pay for college, but the types of financial aid you'll qualify for. So be open to what your student may say.

In most cases, money is going to play a significant role in this decision. Therefore, while you and your son or daughter should by all means consider prestigious, more costly universities, it's also necessary to develop a game plan to ensure your student attends college no matter what happens. To that end, here are four things you need to look at if you intend to cover all your bases.

Local Colleges and Universities

Odds are you have at least one, if not a few, colleges in your area. They may be in your town, a few miles down the road, or within walking distance of your home. You and your son or daughter should consider these local schools as you look at colleges. Granted, most students dream of leaving home and going away to college, but local universities often mean significant savings for the student and parent.

Living at Home

One of the main reasons local colleges are appealing for many families is that the student can continue to live at home. Rather than pay separately for room and board (not to mention things like travel, phone calls, and food), your family doesn't incur any increase in living expenses from this option. In fact, the expenses you'll face if your student remains at home may be significantly less than those same expenses if they were to go away. Naturally, this shouldn't be a deciding factor in your selection of schools, but it is one advantage to commuting of a local school.

Part-Time Work for Students

Another aspect to this game plan is that awful four-letter word: work. Ideally, most people agree that students should focus their time on studies, not babysitting, working the counter at a video store, or waiting tables. However, just a few hours working each week can have a significant impact on college-related expenses. Textbooks can be paid for, gas and car insurance can be bought, and other such incidentals can be covered without you handing over money. Most importantly, disciplined students all over the country work part-time while going to school, with little impact on their grades.

> **Advantages of Working and Studying**
>
> Consider encouraging your student to take on a part-time job while enrolled in college. According to some schools, working can actually be good for your student. "Research has shown higher satisfaction ratings and a better percent of matriculation when a college student is working," says Ellen Frishberg, director of student financial services for Johns Hopkins University.

The Financial "Safety" School

Finally, there's the idea of a "safety" school. Traditionally, this has meant applying to a college that the student feels fairly certain will accept him or her. Yet, a safety school should also be one that you know your family can afford. After all, a college that's completely out of your price range isn't very "safe," is it? In most cases, safety schools are public, located in the family's area (within driving distance), and offer financial aid to the majority of its students. Students who attend their safety school often live at home for the first few years to save on costs.

The bottom line is this: you'll need to discuss each of these options with your son or daughter and identify a safety school as part of your overall plan. Some students attend their safety school (be it a local university or community college) for a few years, then transfer to their dream school to receive their degree. Attending a safety school does not necessarily mean settling, because it's often a temporary compromise on the way to getting a degree.

Does Your Student Understand the Costs Involved in Going to College?

While students may hold a part-time job, file taxes, and/or make car payments, they probably don't have experience dealing with loans for large sums of money, creating a budget meant to last a year, or stretching their money by reducing expenses. Because of this, the high cost of going to college may not be a reality to them. It doesn't take new drivers long to learn that car expenses are costly and gas isn't free. By involving your student in the financial aid process, there's a good chance he or she will quickly learn just how large a sum of money is involved.

"There are parents who give their kids a free ride to college," offers Karon Ray, who has put two children through college, with another one about to start. "The problem is that they graduate from college having never done a budget." Ray and her husband, a Marine Corps officer, gave each of their three children a lump sum of money before they started college, but didn't tell them how to use it. "So really, our kids faced the sticker shock before they started classes. They had to decide if they really needed that high-end computer, or should be saving money for the next semester. Basically, it's about teaching them that things cost money."

> **Who Should Fill out the FAFSA**
>
> Bill Sliwa, vice president of enrollment management at Lees-McRae College recommends that students, not just parents, fill out the FAFSA. "The first question on the FAFSA is name and that name is the student's name, not the parent's. While some parents are afraid to share family finances with children, doing so will help them understand the impact of paying for their college."

Explain to Your Student That Loans Are Going to Be Their Responsibility

Nothing is more frightening to freewheeling college students than seeing how much they owe in student loans. We'll get into loans in more detail later in the book but, for now, it's important for both you and your student to realize that federal loans are going to be in the student's name. The most important reason your student should want to be involved in this process is because the debt he or she is creating is going to be his or her responsibility in a few short years.

Does Your Student Have Realistic Expectations of College?

This is probably the hardest thing for a student to realize. In high school, college represents freedom, choices, independence, and a lot of fun. But, we suggest you remind your student about the consequences of slacking off; don't let your son or daughter forget that studying is a priority, papers will have to be written on time, and exams are going to be difficult.

Although it may not seem obvious at first, you'll probably find that each of these three points leads into a discussion of the next one. Students who have an idea of what they want from college are going to be more willing to take part in the financial aid process. Student who are involved in the process are going learn (very quickly) that much of the cost will be their responsibility, and students who are aware of their financial obligations will have a more balanced expectation of what college is all about.

MOVING ON

This chapter reviewed the types of colleges out there and looked briefly at their comparative costs. We discussed traditional four-year schools, community colleges, and such nontraditional study options as career colleges, online programs, and colleges in a foreign country. We also discussed how the type of college might affect the cost of higher education and recommended having a serious discussion with your student to get him or her involved in the financial side of a college decision. The concept of a financial safety school was introduced, as well as how students can lessen the economic burden by living at home, working, and taking responsibility for student debt.

In the next chapter, we'll talk more in-depth about the difference between a college's sticker price and the actual amount you can expect to pay. You'll begin breaking down individual costs and comparing how these can differ from college to college, as we teach you how to determine the true cost of college for you and your student.

✓ CHECKLIST:

1. Begin talking with your student about the types of college he or she might be interested in:
   - In-state or out-of-state?
   - Public school or private?

2. Begin comparing the costs of colleges in your state, as well as other states your student is interested in. For example:
   - Are universities in your state cheaper than neighboring states?
   - How do out-of-state tuitions in other states compare to in-state tuitions in your state?
   - Are "good neighbor" or regional tuition plans available?

3. Determine and select a safety school with your student. As you do so, discuss the following:
   - Is there a nearby college your student could attend?
   - Will your student be willing to live at home if need be?
   - Is your student willing to work part-time?

4. Talk with your son or daughter about the financial side of attending college. Discuss your student's expectations for college, as well as the possibility that most of the loans and financial burden involved will become his or her responsibility after graduating. Encourage your student to take an active part in this process, and help him or her understand why it is worth the time to do so!

CHAPTER FOUR

Identifying the Costs

So far, we've looked at the big picture when it comes to financial aid, and you should have a good idea of what college costs, as well as what your educational options are. In this chapter we start on the nuts and bolts of paying for college, which means numbers. Fortunately, if you can balance a checkbook, you can do the calculations necessary to get through this process. All right, grab a pencil and some paper, a calculator if you've got one, and read on.

In Chapter 2, we compared the price of college to that of a car, explaining that both have "sticker prices" that usually vary greatly from the actual cost itself. However, in order to compare the sticker price quoted by a university to the actual price you're going to end up paying, you're going to have to break the costs into separate categories (just as the sticker price of a car is broken down into parts).

While you may not look forward to doing this, it's essential to making an informed choice about which college is best for you and your son or daughter. Sometimes costs change, estimates may not include additional fees that impact you, and housing expenses can vary greatly, depending upon the selections chosen by a student and their family. In fact, most housing costs you see are based on an average, which means you may end up paying more or less than that amount depending upon your choices. You wouldn't sign a car loan if you had only an estimate of what you'd be paying, so why do it for a college?

This chapter will help you determine what's needed and what's not when it comes to your student's college education. You'll create worksheets that list all of these costs, so you can do a side-by-side comparison of each school you're considering. Before you actually start crunching numbers, however, let's take a look at the different types of expenses you'll need to consider in your calculations.

Comparing College Costs

As you compare costs from the colleges your student is considering, you should also look into each school's overall financial health. To do this, Edmund Luzine, owner and founder of Adirondack Capital Management, Inc., recommends that "parents and students review the annual financial report of the college. How does it spend its money? Where does it get the money from?"

DIRECT VERSUS INDIRECT

When it comes to college, financial aid administrator use the terms "direct" and "indirect" to define costs. Essentially, every cost associated with college falls into one of these two categories, and they're easy to understand.

Direct Costs

Direct costs are directly related to your student's education and are usually paid to the school itself. There are four types of direct costs: tuition, fees, textbooks, and supplies

What Are Credit Hours?

Many colleges break classes down into credit hours, which reflect how long the class is and how much time it takes out of the student's schedule. Most classes are three credit hours, and most students take an average of four to six classes each semester. Some colleges, however, do not use this system. Classes at these schools are generally worth a half, full, or two credits rather than credit hours.

What Do Colleges Charge?

"Some schools do a really good job of mapping all their costs out," says Connie Gores, vice president for student life and development at Winona State University. "Those kinds of costs should always be in the catalog, or easily available from the school. If a college isn't able to share prices for fees or other costs beyond tuition and room and board, then you should think strongly about that school. This is a good indicator of how helpful a financial aid office can be."

Tuition

This is the amount that a college requires from all students in order to attend class. At some colleges it's a flat rate, while others charge by the number of credit hours (classes) your son or daughter takes. Tuition also varies, depending on whether or not the school is public or private, and whether or not your student is in-state or out-of-state. (For definitions of these terms, see chapter 3.)

Be sure to determine the exact amount of tuition for each college you're considering, because this charge varies greatly. If a school bases tuition on the student's number of credit hours, assume 15 credit hours per semester.

Fees

For every college, there are some fees that must be paid simply because your child will be a student there. They may be named differently from school to school, but most provide funding for the general expenses a college incurs. Other fees can vary greatly, depending on a student's major or their activities.

Student service fees are related to activities that your student may choose to participate in, such as sports, performing groups, or clubs. These fees may be optional, depending upon the college. Class-related fees are most commonly found in the arts and sciences. For example, chemistry majors may pay additional fees to cover laboratory and chemical costs. Likewise, art majors will likely pay a fee to cover costs associated with their materials.

Together, tuition and fees (on the average) account for a whopping one-third of all college costs!

Textbooks

At first, you might not think much about the cost of your student's textbooks. But be aware: textbooks can be very expensive. "When you visit colleges, go to the bookstore on campus," suggests parent Joe Sanseverino. "That was a real eye opener for us! You'll be shocked the first time you see a book cost one hundred and fifty dollars."

What's more, textbook costs are often underestimated and those estimates don't always rise in step with textbook price increases. According to U.S. PIRG (the federation of state public interest research groups), students in 2009 spent an average of $900 on college textbooks, which represents a 400 percent increase over what students were paying just 15 years ago. This amount is equivalent to 20 percent of the tuition at an average university and half of the tuition at a typical community college!

Textbook costs, of course, will vary from school to school. Ithaca College, for example, has estimated that the average cost of books for students there is $968 per year and Vaughn College of Aeronautics and Technology has placed the annual figure at $1,000.

To ensure that you don't come up short, you might want to estimate at least $1,000 a year for textbooks. For some majors this might be far too high but, believe it or not, for other majors it might be too low!

Supplies

These costs usually impact art and science majors, and reflect equipment that the university does not provide for the student. For example, chemistry majors often have to get their own safety glasses and calculators.

> **Shop Around**
>
> There are many ways to cut textbook costs, if you or your son or daughter is willing to shop for the bargains. Several online bookstores and textbook resellers, for example, offer used textbooks, and many of those offer free shipping as well. For an online list of 29+ websites that resell textbooks at bargain prices, go to: www.studenthacks.org/2008/01/23/used-cheap-textbook (be sure to scroll down the page to get to the article).

Indirect Costs

Indirect costs are all the other expenses related to attending college, such as room and board, travel, and personal expenses. There are eight major types of indirect costs: room, board, transportation, travel, computer equipment, personal, medical and dental, and miscellaneous.

Room

Simply put, this is where your student will live. Most colleges refer to this as housing, and there are two types: on-campus and off-campus.

Housing Costs Reality

Many colleges require that freshmen live on-campus, so check with each school you're considering. Also, on-campus housing costs for a college can vary, depending on residence hall. Some dorms may cost more because they're newer or more convenient to campus, so be sure to ask!

On-campus means your student lives in a college residence hall ("dorm" for short), and you pay a lump sum to the college each semester. In turn, the college pays all the bills associated with the housing—heat, hot water, electricity, and so on. Most often, your student will share a room with one or more students.

Off-campus means your student lives in an apartment or house literally off the college's campus. Students living off-campus can expect increased responsibilities, such as monthly bills, grocery shopping, and rent. "Many people don't understand that tuition and room and board are two different things," says Connie Gores of Winona State University. "One of my daughter's friends received a scholarship covering half her tuition and her family thought that it would pay for half of the cost of the college. They didn't realize room and board was in addition to tuition costs."

It may be easier and more convenient for students to live on campus, especially if they are about to start their first year of college. Don't assume living on campus is always cheaper, however. Especially at urban colleges in large cities, campus housing can be limited and expensive compared to local apartments. In addition, find out if close friends of your student are attending the same college. If so, would it be cheaper for them to share an apartment? In rare instances, some parents actually buy a small house or apartment near campus. The student then lives there, and the other rooms are rented out to help make mortgage payments. Parents with experience in real estate can actually make money off such an investment.

Board

You've probably heard the term "room and board" before, and while room is self-explanatory, board refers to food. At most colleges, these two categories (room and board) are paid for separately. When it comes to board, most colleges offer a variety of meal plans, allowing students to eat at campus dining halls without paying out of pocket. Some colleges charge a flat rate for meal plans, while others offer a couple of options, depending on how often the student expects to eat there.

Break it Down

Some colleges combine room and board into one cost on their literature, so check your brochures to see if your prospective colleges have done this. If so, request a breakdown of these two items.

It's important to realize that these plans only cover food your student will eat at the dining hall. So you'll also need to factor in costs for snacks, dining out, and the occasional pizza.

On average, room and board, combined, account for more than 40 percent of a student's college costs.

Transportation

This category covers the costs associated with your son or daughter getting around campus and the area where the college is located. Often, this is minimal, because many students living on-campus simply walk everywhere. However, this could include a bicycle, public transportation, or a car. If your student intends to have a car while in college, you'll need to also calculate the cost of gas and insurance.

Travel

The cost of travel can vary greatly, depending on how far away your student's college is, as well as how often your son or daughter plans to come home. If your student is attending a college in your state, you may choose to drive to campus and pick him or her up for a holiday or long weekend with the family. However, if your student is attending a university on the other side of the country, he or she will likely be flying home for visits. The number of times a year that will happen will vary from family to family. So, unlike other costs, you'll find that travel expenses can vary greatly from school to school.

Computer Equipment

Don't forget to consider any possible hardware or software costs. Even if your student already has a computer, it might not have all the capability that will be needed in a college setting. In addition, there's the possibility that your student's current computer won't meet a particular college's requirements. Check and see if your student's potential colleges expect their

Car Culture

Some colleges do not allow freshmen who live on campus to have cars. If your student plans on having one, be sure to check with your prospective schools. You should also be sure to consider the additional costs involved with having a car on campus. The car will need gas, maintenance, and insurance.

Travel Discounts

Many airlines, trains, and bus companies offer student discounts with a college ID. Have your student look into these discounts so they will gain a better understanding of the costs involved in traveling to and from school. At the same time, your student can investigate other travel policies that could impact ticket prices, such as advance purchase requirements, peak versus nonpeak travel, or additional fees levied during high travel times. You should also investigate credit card mileage or reward programs, especially if your student will have to fly to school. You may be surprised how quickly mileage—and free tickets or rewards—can add up! For a list of websites that specialize in student airfare deals, check out *studenttravel.about.com/od/studentairfare/a/studentairfare.htm*

students to have a certain computer model and/or special hardware and software to make the computer work on the college's network.

Personal

This area is usually one of the most flexible when it comes to determining how much college will cost. Personal expenses can cover everything from long distance phone calls to entertainment, laundry, shopping, and gifts. Most parents look at the student's spending money, and choose a set amount designed to last the semester.

To best determine how much you and your student will need to allocate for personal expenses throughout a semester of college, look at how much your student currently spends per month and multiply by four (because there are just under four months in a semester). You'll probably want to increase this number slightly to cover "non-fun" things like laundry and cleaning supplies.

Medical and Dental

Although it's often overlooked, you'll need to determine how much your student's medical and dental insurance will be. If your student is currently covered by your employer's insurance, you'll need to find out if they are still eligible once they go to college. Depending upon your insurance, you may have to pay an extra fee, or they may not be covered at all.

Most colleges offer health insurance, so if your current health plan will no longer cover your son or daughter, check with prospective colleges to find out what your options are.

Anticipating College Expenses

"To get used to the cost of sending your student to college," says Bill Sliwa, vice president for enrollment management at Lees-McRae College, "Spend his or her senior year living as though you already have the college expenses. This will force you to budget accurately and test your plans for how you will pay for that first year!"

Miscellaneous

While it sounds vague, miscellaneous expenses are everything else that goes beyond the basic costs of attending college. This can include fraternity or sorority dues, athletic expenses associated with playing a sport, clubs, tutoring, and costs associated with summer programs. Students with disabilities would add any additional expenses in this category.

Miscellaneous expenses usually are not as flexible as personal expenses, since reducing this amount means the student must give up sports, clubs, or activities. But while this number can vary from school to school, you'll likely include the same things for each college. (In other words, students planning to try out for the tennis team are likely do so regardless of which college they attend.)

CALCULATING INFLATION

If your student is a senior in high school, inflation won't impact your worksheets. However, if there are still a few years before he or she starts college, you'll need to factor this in.

Inflation is an estimate of how much the cost of something will increase over time. We all know that a pack of gum costs more today than it did 20 years ago. That's inflation, and it affects everything. Therefore, if your student won't be starting college in the immediate future, you'll want to get an idea of how much this education will cost once he or she starts.

The national average increase for the cost of college has been approximately 6 percent every year, so if your student is planning to start college in two years, you should plan to pay at least 12 percent more than what college currently costs. Following is a chart that gives an inflation factor, which you'll use (unless your student starts college next year) on the cost worksheet that's at the end of this chapter.

YEARS BEFORE STUDENT STARTS COLLEGE	INFLATION FACTOR
1	1.06
2	1.12
3	1.19
4	1.26
5	1.34
6	1.42
7	1.50
8	1.59
9	1.69
10	1.79
11	1.90
12	2.01
13	2.13
14	2.26
15	2.40
16	2.54
17	2.69
18	2.85

To use this chart, simply find the inflation factor for the number of years your student has until he or she starts college, and multiply that inflation factor by the total cost of the education. (Not only will the cost of tuition, room, and board go up, but so will everything else.)

For example, if a student has three years until starting college, and the cost of attending a particular college is currently $25,000 a year (including indirect costs, such as travel, personal expenses, etc.), then the estimated costs associated with attending that same college would be $29,750 in three years. How did we calculate that? The chart shows the inflation factor for three years is 1.19, so:

$$\$25,000 \times 1.19 = \$29,750$$

Remember that this is only an estimate. The actual cost may be more or less than this number (but you'll likely be close).

THE ACTUAL COST OF COLLEGE

At the end of this chapter you'll find a worksheet created to help you keep track of all these expenses. It's called the Cost of Attendance (COA) worksheet, and you'll should do one for each college you and your student are considering. You may want to photocopy the worksheet, or create your own on your computer, Maybe you'd prefer to write everything out on a pad or use a calculator online (for example: *toolkit.collegepayway.com/costofattendanceweb/default.aspx*). It really doesn't matter, as long as you have everything written down and accounted for.

How Long For That Four-Year Degree?

An often miscalculated figure when determining the actual cost of attending college is the length of time it will take for the student to complete his or her degree. According to The College Board, it takes a first-time bachelor's degree recipient an average of 6.2 years to complete a degree at a four-year public college. At a four-year private college the average is 5.3 years. The lesson: You might need to budget for more than just four years to pay for that four-year degree!

As you fill out these worksheets, be sure to keep your notes and calculations so you'll remember how you got each number. For example, if personal expenses include the cost of a cell phone, or transportation expenses include the costs associated with your student's car, write that down with the amount you expect to spend for each. As you'll see next, these notes will come in handy.

According to Karen Krause, director of financial aid at the University of Texas at Arlington, schools often offer average numbers to help you fill in your COA worksheet. "Most schools should be able to give you ballpark figures," she explains. "For example, we recently did a bookstore survey that looked at textbooks for six different majors at different years in college. We then used these to get an average cost for our students."

Because you're going to fill out these worksheets for each of your potential colleges, this might be a good time to organize everything you have so far. You've probably got brochures, letters, forms, and notes from each college you and your student are considering. It is easiest to compare the Cost of Attendance worksheets side-by-side, so take a few minutes to organize the bulk of information and papers you've got. Use whatever works best for you: folders big legal-sized envelopes, one of those accordion folders with different sections. Whatever you use, it's a good idea to separate these papers by college so that you'll be able to find things easily later.

STUDENT INVOLVEMENT

Finally, if you haven't already realized it, this is where you really need to make sure your son or daughter is involved. The numbers you come up with on the Cost of Attendance worksheets are going to be largely impacted by the choices your son or daughter makes. Without your student's involvement and input, you might as well be guessing, which will make the process of affording college much more difficult. Some questions you may want to have answered include:

- Does your student plan to join a fraternity or sorority?
- How often will your student eat out (not at the dining hall)?
- If your student wants to attend a college in a major city, will he or she use public transportation to go exploring off campus?
- How many times will your student be traveling between home and school and how will that be done (by plane? train? bus? car?)
- How will phone calls be handled? Does your student have a cell phone that he or she will continue to use while away?
- Does your student plan to participate in a sport or activity that will require equipment or special gear?

By having your student help calculate these expenses for each potential college, you'll have the most accurate worksheets possible. Getting your student involved will also help iron out differences in opinion about what's a necessity and what's not.

COMPARING THE WORKSHEETS

Once you and your student have finished the Cost of Attendance worksheets for your prospective schools, you'll be able to compare all these colleges and see what your student's education is going to cost. Don't worry, yet, about how you are going to pay for that. We'll start you on that process in the next chapter.

You'll realize that all the hard work of filling in the COA worksheets was worth it as soon as you sit down and are able to compare colleges with just a few sheets of paper and a handful of numbers. You'll probably also realize that not only does tuition vary greatly from college to college, but those indirect expenses you spent so much time identifying vary, as well. If nothing else, these comparisons will give you a range on how much your student's higher education will cost. In most cases, you can look at the difference between your safety school and your most expensive private, out-of-state college to get this range. Don't be surprised if it's a big difference. For most families it usually is.

MAKING ADJUSTMENTS

As you compare the Cost of Attendance worksheets for your colleges, you'll find that some schools are much more appealing to your checkbook than others are. Rather than rule out a college at this point, sit down with your student and see if there are any expenses that can be trimmed or reduced. This is where your notes will come in handy, because you can use them as the basis for your changes.

Naturally, tuition can't be changed, but what about personal and miscellaneous expenses, as well as things like travel? Is your student willing to come home only for major holidays if it means he or she can afford going to college in New York City? Would they consider not joining a fraternity or sorority if doing so means they could go out-of-state? Are they willing to attend their dream college so badly that they would give up their car for it?

MOVING ON

To summarize, we began by explaining why it's important to break down the cost of college and introduced the idea of a printed or online worksheet to do this. We then looked at direct versus indirect costs, and learned the four types of direct costs, as well as the eight types of indirect costs. We discussed how inflation can impact the cost of college for students who aren't starting in the near future, and then introduced the Cost of Attendance worksheet. We looked at why it's important that your student be involved in these worksheets and what to do once they are completed. Finally, we touched on how you can compare and adjust COA worksheets to determine better what you can afford.

In the next chapter, we'll talk about just where all this money is going to come from. You'll learn about different types of income and how each can be used to help meet your share of your student's college education. But before you move on, take a look at the checklist for this chapter.

✓ CHECKLIST:

1. Organize the information you have from prospective colleges.
   - Create a folder for each school.
   - Make sure you have all the information necessary to calculate the costs of attending each school.
   - Contact colleges to request any information you need.

2. Review your insurance documents or contact your personnel office to determine if your son or daughter will continue to be covered under your insurance.
   - Will you pay an additional cost?
   - What if your student attends an out-of-state school?

3. Photocopy the Cost of Attendance worksheet at the end of this chapter, or create your own, and add it to your folders for each college.

4. Complete a Cost of Attendance worksheet for each prospective school you are considering.
   - Go step-by-step and refer to this chapter if you have questions.
   - Keep your notes and calculations for changes later on.

5. If necessary, calculate the inflation for each prospective school based on how long it will be before your student attends college.

6. Once your COA worksheets are completed, compare and review their results. If necessary, make adjustments based on your notes and calculations.

Cost of Attendance Worksheet

College: _____

Telephone: _____

Website: _____

Direct Costs:

Tuition $_____

Fees $_____

Books $_____

Supplies $_____

Indirect Costs:

Room $_____

Board $_____

Transportation $_____

Travel $_____

Computer Equipment $_____

Personal $_____

Medical and Dental $_____

Miscellaneous $_____

Total Cost of Attending This College:
(Total of above items) $_____

Inflation (if necessary):

Number of Years Before Student Attends College: _____

Inflation Factor (see chart in this chapter): _____

Cost of Attending This College: $_____

Multiplied by Inflation Factor: ×___

Cost of Attending This College in __ Years: $_____

CHAPTER FIVE

Making the Most of Your Money

By now, you should have a fairly good estimate of how much college is going to cost. While knowing this is better than closing your eyes and hoping everything will work out, you still have to find a way to come up with enough money for it.

To help you, this chapter and the ones that follow look at ways that you—and possibly the federal government, your state, the college, and private agencies—can pay for your student's education. There's no one-answer-fits-all solution, so while everything we'll look at can be of help to families, some of them may not be right for your situation.

In the last chapter we discussed the difference between a student who is going to college in the near future and a student who has a few years before starting. This difference is also going to impact which options are best suited for you and your son or daughter.

College is a life-changing expense, similar to buying a house, getting your first car, or starting your own business. And just as each of those situations require forward thinking and preparation, so does planning for college. Ernie Shepelsky, vice president of enrollment services at Vaughn College of Aeronautics and Technology, says that in a perfect world, parents would start thinking about college and college costs around the time of the first ultrasound! Of course, life isn't perfect, and unless you're incredibly rich, there seldom seems to be enough money to go around. We've all heard that you should have started saving early for your child's education, but rather than focus on the past, let's look at what can be done now.

The College Payoff

Investing in your son or daughter's college education will pay off by providing them with the opportunity for greater earning potential. According to the U.S. Census Bureau, workers with a bachelor's degree currently earn nearly twice as much (an average of $51,206 per year) compared to workers with only a high school degree ($27,915 per year — that's more than $1 million over the course of a lifetime. Even when you subtract the lost earnings while in college and the cost of attending college, that's still quite an impressive payoff for your student.

PLANNING IS ESSENTIAL

If you have a few years until your son or daughter starts college, take advantage of this time. As each year passes, the amount of money you'll be able to provide for your student's education becomes less and less. Just as people plan to have money for retirement, they should also plan to have money for college.

Comments Ellen Frishberg, director of student financial services at Johns Hopkins University, "[A] significant problem we see is lack of planning. For example, a wealthy attorney from New York came in and asked our office for help in planning to pay for college. 'How am I going to do this?' he said to me. Since we don't provide that kind of assistance, I referred him to his financial planner."

Where Will the Money Come From?

A recent Harris Interactive Poll found that while nearly 80 percent of the parents expected to pay for some or all of their child's college education, the majority of them had set little or no money aside to cover those costs.

By the way, it's a common misconception that if you save for college, you won't qualify for as much financial aid. Because you've already learned that financial aid is primarily based on the income you earn, not the amount of money you have, you should understand why this isn't true.* Student aid programs won't care if you have $300,000 in the bank or $300. Instead, they'll care if your family makes $45,000 or $145,000 each year. As far as they're concerned, what you do with your income is your choice.

Keep the cost of inflation in mind, and try to make sure that the money you're putting away at least matches the inflation factor you used in chapter 4. This shouldn't be hard, as you'll soon see.

USING SAVINGS TO PAY FOR COLLEGE

You may have heard the saying, "Make your money work for you, instead of working for your money." It means that if you invest or save your money, it makes more money for you. To calculate just how much you will have to put away in order to meet your student's college goals, look at the following table or use an online calculator, like the one at: *www.savingforcollege.com/college-savings-calculator.*

---

*FAFSA does take into consideration a small percentage of assets if you filed form 1040 (long form) and made over a certain amount, or if you filed 1040A. See chapter 9 for all the details.

MONTHLY INVESTMENT REQUIRED TO SAVE $10,000 FOR YOUR CHILD'S EDUCATION				
Investment Period	Monthly Contribution	Total Contributions	Interest Earned*	Total Saved
18 years	$ 32	$6,912	$3,187	$10,099
14 years	$ 45	$7,560	$2,552	$10,112
10 years	$ 68	$8,160	$1,853	$10,013
6 years	$124	$8,928	$1,144	$10,072
2 years	$401	$9,624	$378	$10,002

*Based on an interest rate of 4%

As the table shows, if you start saving when your student is born, you put away $32 every month after then, and you earned an average of 4 percent interest on your money, you'd have $10,000 (not counting any tax you might have paid on the interest) by the time your student is ready to start college. However, if you only began saving two years ago, you would need to sock away over $400 a month to end up with the same result. Obviously, you get more investment bang for your college savings buck the earlier you start. As The College Board says, "time is the best tool for creating wealth."

To save for college, or anything else, you first have to spend less than you make. For many of us, that is certainly easier said than done. Take a hard look not only at your discretionary expenses (clothing, entertainment, cable TV, etc.) but at your basic expenses (housing, transportation, food, utilities, taxes, etc.) as well. Figure out how much you are spending monthly in each of these categories. Can you find ways to cut back? Could you bring your lunch rather than buy it, check the consignment stores rather than purchasing new, take public transportation rather than your car, use the library instead of buying books, refinance your mortgage? Small cuts can add up to big savings over time.

Once you have identified money you can save for your student's education, the next thing you want to do is grow it. There are a number of ways you can do that, ranging from basic savings accounts to prepaid tuition plans. Each of these plans carries with it different risk levels and tax consequences. We'll describe those next, in our "Savings 101" section.

Savings Don't Reduce Aid

"Whatever you do, plan to save," advises Ellen Frishberg, director of student financial services at Johns Hopkins University. "There's this myth that people shouldn't save because they think it'll keep them from qualifying for financial aid. Yet the odds are, if they make enough money to save for college, they won't qualify anyway because of their income. If you have a significant income, you're not going to get much aid, so you need to save for college."

Savings 101

Traditional Savings Accounts

The most common way that people save is by putting their money in a bank account for use later. A minimal amount of interest is paid, and although you won't make much in savings, there is less risk involved than with investments. The interest you receive, though, is probably going to be taxed.

Stocks

Stocks are a way you can invest in companies, and when you buy a stock you actually own a tiny piece of that company. Hopefully, when you sell, your stock will be worth more (remember, though, that you will have to pay tax on the gain). But, there is a risk. It's doesn't always happen that way. And, when stocks go down, there goes part of your savings. Although they charge a fee, stockbrokers and financial advisers can work with you to pick stocks and other investments to suit your needs. Or you can buy and sell stocks online yourself, using a discount brokerage; for a list of some of these, see *www.fool.com/investing/brokers/index.aspx* or *www.tradewiser.com/brokers.html*.

Bonds

When you borrow money from the bank, it's called a loan. When companies or the government borrow money from people like you, it's called a bond. There are basically two types, government bonds and corporate bonds. In both cases, you loan money to the government or business, and they agree to pay you back in the future with interest. Government bonds can be bought from banks, and corporate bonds are available through stockbrokers.

All of us can remember getting government savings bonds as gifts when we were kids. While we probably didn't appreciate them then, we certainly could recognize their value when we cashed them in later. Now that you are planning for your own child's education, keep these savings bonds in mind. The interest earned on Series I bonds and EE bonds issued after 1989 can be tax free if used for educational purposes, but only if you meet these requirements: you bought the bonds when you were at least 24 years old, you registered the bonds in your name or your spouse's name, and your modified adjusted gross income (as of the 2008 tax year), is less than $82,100 if you're filing single or less than $130,650 if you are filing jointly. Unfortunately, bonds purchased for your child (or by your child) won't meet these requirements and the interest earned is taxable. To learn more, go to www.savingsbonds.gov.

> **How Everyone Else Is Saving**
>
> Parents who expect to pay some or all of their child's college expenses plan to use the following savings vehicles:
>
> - Traditional savings accounts (32%)
> - 529 college savings plans (28%)
> - Mutual funds (18%)
> - Stocks (17%)
> - CDs (13%)
>
> *Source: 2006 Harris Interactive Poll.*

Mutual Funds

The easiest way to understand mutual funds is to imagine that you want to buy a bunch of stocks but you only have enough money for one or two of them. That's where mutual funds come in. They are bought and sold like stocks, but instead of investing in one company, you are investing in several similar companies at once. These companies may all be in the same business, they may be the same size, or share other traits in common. Mutual funds can also represent the entire stock market, and these are called "index funds." A fund manager is paid by investors in the mutual fund to select stocks to buy and sell, and it's their responsibility to make sure the index fund makes money.

"If a family plans to use some of their investments to pay for college," advises parent Clark Ray, "I'd suggest moving that money into a good U.S. index fund three or four years before they'll need it. It's a good way to stay in the market and still be conservative. At that point, you should be looking to preserve what you've got invested, not trying to beat the market."

CDs

We're not talking about silver disks that play music here, but Certificates of Deposit (hence the abbreviation "CD") usually offered by banks. When you get a CD, you give the bank money, which they agree to return to you on a set date in the future (called a "maturity date"), with interest. CDs, like savings accounts, are not investments, yet the two differ in one important way. When you have a savings account, you can take the money out of the bank whenever you need it. With a CD, you agree to leave the money in the bank until the maturity date and, if it turns out that you do have to withdraw funds before then, you agree to lose some of your interest as a "penalty." Check what the penalty for early withdrawal would be before committing to any CD. After all, you never know what could happen in the future. . . .

CDs are offered for anywhere from a few months to a few years. The longer the CD, the more you'll make in interest (but keep in mind that the interest is usually taxable).

Treasury Notes

Often called "T-bills" or "treasuries," treasury notes are a way of investing money with the U.S. government. Treasury notes mature anywhere between two and ten years; while shorter treasury bills mature in under a year. One advantage of treasuries is that they're exempt from both state and local taxes. But like CDs, if you need the funds back before they mature, you can expect to lose money.

529 Savings Plans

In 1997, Section 529 plans were created for the sole purpose of giving families at any income level a way to save for college. All 50 states offer at least one of these plans, and contributions to a 529 savings plan are made with after-tax dollars. Since 2002, earnings on these plans have been granted federal tax exemption when used to pay for qualified higher education expenses. This means that earnings are no longer just tax-deferred, but tax free, and when the plan makes a distribution to pay for the beneficiary's college costs, the distribution is currently free from federal taxes as well.

With a 529 savings plan, families invest money as they would through other investment plans, but unlike a brokerage account or mutual fund, these state-supported plans remain tax free as long as their funds are used for such required college expenses as tuition, room, board, books, and fees at an accredited college or university in the United States. Most plans are administered through an outside firm.

Section 529 savings plans often offer several investment options. Because you can invest in a plan in any state (not just your own) and because some states welcome out-of-state investors, you should shop around. But be sure not to overlook your own state, because it may offer better tax advantages to its residents than the out-of-state plans. Most plans permit lump-sum contributions of over $100,000 (unlike other tax breaks, high earners are not excluded; benefits are available to all taxpayers) and you are allowed to contribute up to $300,000 per beneficiary or possibly more, depending on the state. In addition, 529 plans can now be transferred to a close relative as a beneficiary, meaning that if your child chooses not to go to college, the money can go to someone outside the immediate family (until this change, 529 plan beneficiaries could only be transferred to a sibling). In a 529 savings plan, the parent remains in control of the account and decides when withdrawals are made. Most plans allow funds to be withdrawn for noncollege purposes, although you would then be responsible for federal income tax, a 10 percent penalty tax, and any state penalties that may apply.

Your 529 savings account is treated as an asset in determining eligibility for federal financial aid. This means that your expected contribution (see chapters 7, 8, and 9) to the cost of college will include 5.6 percent of the value of your account. Compared to the 20 percent assessment made against assets in your student's name or a custodial account, this is quite a deal! Here's another plus: when you take a distribution from the plan to pay for your beneficiary's education in one tuition year, it will not reduce the student's financial aid eligibility in the next year (that's because those distributions are not considered to be part of your base-year income).

While this sounds great, we should inject a note of caution: 529 plans are investments, and investments mean risk. Consequently, if the stock market tumbles, your 529 plan could take a hit, too.

Another disadvantage is the possible confusion associated with these plans. Because of the many choices available to parents and investors, understanding and selecting the best 529 plan isn't easy and there's lots of room for mistakes. That's why these plans work best when incorporated into your overall financial planning. For example, 529 plans affect tax planning by changing how investors treat earnings and withdrawals from accounts. These plans can also affect estate planning for everyone involved. Situations differ from state to state, so be sure you're informed before you select a 529 plan for your student.

Because you can participate in any number of 529 savings plans—in your state or outside—it is sometimes difficult to choose among them. Here are some questions to think about as you review the various plans:

- What fees (transfer fees, commissions, maintenance fees) are involved and what is the expense ratio for each plan (look for plans with expense ratios under 1.5 percent per year)?
- How easy is it to change the account's beneficiary (just in case your student decides not to go to college)?
- What tax or other benefits will you get with each plan?
- What investment options are offered by each plan?
- What's the least and the most your can contribute to the plans? When can those contributions be made?

529 Prepaid Tuition Plans

There are actually two types of 529 plans: savings plans (discussed above) and prepaid tuition plans. Both of these plans are state-operated and offer a way, federal tax free, to save money for college. Every state has at least one of these options, and some states have both. But, while the 529 savings plan option lets parents use the funds at any college, the 529 prepaid tuition plan is different. With the 529 tuition plan, families prepay all or part of the future costs of an in-state public college education. Generally, you are required to establish this type of plan before your student becomes a high school freshman. The way the plan works is that you buy tuition credits for certain colleges at current prices. This means that if you buy five credits through a plan, it doesn't matter how much they cost when your son or daughter actually attends college, because you'll have already paid for them. The state agrees to pay the difference, as long as your son or daughter attends an in-state public college. States offering prepaid tuition contracts covering in-state tuition will also often allow you to transfer the value of your contract to private or out-of-state schools (although you may not get full value, depending on the particular state). Tax law now allows colleges to offer their own 529 prepaid programs, a development that permits families (from any state and at any income level) to target their financing to a specific school or group of schools.

> **529 Links**
> Two of the best websites to learn about 529 plans are *www.savingforcollege.com* and *www.collegesavings.org*. These sites also provide links to state-supported websites for 529 plans.

Prepaid tuition lets you lock in the cost to attend certain colleges, but if your account earns more than the rate of inflation or the cost of attending your colleges, you don't come out ahead. In contrast, in a 529 savings plan, you benefit when your investments earn more than the rate of inflation. However, if the cost of college continues to rise as dramatically as it has been, above the rate of earnings for most investments, a prepaid tuition plan holder is a big winner.

While prepaid plans (either from a state or a specific college) are low-risk and possibly high-return investments, there are some downsides. Not every state, or even college, offers this plan. The plan locks you into a particular school, or set of schools, or schools in a specific state, and when your student is ready for college, he or she may not want to go there. Finally, most of these plans only cover tuition; you still will have to look for money to pay for other college-related costs.

Coverdell Education Savings Accounts (ESA)

Instead of, or in addition to, 529 plans, you can set up an Educational Savings Account (ESA).This type of savings account (which was formerly known as an Education IRA) is specifically designed to help parents plan for college. ESAs allow contributions (not tax deductible) of up to $2,000 each year per student, and withdrawals for qualified educational expenses are federal tax free. Your account grows federal income tax free, and annual investments are allowed until a college-bound beneficiary turns 18. But, unlike the 529 savings plans, there are income restrictions in making contributions to an ESA. Currently, you can make a full contribution to this type of account only if you do not make more than $100,000 for a single tax filer or $200,000 for married couples filing jointly.

Contributions aren't deductible, but there are no tax penalties on earnings or withdrawals. Even better news: you can now take tax-free withdrawals to cover your student's grade school to high school (K–12) costs. Eligible expenses include private school tuition, room and board, and even transportation. Public school students can use withdrawals for books, tutoring, computer equipment and software, and even Internet fees.

This is an investment, because parents decide how the money in their account will be invested and how much risk they will assume. You may want to consult a finance professional to help you determine the best way to establish an ESA, because there are a number of variables that could impact your student's financial aid package. For example, as with 529 savings plans, ESAs are considered assets of the account owner. If the owner is the student, it could reduce financial aid eligibility, but there are exceptions. If the owner is a parent, however, the impact on financial aid eligibility is less, in part because qualified distributions are not counted as income on the FAFSA. You should also be aware that coordinating ESA withdrawals with other tax benefits can be challenging.

Individual Retirement Accounts (IRA)

If you have an IRA, it might be tempting to tap into that pool of money to pay for your student's education. You won't even have to pay the usual 10 percent penalty for early withdrawal (before age 59 1/2), because the federal government waives that as long as the money is going to be used for and does not exceed the amount spent on eligible college expenses. But, before you make that withdrawal, think about this: you'll probably have to pay tax on the money you take out of a traditional IRA (with a Roth IRA, you won't). Even with a Roth IRA, you'll have to pay tax on the earnings portion after it's withdrawn. More importantly, you've reduce the amount of money that will be available to you in retirement. It's best to consider tapping into your IRAs only after you've exhausted all the other options available.

Custodial Accounts

If at this point you expect to pay for college yourself or you think your income is too high to receive federal or college student aid, you might consider establishing a custodial account for your student. These accounts are set up for a minor (under the age of 18 or 21), managed by an adult, and taxed at the minor's lower income tax bracket. They are usually opened at a bank, brokerage firm, or mutual fund. There are two basic types: 1) the Uniform Gifts to Minors Act (UGMA) account, which permits any adult to place up to $13,000 a year in the account without incurring a gift tax and 2) the Uniform Transfers to Minors Act (UTMA) account, which is similar to the UGMA but allows an adult to control the account for a longer period of time.

As tempting as it might be, from a tax point of view, to move money out of your name and set up a custodial account for your student, you should think carefully before you do so. Keep in mind that when it comes to financial aid, students are expected to contribute about 35 percent of their assets (including money in accounts like these) toward the cost of education, whereas parents need only put up 5.6 percent of their savings. Beware of unintended consequences. If you do decide later to apply for student aid, you may find that the amount of tax savings over the years from the custodial account does not make up for what was lost in your student's aid award.

USING PRESENT INCOME TO PAY FOR COLLEGE

Up until now, we have focused on "past" income—money that you put away earlier that you can use for college. Now, let's take a look at your present income: money you're earning now. Depending upon your financial situation, this may be coming from more than one source.

Wages

The most common source of income, wages are the money you make from your job. Your employer pays your wages by paycheck. For most people, this is their major, if not only, source of present income.

If you have a few years before your student goes off to college, and you live near a college, you may want to investigate job opportunities there. Bill Sliwa, vice president for enrollment management at Lees-McRae College in North Carolina points out that "many colleges participate in tuition exchange programs that offer scholarships or free tuition to the children of faculty and staff members of other participating institutions. If a parent has a particular skill set that could be used at a local college that participates in a tuition exchange, getting a job at that school could save tens of thousands of dollars in tuition."

There are a wide variety of jobs available at colleges. A marketing professional might be able to get a job in a college's fund development, communications, or marketing departments. Someone with a finance background could look into the accounting or financial aid departments. A tech expert might find a position in a college's IT department. Alternatively, depending on your skill level, maybe a better fit would be to join the faculty as an adjunct, teaching one class a semester (these positions usually require an advanced degree).

Regardless of your particular skill, it could pay to consider pursuing a job at a college. The requirements of the programs, such as length of time you must be employed and type of aid you may qualify for, will vary from school, to school so be sure to look into all the details before committing to a new job!

You can get information about participating schools as well as program requirements and benefits for the major exchange programs online. Here is a list of some of the major coordinating agencies:

The Council of Independent Colleges, *www.cic.org/tep*

The Tuition Exchange, *www.tuitionexchange.org*

Catholic College Cooperative Tuition Exchange, *www.cccte.org*

Council for Christian Colleges & Universities, *www.cccu.org*

ROI

When you sell stocks or other investments and you make a profit, that amount is considered your return on investment (ROI). Parents who own stock sometimes sell some or all of their shares to help pay for their student's college. While stocks themselves reflect past income because they were bought in the past, the money someone gets when they sell investments is considered present income.

Dividends

Another source of present income can come from investment dividends. Some companies choose to pass along the money they make to people who own stock in the company (called "shareholders"). Not all companies pay dividends, but those that do send checks to their shareholders four times a year (unless the company did not make a profit). A set dividend is paid to each share of stock, so those who own more shares of stock in that company receive more dividends. Dividends can range from a few cents to dollars per share.

Other Income

Any other way you receive money on a regular basis would count as other income. Child support is an additional source of income for parents who receive it, as are payments from the military received by retired members of the armed forces. A family may rent out an apartment above their garage, or receive rent from people living in a second home they own. Anything that you claim on your taxes as additional income could be very helpful in affording college.

BORROWING TO PAY FOR COLLEGE

Student loans, credit cards, lines of credit, and mortgages are all examples of borrowing, or using future income for needs in the present. Getting a loan to afford college may seem risky, but unlike loans for some other purchases, it's actually a good idea. Loans are a way of deferring payment on something you're getting now, and if what you're getting is going to increase in value, like an education, then this is referred to as "good" debt. When you use loans to buy something that is going to decrease in value, such as most credit card purchases for things like clothes and electronics, it's referred to as "bad" debt.

Consider a home mortgage. When buying a house, you borrow from a lender to afford a costly house, and then agree to spread out repayments of this amount over a number of years. You pay interest, but often the value of the house increases beyond the interest you are paying. With college, it's a similar situation. College graduates will also pay interest on student loans, but they can expect their earnings to increase in the future far beyond the interest they are paying.

College loans are truly an investment in your student's future. We'll cover the educational loans available to you and your student in Chapter 6. But, for now, if you compare the difference in income between high school graduates and college graduates, you'll see why student loans aren't only "good" debt—they're the best debt you can have.

AVERAGE STARTING SALARIES BY MAJOR	
Accounting	$48,334
Business administration	$47,641
Computer science	$58,419
Chemical engineering	$65,486
Civil engineers	$50,785
Construction science/management	$52.837
Economics/finance	$49,794
Electrical engineering	$57,404
Liberal arts	$36,445
Logistics/materials management	$49,398
Mechanical engineering	$58,648
Nursing	$46,655

Source: National Association of Colleges and Employers Winter 2009 Salary Survey.

MOVING ON

We began this chapter by explaining how planning for your student's education is just as important as planning for retirement. We then learned about the three different types of income—past, present, and future—and about several sources for each of these incomes. We reviewed the difference between "good" and "bad" debt, and learned why student loans are considered good debt to have.

In the next chapter, we'll look at the role financial aid will play in your student's education. You'll learn about the three basic types of aid and the various programs available, as well as your rights and responsibilities when applying for financial aid. Before you move on, take a look at the checklist for this chapter.

✔ **CHECKLIST:**

1. Decide if there are sources of income you can use to help pay for college. To get the best results, begin by looking at savings, then present income, then borrowing options.

2. Do you have savings or investments that could be used for college?

3. Do you receive dividends or other sources of current income that can be saved or invested for college?

4. Could you find a job at a college that participates in a tuition exchange program?

5. Review your household budget to look for ways you can set money aside for your student's college.

6. Depending on your student's age and income, consider if investments would help college expenses down the road. Stocks and bonds can help long term, while short-term CDs may provide a better return than a savings account.

7. Consider opening a separate account for your student's college fund, if you don't already have one. Doing so helps keep track of how much you have for these expenses. Look at 529 plans and education savings accounts to see if they are right for you.

8. Begin educating yourself about various types of student loans. You won't need to apply for them until you have completed the financial aid paperwork, but the more you learn now, the easier the process will be later.

CHAPTER SIX

Getting Your Share of Student Aid

Once you've reviewed your income and know how much you have available to contribute to your student's education, you're ready to begin looking at your financial aid options.

When you think of financial aid, you probably think first of funding from the federal government. That's not surprising. The lion's share of student aid (nearly $70 billion each year) comes from your Uncle Sam. But, another $23 billion comes from the colleges themselves, $7 billion from the states, and over $7.5 billion from private and employer aid.

Before addressing how you can get your share of this funding, it's helpful to have an understanding of the types of aid available, as well as the differences among them. By understanding both the basics of financial aid and the programs out there, you and your son or daughter will be able to find assistance that best suits your needs and budget.

CATEGORIES OF FINANCIAL AID

There are two primary categories of financial assistance: need-based aid and merit-based aid.

Need-Based Aid

As the term suggests, need-based aid looks at a family's financial resources to determine how much money the student needs to attend college. Examples are government-supported student loans and grants offered to low-income families and private scholarships awarded to students on the basis of documented financial need.

Financial aid offices at colleges and universities look at your income and financial situation to determine how much you should be able to contribute to your student's education (your expected family contribution, or EFC). This involves a mathematical calculation referred to as need analysis. This need analysis will be done by both the federal government and the financial aid offices at each school to which your student is applying. Usually, the government calculates its need analysis for your student, and then informs each of your potential colleges of its decision. This, in turn, may influence the need analysis calculated by those schools. For those of you who are interested, we'll look at this calculation in depth in chapter 9. For now, though, you just need to be aware that this process exists.

"Every parent should ask prospective schools if they meet students' full financial need, and what formula they use to determine need," says Ellen Frishberg, director of student financial services at Johns Hopkins University. "Schools can use liberal calculations to determine need, but those results are useless if they don't have the money to back them up."

Merit-Based Aid

Merit-based financial aid is not based on financial need but on a student's personal characteristics (achievements, abilities, contributions, potential, etc.) and is awarded regardless of the recipient's financial status. For example, athletic scholarships are merit-based aid, as are grants awarded to top academic students for their grades. Merit-based aid, also commonly referred to as "no-need" funding, is usually awarded by colleges, organizations, or businesses and corporations.

The factors involved in awarding merit-based aid depend upon the school itself, as well as the type of aid given. If an academic scholarship pays for the tuition of a student who majors in biology and is a minority, qualifying students must not only have good grades, but obviously major in biology and be a minority. Not all merit-based aid is so narrow in scope. Corporations may offer scholarships to students based solely on GPA, or a local organization may provide a grant to an exceptional student in the area. Scholarships and grants are also available based upon artistic talents and other abilities beyond academics and athletics.

Because of the nature of merit-based aid, colleges use these types of assistance to remain competitive with other schools. For example, a well-known state school with a good academic reputation may try to compete with Ivy League schools for top students. In this situation, the public school may offer to give a top student a free education in hopes of luring the student away from an Ivy League school. Likewise, schools that are trying to become more diverse may award scholarships to minorities or persons with disabilities in hopes of creating a more diverse student body.

Although this book focuses primarily on need-based aid, you and your son and daughter should actively look for merit-based aid regardless of academic grades, SAT scores, or your financial situation. You should ask prospective schools about merit-based aid, as well as your employer, local businesses, and organizations to which you belong. You'll find more information about this in chapter 12.

It's also important to note that some financial aid can be a combination of both need- and merit-based aid. For example, a college may offer a scholarship to a student with high grades and an excellent GPA, but may also require the recipient to come from a low-income household.

Non-Need-Based/Non-Merit-Based Aid

The good news is that it exists. The bad news is that it is primarily granted in the form of loans. This unrestricted aid is offered without any special stipulation regarding achievement or potential and is granted irrespective of the family's financial status. Unsubsidized Stafford loans (we'll talk more about them later in this chapter) are not need or merit based, so any student is eligible for them. Similarly, any parent is eligible to apply for Parent Loans for Undergraduate Students (PLUS loans); good credit is more important than any other factor—but more on that later.

> **Limits on Merit-Based Aid**
>
> Bill Sliwa from Lees-McRae College cautions parents and students against relying on merit-based scholarships. "Many schools are cutting back on the number or merit scholarships that they offer. Some are eliminating them completely. Hamilton College, for example, announced that it ended merit scholarships for students entering in 2008. They are putting the money toward need-based scholarships instead."

THE THREE TYPES OF AID

While need- and merit-based aid define the two categories of assistance, there are three basic types of financial aid that can be offered in each of those categories: grants and scholarships (gift aid), loans (self-help aid), and work-study programs (work aid).

Grants, Scholarships, and Tuition Discounts (Gift Aid)

Any financial aid that does not need to be repaid is, by definition, gift aid. Grants, scholarships, and tuition discounts are examples of financial gifts that do not need to be given back or returned at a later date. Some gift aid is given to students one time only, while others are renewed each year.

Loans (Self-Help Aid)

Financial aid that must be repaid to a lender is considered self-help aid. The vast majority of this type of aid consists of loans borrowed by either a student or parent.

Work-Study Programs (Work Aid)

Often called work-study, work aid is money earned by the student to help afford college. Most colleges offer work-study programs, where students work on campus parttime (generally 10 to 15 hours per week during the semester). Depending upon the school or program, students may receive paychecks, or the money may be subtracted from their tuition and fees. The money will only be subtracted from tuition and fees if you and your student opt to sign your student's paychecks over to the college. The exact process for this option varies from school to school, so be sure to find out the details from the financial aid office if you plan to use a work-study program to cover a portion of your student's tuition. If your student receives a paycheck from a work-study job, you may want to consider that his or her spending money for each week.

Aid Is More than Just Loans

"There's a myth that student aid just means loans," offers Jack Toney, director of financial aid at Marshall University in West Virginia. "People think loans are the only thing available to them, and it often discourages them from getting involved."

Not surprisingly, there are pros and cons to each of these types of aid. Gift aid is obviously the most desired type of financial aid, but scholarships and grants may require a student to maintain a certain grade point average, attend a particular college, or major in a particular discipline. Self-help aid, unlike gifts and work aid, has to be repaid at a later date. And while helpful, work aid requires participating students to add the additional responsibility of part-time work to their schedule, which may prove difficult.

Most families need to use a combination of these three types of aid to be able to afford college, although loans and self-help aid are increasingly making up the majority of financial aid offered to students. Work aid can greatly help disciplined students, but it can also create additional stress for students who must maintain a high GPA to keep their scholarship. Academic scholarships are extremely helpful, but some, like athletic scholarships, require a major time commitment. Once your son or daughter is offered these various types of financial aid, the two of you will be able to decide which are best to use.

FINANCIAL AID PROGRAMS

"Financial aid programs at public and private colleges aren't all that different," says Karen Krause, who has worked in financial aid offices at both public and private schools. "Sometimes funding sources are different, especially in the area of grants, but that's the major difference."

In order to find the best financial aid options for you and your son or daughter, you will need to understand the different types available and which you qualify for. To help, the following chart lists the major need-based and merit-based programs offered. In a moment, we'll look at each of these programs in more depth.

NON-NEED OR MERIT-BASED AID	NEED-BASED AID
Federal Aid	**Federal Aid**
	Federal Pell grant
	Federal academic competitiveness grant
	National SMART grant
	Federal SEO grant (FSEOG)
Student employment program	Federal work study
	Federal Perkins loan
Unsubsidized federal Stafford loan	Subsidized federal Stafford loan
Federal parent PLUS loan	Federal parent PLUS loan
Unsubsidized federal direct student loan	Federal direct student loan
State Aid*	**State Aid***
State grant program	State grant program
State loan program	State loan program
State scholarships	State scholarships
Institutional Aid	**Institutional Aid**
Academic incentive awards	Need-based grants
Merit-based scholarships	Tuition discounts/waivers
Combination merit & need-based awards	Combination merit & need-based awards
Other	**Other**
Private scholarships	Private scholarships
Private loans	Private loans

*Since state aid programs vary from state to state, not all options may be available in your state. You'll need to contact the agencies in your state to determine what is available to you. See chapter 11 for a listing of state aid agencies.

You'll notice that every option listed in the chart is a grant or scholarship (gift aid), a loan (self-help aid), or a work study program (work aid). In order to better understand the options within each of these three types of aid, let's look at each type separately.

Grants, Scholarships, and Tuition Discounts (Gift-Aid Programs)

When it comes to grants and scholarships, there are three basic types of gift aid programs.

Institutional Grants and Scholarships

Institutional aid is the term used to describe money offered to students from a school's own funds. The criteria and policies for these types of awards vary from college to college, but if your student is eligible for federal financial aid, these institutional funds are linked to the federal financial aid he or she will receive. These institutional awards may require additional application forms, which must be turned in by a set deadline, often with the student's application to attend the school. The majority of institutional aid is awarded to full-time students.

> **Tuition Discounting**
>
> In its latest report on tuition discounting, the College Board reported that public four-year colleges discounted their tuition an average of 14.7 percent and private four-year colleges discounted theirs an average of 33.5 percent. To read the report in its entirety, go to: *professionals. collegeboard.com/data-reports-research/trends/tuition-discounting*.

While academic record isn't the only selection criterion considered, it's always a plus to have a strong GPA or standardized test scores. "Good academics are essential to getting scholarships," Samuel Ellison of Morehouse College comments. "To be considered for our academic scholarships, a student needs a minimum GPA of 3.5."

An increasingly popular form of gift aid, tuition discounting, began to soar about a decade ago. Typically offered to recruit the brightest students, high SAT scores or a solid GPA can lead to thousands of dollars off the price of tuition. Athletic ability can also. But, check with the colleges your student is considering. You may be surprised at the other types of discounts offered. For example, Mercy College of Health Sciences recently announced a discount plan to assist unemployed workers interested in a health career, Canisius College gives discounts to undergraduate students from Canada, and Kaplan University in Davenport, Iowa, provides a 53 percent discount for active-duty military personnel. For more on these "alternatives" to financial aid, see chapter 13.

Government Grants

State Grants.   Every state offers grants and scholarships, and to be eligible for these awards, a student usually must be a resident of the state. Most state grants also require the student go to school in-state, as well, although a handful do not. While the bulk of state grants are geared toward need-based students, some are merit based and awarded regardless of financial need or a family's income. To learn more about gift aid offered by your state, you'll need to check with your state's higher education agency. You'll find complete contact information in chapter 11.

Federal Pell Grant. The largest grant program offered by the federal government, Pell grants, like the other federal grants, are need based. The amount of aid a student receives is based upon his or her need analysis and whether the student will attend college full or part time; generally the awards range from zero to $5,350. Other student aid received will not reduce a student's award amount. You do not apply for these grants. When you file your financial aid forms with the federal government, your student will be automatically considered for a Pell grant. When your student receives the awards packages from the colleges, you'll find out if your student qualified for the grant or not. Millions of students from low-income families receive Pell grants each year, but the vast majority of middle-income families do not qualify for this aid, because awards are related to EFC.

Academic Competitiveness Grant (ACG). This federal grant was first introduced for the 2006–07 academic year and it awards up to $750 for the first year of undergraduate study and up to $1,300 for the second year (but the amount of the ACG when combined with a Pell grant cannot exceed the actual cost of attendance). To be eligible for this grant, students must be U.S. citizens, enrolled in college at least half time, and eligible for a federal Pell grant. Most important, students must have completed a rigorous high school program. Each state has a program that is recognized by secretary of education and the details of these programs are available on *www.studentaid.ed.gov.*

National SMART Grant. The National SMART (Science and Mathematics Access to Retain Talent) grant provides up to $4,000 for each of the third and fourth years of undergraduate study for students with at least a 3.0 GPA who are majoring in physical, life, or computer sciences; math; technology engineering; or a foreign language that is critical to national security. As with the Academic Competitive grant, students must be enrolled at least half time, U.S. citizens, and eligible for the federal Pell grant.

Federal Supplemental Educational Opportunity Grant (FSEOG). The FSEOG is a federal grant awarded by colleges (so it's called a campus-based program) to the neediest students who will be attending the school. Because of this, FSEOGs are often given to Pell grant recipients. The award amounts range from $100 to $4,000 per year. Note: not all schools participate in the FSEOG program. But, if your school does, be sure to apply early. Only a certain amount of money is allocated to each school and it is disbursed on a first-come first-served basis. When the money is gone, it's gone. So, not everyone who qualifies will end up receiving the grant.

Other Federal Grants. The federal government awards a handful of merit-based grants and scholarships each year. The majority of these awards are specific to a field or major, such as science or nursing, or to honors students. Some are designed to be given to graduate students. Although these grants are funded by the federal government, they are awarded by state scholarship agencies or require students to apply to the federal government separately for them.

Private Grants and Scholarships

Many corporations and organizations offer financial aid to students all over the country, and this type of gift aid exists outside the governmental and institutional types of aid offered. For example, high schools may offer small grants to exceptional seniors, corporations may offer scholarships to children of employees, minority groups may offer assistance to minority students, or college alumni associations may offer grants to exceptional students attending their university. There are many kinds of aid offered by private organizations and corporations, so don't assume it's not worth the effort—some are need based, some are merit based, and some are a combination of both. These types of aid require a bit of legwork and research, but are worth the time and energy. We'll give you tips on how to search for these scholarships in chapter 12.

"The ideal time to start looking for these kinds of grants and scholarships is early in the student's junior year," says Jack Toney, director of financial aid at Marshall University. "The students won't be able to apply then, but they'll learn which scholarships they're interested in, and when the deadline is for the following year when they'll apply."

Make sure you and your student remain realistic when applying. "Lots of people oversell themselves in this area," says Barry Simmons, director of financial aid at Virginia Tech. "Many believe that a solid B student is going to receive a significant amount of scholarships. Some scholarships can be competitive," he acknowledges, "and parents need to be realistic about competition for them."

Loans (Self-Help)

When it comes to federal self-help programs for college, there are three major loans available: Perkins loans, Stafford loans, and PLUS loans. But, before we discuss each of these loans and their specific requirements, we want to review some basic terms and ideas behind those loans.

Loans 101

Interest Rate. Just as banks pay interest when you put money into a savings account or CD, you have to pay lenders interest when you borrow money from them. Interest on loans can be a fixed rate or a variable rate. A fixed rate means that you pay the same percentage of interest throughout the length of your loan. A variable rate means that the amount of interest you pay will change at certain times during the length of the loan. A fixed rate gives you the security of knowing exactly how much you'll have to pay each month, but if the interest rate drops in a few years, you'll be paying higher than that reduced amount. With a variable rate, there is some uncertainty regarding just how much your interest will be, but when interest rates drop, so will the amount of interest you'll pay (of course, if it goes up, your payments will, too).

Repayment Terms. This refers to how long you will be required to pay back the loan, as well as when you will be expected to start making payments. Just as car loans can be five or seven years long, repayment on student loans can be anywhere from 10 to 30 years. In addition, some student loans may release the student or parent from making any payments until the student graduates from college, while others may require that repayment start while the student is still attending school. The terms of repayment, along with the interest rate, are the two most important things you should know when considering a loan, because they will impact how much you will pay each month and over the life of the loan.

Fees. You've learned that colleges charge fees in addition to tuition, room, and board. So do banks and lenders. These can include administration fees, application fees, and other kinds of charges. These fees are not included in the amount you borrow, but are subtracted from the amount you actually receive. This means that the more a lender charges in fees, the less you actually get to use for college. Because of this, families often borrow more than the actual amount they need, so that there will be enough to pay for school once fees are taken out. Before applying for any loan, make sure you ask about any fees associated with the loan so you won't be surprised later.

Net versus Gross. Gross refers to the total amount you are requesting when applying for a loan, while net refers to the amount you will actually receive after fees are taken out. If you ask for a $10,000 gross loan, and the bank lending you the money charges $850 in fees, your net (the money you get) would be $9,150.

Monthly Payment. Your monthly payment simply means the amount you will owe the lender each month. Educational lenders will often offer examples of various pay-back times or other options, to help you estimate what you will have to pay each month.

Forbearance. Sometimes, because of personal problems (like unemployment or hospitalization) a borrower needs to stop paying on a loan temporarily or needs to have the amount of the loan payments reduced. When the lender agrees to these changes, this is referred to as forbearance. During the forbearance period, interest owed on the loan continues to accrue and must be paid later.

Don't Even Think about Defaulting

If you or your student is having trouble paying on a loan, it is important to check with the lender to see if it is possible to postpone payment (deferment) or put loan payments on hold (forbearance). But one thing you don't want to do is fail to make your payments (default on the loan). If you do, your school, your government or private lender, and your loan guarantor (if there was one) can all take action against you. Here are some of the possible consequences of a default:

• Your credit can be negatively affected.

• You would not be eligible for other loans, if you decide to return to school.

• Loan payments can be deducted from your pay check.

• If your loan came from the state or federal government, your income tax refunds can be withheld.

• You will be charged for late fees and collection costs, in addition to the principal you owe.

• You might even be sued.

Deferment Options. Deferment means the borrower may postpone making payments on the loan during certain situations. For example, many educational lenders allow borrowers to defer monthly payments while a student is in college. Other options allow borrowers to make payments on their interest only, meaning the payment of principal (amount borrowed) is deferred. Deferment options vary from loan to loan, and you'll need to know what these are.

Prepayment Penalty. Some lenders charge a fee if the loan is repaid early, and this is called a prepayment penalty. Try to avoid loans with this penalty, because without it you and your student will have the option of paying the loan off early at no extra charge. If you can afford to pay the loan off early, try to do so. You'll save money, because you'll pay less interest.

Consolidation. This is simply combining several loans into one. If you and your student take out a loan for each year for college, you'll find yourself with several different loan payments due each month. By consolidating those loans, you'll then only have to make one payment. In addition, consolidating often reduces the amount you'll pay each month, because the final monthly payment you'll owe will probably be less than the separate checks you write otherwise. If you expect to take out loans each year, it may be a good idea to try and use the same lender for each loan, because that will make consolidation more convenient in the future.

To make consolidation easier, the federal government has created the Federal Consolidation Loan Program, which lets Federal Stafford and Federal Perkins loans be consolidated under one lender and interest rate. It also offers extended repayments, although this will increase the interest you owe. For more information, go to *www.loanconsolidation.ed.gov*.

Federal Perkins Loans

Perkins loans are need-based loans offered to students who are or will be attending school at least half time. The interest rate charged is around 5 percent—the lowest of any educational loan program. This is a campus-based program; colleges have set funds designated for Perkins loans and select recipients to receive them. Interest on a Perkins loan does not accrue while the student is in college, and repayment doesn't begin until nine months after the student graduates. To be eligible for this program, students must have applied for a Pell grant. Undergraduate students can borrow up to $5,500 a year for up to five years, depending on eligibility. Other than interest, no other fees are charged for this loan (unless you incur late payment charges). Monthly payments can be as low as $30 and borrowers have up to 10 years to repay the loan.

Stafford Loans

The U.S. Department of Education administers the Federal Family Education Loan (FFEL) Program and the William D. Ford Federal Direct Loan (Direct Loan) Program, both commonly known as Stafford loans. The FFEL program is often referred to as the federal Stafford loan and the Direct Loan program is referred to as the Direct Stafford loan. Most colleges participate in one program or the other, some colleges participate in both. Each can be subsidized or unsubsidized and while they are quite similar, there are differences that you should be aware of.

Federal Stafford Loans (FFEL). The funds for this program will come from a bank, credit union, or other lender of your choosing. You can contact your student's college for a list of preferred lenders or look into your own lender. After your student graduates, the loan will be repaid to that lender.

Direct Stafford Loans (Direct Loan). For this program, the funds come directly from the federal government, provided by the U.S. Department of Education. If your student has this type of loan, he or she will make payments directly to the federal government.

Subsidized versus Unsubsidized Stafford Loans. Depending on eligibility, you will qualify for either a subsidized or an unsubsidized loan. Subsidized Stafford loans are need based and your student's college must certify his or her eligibility on the loan application, so you can expect to turn the bank's form over to your college for verification. Like the Perkins loan, interest does not accrue while your student is in school at least half time (it's paid by the U.S. Department of Education) and repayment begins six months after graduation. There are fees associated with subsidized Stafford loans, and the remaining balance is paid directly to your student's college. Unsubsidized Stafford loans are similar to subsidized Stafford loans except that they are not need based, so any student is eligible for them. In addition, interest accrues on these loans while the student is in college. As with the subsidized Stafford loans, there are fees associated with unsubsidized Stafford loans, and the remaining balance is paid directly to your student's college.

Loan Amounts. Because subsidized loans are awarded based on need, if you qualify for one you will be given a maximum that your student can borrow under the program. If that amount does not meet the following maximums listed, you can supplement it with an unsubsidized loan. If you only qualify for an unsubsidized loan, you may borrow up to the full maximum through that program.

For the 2009–10 academic year, dependent students can borrow up to the following maximums:

- $5,500 (no more than $3,500 of this can be in subsidized loans) for first-year students
- $6,500 (no more than $4,500 of this can be in subsidized loans) for second-year students
- $7,500 (no more than $5,500 of this can be in subsidized loans) for third- and fourth-year students

The interest charged for the subsidized Stafford is currently 6 percent and is expected to go as low as 3.4 percent by 2011. The interest rate charged for the unsubsidized Stafford is currently set at 6.8 percent. Stafford borrowers have between 10 and 25 years to repay their loans, depending upon the amount owed and the type of repayment plan selected. In addition, a fee of up to 2 percent is charged for each loan.

Federal PLUS Loan

Parent Loans for Undergraduate Students (PLUS) are federal loans for the parents of undergraduate students only. Like the Stafford loan, they may be borrowed either directly from the federal government (Direct PLUS loans) or through private lenders (FFEL PLUS loans). These are unsubsidized loans and they are not need based, so any parent is eligible (as long as they are deemed "creditworthy"). Repayment begins 60 days after the money is loaned, and parents can borrow up to the cost of the college (minus any financial aid), as long as their student is enrolled at least half time. Fees are charged, and because lenders check the parent's credit history, a cosigner may be required or the loan may be denied if there are credit problems. The current rate is 7.9 percent for Direct PLUS loans and 8.5 percent for FFEL PLUS loans. There is also a 4 percent fee charged, so be sure to borrow 4 percent more than you need to cover that.

State Loans

As with state grants, the types of state loans available vary from state to state, so you'll need to find out what is available. To learn about the loans offered by your state, check with your state's higher education agency. See Chapter 11 to get complete contact information.

Other Loans

While the federal and, to a lesser extent, state governments are the major sources of educational loans, there are a number of other ways that you and your student can borrow for college:

- get a personal loan
- take money out of your home, by refinancing or getting a home equity loan
- borrow funds from your retirement accounts
- take a loan from the cash value in your life insurance policy
- borrow from relatives or others that you know

Each of these options has its own unique set of advantages and disadvantages, so you'll want to think carefully before taking money from any of these.

Who Should Borrow: Parent or Student?

Many families wonder if student loans should be in the student's name or the parent's name. In reality, every family is different. Often, this burden is split between parent and student, although sometimes parents shoulder their student's entire loan debt and sometimes students have all their student loans in their name. Opinion regarding this is divided, with some parents insisting that their student pay as much of his or her education as possible, while others believe it's best to keep their student's debt at a minimum.

Regardless, student borrowing differs from other loans. When you are the one applying for a loan, lenders use your monthly income to estimate your loan payments. Students, on the other hand, must rely on estimates of their future income in order to indicate their potential to pay back a loan for college. Unfortunately, you can't predict your son or daughter's income after graduation, but you might be able to estimate his or her average salary based on entry-level incomes in that field.

> **Students Rather Than Parents Should Borrow**
>
> Finance expert Edmund Luzine, owner and founder of Adirondack Capital Management, Inc., states that "A college education is a vast investment in human capital that yields results (dividends) in the form of higher wages for a long period of time." As such, he recommends that parents place "most of the burden on the child, and provide the incentive to them to fund their own human capital investment. They will then learn how to manage their finances and payoff their debts (student and other loans) through the generation of cash flow (a job)."

LOAN REPAYMENT PROGRAMS

Although most students are not aware of this, there is a way to have their educational loans repaid for them after their graduate. To do this, they must accept jobs which offer loan repayment or loan forgiveness as part of their employment package. Most of the jobs that offer this benefit are in government agencies or professional organizations in the fields of education, law, health care, and military service. For example, the federal government's Teacher Loan Forgiveness Program repays the outstanding federal loans (up to $17,500) for teachers who are willing to work in eligible elementary or secondary schools.

"I always joke with my kids that the Marine Corps is always hiring," laughs Clark Ray, an officer with the Marines in West Point, New York. "When it comes to paying for their share of college, there's a lot of financial support in the armed forces. That's not for everyone, but there are other loan forgiveness programs out there that can also make a big difference."

> **Debt Forgiveness Information**
>
> Practically every state offers some type of loan forgiveness or loan repayment program. For links to each of these state programs, go to the Debt-Free College Guide at *debtfree.elearners.com*.

LOAN REPAYMENT PROGRAMS

Here is just sampling of the many loan repayment programs available:

- **Community Service**—Serve for 12 month in AmeriCorps and receive a living allowance and, at the end of your term of service, $4,725 to be used to repay qualified student loans. Call 1-800-942-2677 or go to *www.americorps.org.*

- **International Service**—Volunteers in the Peace Corps may apply for deferment of Stafford, Perkins, and Consolidation loans as well as partial cancellation of Perkins loans (15 percent for your first two years of service, 20 percent for your third and fourth years). Call the Peace Corps at 1-800-424-8580 or go to *www.peacecorps.gov.*

- **Military Service**—There are a number of loan repayment programs available to student who are willing to serve in the military. For example, the Air Force College Loan Repayment Program repays the federally-insured student loans of enlistees (one third of the loan or $1,500, whichever is greater, for each year of active-duty service) who sign up for 4 years of active duty. For more information, go to *www.usmilitary.about.com/cs/joiningup/a/clrp.htm.*

- **Teaching**—Students who become full-time teachers in an elementary or secondary school that serves students from low-income families can have a portion of their Perkins loan forgiven. The AFT maintains an excellent list of loan repayment programs for teachers. Go to *www.aft.org/tools4teachers/loan-forgiveness.htm.*

- **Legal Field**—There are 22 state loan repayment assistance programs for students who take jobs in legal aid offices after graduation from law school. The American Bar Association maintains a list of these. Go to *www.abanet.org/legalservices/sclaid/lrap/statelraps.html*

- **Health Care Workers**—Up to $50,000 in loan repayment funds are available to primary care physicians, primary care nurse practitioners, certified nurse-midwives, primary care physician assistants, dentists, dental hygienists, and behavioral and mental health providers if they are willing to work for two years within a designated Health Professional Shortage Area. This payment is tax free and made in a lump sum, so you will be able to pay down your loans fast. For more information, go to *nhsc.bhpr.hrsa.gov/applications/lrp.*

- **Public Sector Workers**—Under the Loan Forgiveness for Public Service Employees program, a borrower's remaining outstanding loan balance and accrued interest on an eligible Direct Loan can be eliminated if the borrower works full time in public service. To learn more, go to *studentaid.ed.gov/students/attachments/siteresources/LoanForgivenessv4.pdf.*

Work-Study Programs (Work Aid)

There are basically two types of part-time work aid programs available to college students: work-study programs supported by the federal government and work-study programs supported by the state government.

Federal Work-Study Program (FWS)

FWS provides jobs for students who have demonstrated financial need. Participants earn at least the federal minimum wage. However, the amount might be higher, depending upon the work assigned and the skills required. Most of the FWS jobs are on campus, with students often working in cafeterias, libraries, or campus offices. An attempt is made to provide work assignments related to the student's course of study. Most colleges will ask if your student wishes to be considered for work-study when you apply for financial aid, and positions are awarded based on your need analysis.

State Work-Study Programs

A small number of states offer work-study programs that are similar to the federal program, except that state programs are funded with state rather than federal funds. To learn if your state offers a work-study program, contact your state's higher education agency. Chapter 11 provides the information you'll need to do that.

> **Other Work Options**
> If your student is not eligible for a state or the federal work-study program, he or she can still seek part-time work while enrolled in college. Many colleges offer part-time jobs that are not part of a work-study program, and nearby businesses, especially those that cater to students, may be very interested in hiring students to supplement their workforce during the school year.

RIGHTS AND RESPONSIBILITIES

Now that you've learned about the numerous types of financial aid programs available to you and your student, you'll also need to know what your rights and responsibilities are when applying for financial aid. Refer to the following list as you begin the financial aid process.

Your Rights

You have the right to:

- Privacy—all records and data you submit with financial aid applications should be treated as confidential information
- Accept or decline any offer of financial aid
- Be notified before any financial aid is canceled, as well as the reason for the cancellation

You have the right to know:

- What financial aid is available from federal, state, and institutional resources
- Procedures and deadlines for submitting financial aid

- How financial aid recipients are selected
- How your financial aid eligibility is determined, including all resources considered, with this information made available to you by the financial aid office
- How and when your financial aid funds are going to be dispersed
- The full details of each financial aid award you receive
- The criteria used to determine satisfactory academic progress for keeping financial aid awards
- How to appeal a decision by the financial aid office concerning a financial aid award

For student loans, you have the right to know:

- The interest rate
- The total amount you must repay (including all charges and fees)
- When repayment begins
- The length of the repayment period
- The cancellation or deferment options
- The consequences of defaulting
- The available options for consolidating your loans

For work-study programs, you have the right to know:

- A description of the job
- The hours the student must work
- The rate of pay
- How and when the student will be paid

Your Responsibilities

You are responsible for:

- Reading and understanding all financial aid documents
- Filling out all applications completely
- Complying with any deadlines
- Keeping copies of any form you are required to sign
- Providing correct information on all financial aid applications and forms (misrepresentation can be considered a criminal offense)

- Providing documentation to support your application
- Repaying any student loans you receive
- Reporting any change in the student's enrollment, housing, or financial status (including scholarships or grants from outside sources), as well as changes in personal status (including address, name, and marital changes)
- Reporting any personal or enrollment changes to your lender
- Completing an entrance and exit interview if you receive a student loan
- Using financial aid funds for educational-related expenses only

MOVING ON

This chapter began by comparing need-based and merit-based kinds of financial aid. Building upon that, we discussed the three basic types of financial aid: gift aid, self-help aid, and work aid. We then reviewed how most families use a combination of these three types in order to afford college.

Next, we looked at the different financial aid programs, separating them by need-based and merit-based programs. We then examined the programs by breaking them down further into gift aid programs, self-help programs, and work aid programs. The section on gift aid programs covered various grants and scholarships, while the self-help section discussed the loans available to pay for college. Then, the work aid section examined ways students can reduce college expenses by working on campus.

Finally, the chapter provided a quick list of rights and responsibilities every parent and student should keep in mind when applying for financial aid.

In the next chapter, you'll learn how to navigate the financial aid process. We'll be discussing the applications, forms, and documents involved in applying for financial aid, as well as what you can expect once the paperwork is completed. Before you move on, take a look at the checklist for this chapter.

✓ CHECKLIST:

1. Have your student begin looking for merit-based financial aid opportunities.
   - Contact prospective universities to find out what they offer.
   - Check with your state's higher education office.
   - Ask your employer if they offer scholarships. Similarly, if your student has a part-time job, he or she should look into scholarship opportunities there.
   - If you belong to a union or a civic organization, find out if they offer a scholarship.
   - Contact local businesses and organizations to find out what they offer.
   - Use the Internet and your student's high school for assistance.

2. Begin learning about federal financial aid opportunities you may be interested in.
   - What programs do you qualify for?
   - Are you eligible for grants as well as loans?
   - What are the advantages and disadvantages of various loans?
   - How much can you borrow?
   - What are the program's deadlines for application?

3. Contact your state's higher education agency to find out what state grants and loans are available. Request paperwork or have your student apply online for any programs that look interesting.

4. Discuss work-study programs with your student.

5. Begin contacting lenders about various types of student loans. Be sure to compare interest rates and fees, as well as repayment terms and deferment options to find one that best suits your needs. Compare the differences in taking a loan out in your name versus your student's name.

CHAPTER SEVEN

Navigating the Process

There's no doubt that applying for financial aid can be an overwhelming and confusing process. But, now that you know what college will cost and the types of financial aid programs available, you'll find that applying for aid will be much easier than you thought.

The process of applying for financial aid can vary from school to school, although the same basic forms are used by almost every college and university. To start, we'll introduce you to the various forms, and then we'll take a look at each one individually.

FINANCIAL AID FORMS

There are essentially nine kinds of financial aid forms. They can be grouped into three basic categories (core forms, supplemental forms, and verification forms) with, coincidently, three separate forms in each of those categories.

Core Forms

Core forms are the mandatory forms that you and your son or daughter will need to fill out and file before doing anything else. Because they form the core of your financial aid applications, they're the first step in the financial aid process. These forms are the Free Application for Federal Student Aid (FAFSA), the College Scholarship Service (CSS) PROFILE Form, and the State Grant Application.

Free Application for Federal Student Aid (FAFSA)

The Free Application for Federal Student Aid (FAFSA) is the basic form required to apply for any federal financial aid. In previous chapters, you learned that the federal government uses your income tax information to determine how much aid your family qualifies for. The FAFSA form is what you use to provide that income tax information to the government. In turn, those numbers are used in the government's need analysis process to decide how much your EFC will be, as well as how much aid you can receive. When filing the FAFSA, your information can be forwarded to potential colleges, which will help in their financial aid process. A new FAFSA must be completed every year and is required by all colleges.

College Scholarship Service (CSS) PROFILE Form

The College Scholarship Service (CSS) is part of The College Board, a private educational organization best known for developing college entrance examination tests like the SAT, and the PROFILE form is a financial aid form required by hundreds of colleges, universities, and scholarship programs. It is designed to provide more complete and accurate information than the FAFSA, and because the CSS is not part of the federal government, this form is separate from your FAFSA information. The PROFILE form is most often used by private colleges, which have their own funds to award and need additional information in order to make their financial aid decisions.

State Grant Application

In chapter 6, you learned that some states offer grants and student loans supported by state funds. The FAFSA is used only for federal financial aid, so if you're interested in applying for any state-supported aid, you'll need to file the necessary forms to do so. You'll find contact information for your state agency in chapter 11.

Supplemental Forms

In addition to these essential core forms, you may also have to file some of the following supplemental forms, depending upon your financial status and family situation.

Institutional Aid Application

As we discussed in the previous chapter, institutional aid is financial aid offered by the college or university itself. Although colleges use the FAFSA and PROFILE forms in their need analysis of your family, some schools may require you to fill out their own institutional aid form. You will need to contact each prospective college to find out if they require an institutional aid application.

Not all will. "We don't have a separate application for institutional aid," explains Jade Kolb, manager of financial aid at New York University. "But everyone is considered for those awards."

Divorced/Separated Parents Form

The Divorced/Separated Parents form is a supplement to the CSS/PROFILE. If a student's parents or custodians are divorced or separated, the parent who does not have custody of the student will be required to fill out this form. The instructions for the PROFILE form explain the Divorced/Separated Parents form in more detail.

Business/Farm Supplemental Form

The Business/Farm Supplemental form is also a supplement to the CSS/PROFILE. Parents who are farmers or who own their own businesses will be required to fill out this form. The instructions for the PROFILE form will explain the Business/Farm Supplemental Form in more detail.

Tax Documents

You'll need to have your tax documents handy in order to fill out the core and supplemental forms. Since these forms often refer to specific line items on your income tax forms, such as your 1040, you'll need to be able to look that information up as you complete your applications. If you have your completed tax forms handy as you fill out the FAFSA and PROFILE, you'll probably be able to simply copy numbers from one form to the other.

Parent's Federal Tax and W-2 Forms

Naturally, you'll need your federal tax forms for the previous year, as well as any W-2 forms provided by your employer. If you're filing the FAFSA and PROFILE forms in a timely manner, you'll probably have already pulled these tax-related materials together.

Student's Federal Tax and W-2 Forms

If your student filed an income tax return for the previous year, you will need his or her income tax forms and W-2s as well.

Other Forms

Depending upon your financial situation and income tax filing, you may need to refer to other tax documents for verification. For example, 1099 forms used to represent interest on savings accounts or dividends received from stocks will have information you'll need to list on your financial aid applications. In most cases, any additional or supplemental forms you filed with your income tax will also be needed as you fill out the FAFSA and PROFILE forms.

> **Tax Reality 101**
>
> "One of the best ways a student can learn how to become responsible for their own money and job is for them to do their own income tax," says parent Karon Ray. "It's a real eye-opener."

Just as your income tax must be filed by April 15 every year, these financial aid forms have deadlines and timetables as well. Many students and parents assume that the financial aid deadlines for these forms are the same as the deadlines for applying to attend the college, but that's not the case. Financial aid applications are based on the academic calendar, which starts when college begins in either August or September and ends when college lets out for the summer in May or June of the next year, rather than a calendar year of January to December. Because of this, you'll find yourself filing for financial aid in the fall before your student starts college (for the PROFILE), or early in the year that they will start college (for the FAFSA).

If you will need to fill out the CSS PROFILE form, this can be completed first. Because your student will be applying to colleges in the fall before they graduate from high school, the PROFILE form should be filled out and filed at the same time they are completing their college applications. Most students and parents start the PROFILE form after October of their student's senior year.

"We filled out the PROFILE first," says Joe Sanseverino, whose daughter recently applied to state and private schools that required the CSS PROFILE. "The PROFILE didn't rely on your tax information, so we could get it out of the way earlier. Besides, after doing that, the FAFSA was a breeze."

The FAFSA form should be completed early the next year, ideally as soon as possible after January 1. You'll need to find out what your college's deadlines are for these forms and attempt to finish the process as soon as possible. Although many families don't realize it, most financial aid is awarded on a first-come, first-served basis, so the sooner you and your student apply for financial aid the more financial aid he or she is eligible for.

"Not meeting deadlines for filing is the biggest concern at most colleges," insists Jack Toney, director of financial aid at Marshall University in West Virginia. "Many families wait so long to file the FAFSA that they don't file the school's financial aid form in time. When that happens, students lose out on aid they could have been eligible for."

THE PROCESS

Now that you understand the types of financial aid applications and how they work, it's time to look at the process itself. To make things easier, we'll go over how to apply for financial aid, step-by-step, in the order you should follow.

Selecting Schools for Application

The first step in applying for any financial aid is to know which schools your student is applying to. This certainly doesn't mean that your son or daughter must have selected a college, but any school that you and your student are seriously considering should receive your FAFSA results, as well as a CSS/PROFILE form if necessary. Be sure your list of prospective colleges includes your safety school, as well as your student's dream school, and everything in between.

Is the CSS/PROFILE Necessary?

You already know that the CSS/PROFILE form should be filled out before the FAFSA form, so you'll need to find out which prospective colleges, if any, require it. The best way to do this is to contact the financial aid offices at your colleges directly and ask them. This is also a perfect time to ask about supplemental and institutional forms they may require, and request that they be mailed to you. If any of your prospective colleges require the CSS/PROFILE form, then you'll need to complete step 3. If you don't need to file a PROFILE form, you can skip ahead to step 4.

Filling Out the CSS/PROFILE

There are five easy steps to completing the CSS/PROFILE form, and you'll need to do them in the following order:

Step 1. Complete the Registration Worksheet

The first thing you're required to do for the PROFILE form is complete a worksheet. It's called the PROFILE Registration worksheet, and it asks for basic information about yourself and your student. On it, you also list which schools you want to receive the results of your PROFILE. This worksheet is used to provide you with a customized PROFILE form and is available only online, at *www.collegeboard.com.*

Step 2. File the Worksheet and Pay the Fee

Once you have filled out the PROFILE Registration Worksheet online, you need to pay a registration fee ($9), as well as a processing fee ($16) for each school receiving your PROFILE. A limited number of fee waivers are granted automatically to first-time applicants from low-income families, based on financial information provided on the PROFILE.

Step 3. Complete the PROFILE Form

Next, you have to fill out the PROFILE form online. Each form is customized, based on your financial situation and needs, as well as questions or information that may be specific to your prospective colleges. You can complete the form immediately after paying your fees, or return to it at a later time. But, in either case, you should finish the process at least two weeks before the earliest college or scholarship program priority filing date you need to meet.

Step 4. Provide Additional Information If Necessary

If you are divorced or separated, or own your own business, you'll be required to fill out and file the supplemental forms we discussed earlier in this chapter. Also, some of your prospective colleges may include additional questions or sheets. These forms will need to be completed and filed with the PROFILE form.

Step 5. File the Form and Receive Your Summary

Once the PROFILE form and any supplements are filed (this has to be done before the earliest priority filing date specified by your colleges), the CSS will automatically share this information with the institutions you selected. This means that after you finish the PROFILE form, it's not necessary to give it to colleges yourself. Once the process is complete, you'll receive an acknowledgment or confirmation from the CSS which will summarize your information and let you know that it has been sent to your prospective schools.

Filling Out the FAFSA

Next, you will need to file a FAFSA to apply for any federal aid, including the PLUS or Stafford loans as well as any federal grants you and your student might qualify for. Even if you don't think your student can qualify for the federal programs, it is a good idea to fill out the form anyway. Many college and private scholarships require applicants to have filed the FAFSA and, if you haven't done that, those other options will not be available to your student.

There are five (or sometimes six) steps to completing the FAFSA, and you'll need to do them in the following order.

Step 1. Get a Form

No matter where your son or daughter decides to go to college, you need to fill out a FAFSA and, thanks to the Internet, you have a few options as to how you do that. Most high school guidance offices offer the paper form, or you can request one by calling the Federal Student Aid Information Center at (800)4-FED-AID. The easiest and fastest way to complete the FAFSA is online at *www.fafsa.ed.gov*. An added benefit of completing the form online is that if you need to make a correction after the FAFSA has been processed, you can do so rather easily. You will also be able to complete the renewal FAFSA online each year, instead of starting the process from scratch.

Step 2. Fill Out the Form

If you request a paper FAFSA, follow the directions included to complete the form. If you're going to fill out the FAFSA online, you'll want to print out and complete the website's worksheets beforehand. This makes the online process less time-consuming. Instead of sitting in front of a computer while you sort though papers hunting for a particular amount or number, a completed worksheet allows you to type everything online in much less time. Regardless of which method you use, you'll need your tax documents to complete a FAFSA. You'll also want to indicate which prospective colleges and universities should receive this information.

Because the FAFSA is the form most likely to be submitted by students and their families, we've devoted the entire next chapter to detailing, line by line, exactly how to fill out the form. You'll also find a copy of the form online at *federalstudentaid.ed.gov/docs/bw_English_fafsa_2009_2010.pdf*.

Step 3. Review the Form

When you finish the FAFSA, take a few minutes to double-check all your information. Corrections can be made to your FAFSA later, but doing so will slow down the financial aid process and may impact how much financial aid you qualify for. "One common problem we see is when parents put the wrong information on the FAFSA form," explains Samuel Ellison, a financial aid adviser at Morehouse College. "If parents and students file for extensions, they may end up putting incorrect information on the FAFSA without knowing it."

Ellison also reminds students to make sure they've selected the correct school codes for prospective colleges. "Other students forget to put school codes on the form, and when that happens we never get their information. Luckily, if they forget, they can call or go online to correct that."

Step 4. Submit the Form

Once you're satisfied with your information, you need to submit the FAFSA. If you're using a paper form, sign it and send it in with the included postcard. This postcard will be mailed back to you to let you know that your FAFSA is being processed. If you're filing your FAFSA online, you have two options. You can print out the FAFSA, sign it, and mail it in, or use a government-issued PIN number that works much like the PIN numbers for ATM cards.

Anyone who has a valid social security number and is a U.S. citizen or eligible noncitizen may apply for a federal student aid PIN. If you decide to use a PIN number, you need to register for this online at *www.pin.ed.gov*. There are three ways you can get your PIN: online, in an email, or by postal mail. Because your social security number will have to be verified, it takes up to three days before you can use your PIN and begin filling out the FAFSA. Still, this is faster than mailing in your signature. The earliest a FAFSA can be submitted is January 1. Try to submit your form as soon after then as possible, since some federal aid is awarded on a first-come first-served basis, and you don't want to miss out on your share.

"We want students to be able to make an informed decision when considering which college to attend," explains Frishberg of Johns Hopkins, "And knowing their financial aid options are part of that, we've set a school deadline of February 15 for students to file their institutional aid form and have completed their FAFSA, because we're then able to give them our package to help their decision."

"Families with unique situations should provide additional financial information to colleges as soon as possible," adds Connie Gores, who is both a vice president at Winona State University and a parent.

File the FAFSA as Early as Possible

"Don't wait until summer to file your FAFSA," insists Jack Toney, director of financial aid at Marshall University. "File it as soon as possible after January 1. You can always make changes to it later, but schools need your FAFSA as soon as possible if you don't want to miss the deadlines for certain aid opportunities."

"I recommend they don't wait until after they receive their aid package, but instead, send a letter to the college's financial aid office right after submitting their FAFSA. If a family has a significant event, such as a parent losing a job, caring for an additional family member, or even something like a significant one-time bonus that might increase their income more than usual, it's smart to let schools know early on."

Remember, however, that no matter how much you've put off applying for financial aid, it's never too late to start. In fact, you and your son or daughter can file a FAFSA even after he or she has already started college. Granted, you'll have to work a little harder and cram some things into a short period of time, but it's worth it. Don't give up because you think you waited too long, but don't use this as an excuse to put things off. Some financial aid is campus-based; so, if you wait you may lose out on other significant sources of aid that might otherwise have been available to you.

Step 5. Receive Your SAR

After your FAFSA is processed, you will receive a Student Aid Report (SAR) in the mail. This report tells you the results of your need analysis and lets you know how much your Expected Family Contribution (EFC) is. This same information will be reported to your prospective colleges. As we discussed earlier, your EFC is not negotiable, so even if the amount is more than you can afford, there is no way to change this number (unless some of your information is incorrect and you correct those amounts on your FAFSA).

"For me, the troubling thing about my FAFSA was that the calculations don't take your cost of living into consideration," says Joe Sanseverino. "We live on Long Island, close to New York City, and our SAR certainly didn't seem to reflect how expensive it is to live here." As anyone who has visited New York knows, a dollar isn't always worth a dollar. "It just didn't feel accurate for where we live," he admits.

Ellen Frishberg of Johns Hopkins acknowledges the sentiment. "Unfortunately, the FAFSA doesn't take your cost of living into account," she says.

Step 6. Verify Your Information

About 30 percent of all FAFSA applications are randomly selected for verification, and if it happens to you, don't worry. Unlike a tax audit, this doesn't mean that you've made a mistake or that you have incorrect information. Your prospective colleges will send you a verification worksheet and ask for copies of certain documents. These may include tax returns, bank statements, statements from investment accounts, or other supplemental information. You should make every effort to provide the colleges with those documents and information as soon as possible. When colleges request additional information, it means that your need analysis has not been completed, and the longer the process takes, the less financial aid you may receive. Verification is usually a simple, straightforward process. "When we verify students, we'll ask for tax documents from the families," says Jade Kolb of NYU. "If we think something like a family's amount of tax paid is wrong—for example, if someone got a refund and wrote 'zero' on their form—we'll correct that for them."

"Students are selected for verification by the Department of Education, not by colleges," explains Karen Krause of the University of Texas at Arlington. "We verify those students, and it can be more than 30 percent of applicants, or less." Krause also notes that while the Department of Education can flag a student for verification, colleges are also able to do so. "We have the option to do it as well, if something doesn't seem right. It's really about quality control."

Filling Out State Forms

Once you and your student have filed a FAFSA (and a CSS/PROFILE form, if necessary), your next step should be applying for state-supported financial aid. You've learned that financial aid opportunities vary from state to state, so you'll need to research what's available in your state and what you qualify for. Some states provide grants for students attending an in-state private college, while others offer loans to supplement federal programs. Use the information in chapter 11 to contact your state's higher education agency and request forms.

Filing Institutional Forms

If your prospective colleges offer institutional aid, be sure to fill out and file those forms as well. These may rely on your FAFSA and CSS/PROFILE information, so once those forms are completed, institutional aid forms are often easier and faster to complete.

Applying for Private Aid

Private aid includes grants and scholarships from businesses and corporations, as well as other sources beyond the federal government, state governments, and academic institutions. Ideally, you and your student should be constantly seeking and applying for these types of aid throughout the whole financial aid process. However, once the federal, state, and college forms are completed and filed you'll be able to focus solely on other sources.

"You need to go out and beat the bushes," insists Barry Simmons, director of financial aid at Virginia Tech. "Even if you ask a local organization, and they don't have a scholarship, sometimes they'll decide it's a good idea to start one. I've seen that happen,

Be on the Lookout

Your student should constantly be on the lookout for local and national scholarships that can help them afford college. Some may be as little as $100, but they may not require a lot of time or energy to apply. Local clubs, service organizations, businesses, and groups should all be contacted. For most students, a few inquiries a week can lead to a steady number of opportunities without overburdening them.

and the student who first asked about the scholarship ended up receiving it because they got the organization started."

To help you "beat the bushes," we've devoted all of chapter 12 to a discussion of the strategies and tools you'll need to search for over $6 billion in private scholarships.

WHAT HAPPENS NEXT?

After you fill out all these forms, you'll probably be sick and tired of forms, pencils, and more acronyms than a spy movie. But give yourself a pat on the back. You've stuck with the process and, hopefully, you're about to reap the rewards. So, what can you expect next?

Acknowledgment Letters

First, you'll start to receive acknowledgment letters from the programs you applied to: FAFSA, CSS/PROFILE, institutional aid, private scholarships, and so on. These will confirm in writing that you have applied for the programs and may review the information you provided. As we mentioned earlier, you may also be asked for additional information. If so, be sure to provide that information promptly. Now is not the time to procrastinate; certainly not after you've worked so hard!

Some colleges or financial aid programs may send letters stating that they are missing information. When this happens, the college or program cannot complete your need analysis, which means you can't get any financial aid. If you receive one of these letters, address it immediately. If you're confused or have already supplied the information they are requesting, call the college or program and clarify what is needed. These kinds of letters should always be treated as high priority.

Award Letters/Financial Aid Packages

All this labor will pay off when you and your student receive your award letters. These are sent out by the programs and colleges to let you know how much financial aid your student has received. They are not mailed until your student has been notified that he or she has been accepted to that college, and they'll list the financial aid awards offered to your student in detail.

The amount offered to students is often called a financial aid "package" because it is a combination of gift aid, self-help aid, and work aid. This package is the total amount of financial aid your student receives (unless there are grants and scholarships from outside sources, such as corporations, being paid directly to your student).

Ideally, your student's financial aid package will cover the complete amount of money you'll need to afford college (in other words, whatever the difference is between the cost of this college and what you can afford to pay). Unfortunately, this is seldom the case. When the combination of your student's financial aid package and the amount you can pay falls short of the cost of that college, you're faced with a few choices.

When this happens, you and your student may decide to take out loans to cover this difference, you may try to appeal to the college to increase its award, or you may decide that your student shouldn't attend this particular college. Most families don't make these kinds of decisions until the student has received all the financial aid packages from every prospective college. Because of that, we'll look at these choices in more detail later, including how you can attempt to negotiate your financial aid package if it's less than

College Financial Aid Information Online

Check out the financial aid pages on your prospective colleges' websites. "We send out financial aid information with our acceptance letters," says Jade Kolb of NYU. "But we also encourage and refer students to our website. It's comprehensive and up to date, and can provide a lot more information than the packets we send out."

what's offered by other colleges. For now, remember that an informed decision will be based on the offers from all your prospective colleges, not just one award letter.

Filling Out Loan Applications

Once your student has decided which college he or she will be attending, the last forms you may need to fill out are federal loan applications. If you qualify for a federal Stafford loan, a direct Stafford loan, or a Perkins loan, you will have to fill out a supplemental loan application. In addition, students receiving a Stafford loan are required to take an entrance interview, which explains the rights and expectations involved in the loan. Federal Stafford loans will also require you to select a lender, so if you've done some research, you may already have a lender in mind. If not, ask the school's financial aid office for assistance.

MOVING ON

This chapter began by comparing the three types of forms involved in applying for financial aid: core forms, supplemental forms, and verification documents. Within each of these categories, we looked at the various forms involved, learning the difference between the FAFSA and the CSS/PROFILE form. We also discussed how business owners and farmers may have to file additional forms in this process. Next, we went through the process of applying for financial aid step by step. We looked at why the CSS/PROFILE form should be completed before the FAFSA, and what steps are involved in completing each. We also discussed where state, institutional, and other forms fit into this process.

Finally, we reviewed the importance of providing additional information when it's requested, and what is involved in the award letters you can expect to receive. Once your student selects the college he or she will attend, you'll need to fill out loan applications if you qualify for federal self-help aid.

In the next chapter, we're going to focus specifically on how to fill out the FAFSA, because more students use that form than any other. We'll provide you with a line-by-line tutorial, so when it is time to fill out the real form, you'll feel like a pro! Before you move on, take a look at the checklist for this chapter.

✓ CHECKLIST:

1. Determine which (if any) potential colleges need the CSS/PROFILE form (you will only be able to fill that form out online). Request institutional aid forms at this time, as well.

2. Request FAFSA forms in paper, download an electronic copy of the form, or fill out the form online.

3. Collect federal tax returns and W-2 forms for both you and your student.

4. Find out the filing deadlines for the FAFSA and CSS/PROFILE, including any deadlines at your prospective schools.

5. Complete and submit the CSS/PROFILE form (if necessary).

6. If you want to file your FAFSA online, request a PIN number from *www.pin.ed.gov*.

7. Complete and submit your FAFSA form.

8. Complete any state, institutional, and private financial aid forms necessary.

9. Review your acknowledgement letters from various programs and submit additional information for verification (if necessary).

10. Review your award letters.

11. Begin the student loan application process, if appropriate, once your student has selected his or her college or university.

CHAPTER EIGHT

Filling Out the FAFSA

If you and your student are looking for financial aid to help pay for college, there are many different forms you may have to fill out in the process, including applications from colleges, your state, private lenders, scholarship sponsors, and the federal government. Of these, the most important document you'll ever complete is the Free Application for Federal Student Aid (FAFSA). There are many reasons why:

1. This form is required for your student to be considered for a whole host of funding opportunities from the federal government, including grants, loans, and work-study options (for more information, see chapter 6).

2. The FAFSA is required to apply for most state and college aid.

3. A number of private scholarships will not consider your application unless you have filed the FAFSA.

4. Once you have completed this form, other ones (like the CSS/PROFILE form) will go much faster, because you will be able to reuse the information you gathered for the FAFSA.

You Can Do It

With its 109 questions, the FAFSA form looks daunting. But, don't let that stop you. Last year, nearly 15 million students submitted the form. You can do it, too!

While the FAFSA is the most important form you will fill out in your quest to find financial aid, it is also one of the most complex. That's why we've devoted an entire chapter to detailing, line by line, how to fill out the form.

The easiest and most accurate way to fill out the FAFSA is to work with completed income tax returns for the previous year. If you haven't already done your taxes, you can estimate your adjusted gross income (AGI) and tax liability on the FAFSA. But, if that estimate doesn't match the figures on the tax returns you actually file, you will have to correct the information on the FAFSA online or by mail. That could mean that a delay in your student getting financial aid.

FAFSA TUTORIAL

For the purposes of this tutorial, we are using the 2009–2010 FAFSA. Even if you are just going through the process for practice right now, you will still need to have this form at hand, as you read through this chapter. If you haven't already obtained a copy of the FAFSA, you can either use the sample we've included at the end of this chapter or download one from: *www.federalstudentaid. ed.gov/fafsa/fafsa_options.html#pdfFafsa*

Before You Begin

When you're ready to start, set aside a block of time. Filling out the FAFSA can be time consuming (there are 109 questions on the form!). Have your copy of the FAFSA in hand and then gather together the documentation and the IRS tax forms you'll need. Here's a list:

FAFSA Tips

Keep these tips in mind when you are filling out the FAFSA:

- When entering numbers on the FAFSA, never leave a field blank when your answer is zero. In those cases, always enter "0."

- If you are filling out the form online (www.fafsa.gov), always click the "Save" button when you see it, so you don't lose any information.

- File as early after January 1 as you can. You don't want to miss out on any campus-based financial aid that's distributed on a first-come, first-serve basis.

- You must file no later than June 30. That's the deadline. After that, no applications will be accepted.

- Report only dollar amounts and don't use decimals. Round to the nearest dollar. So, $101.26 would be reported on the form as $101.

- The student's and parents' social security numbers (or, if not a citizen, then an alien registration or permanent residence card).

- The student's driver's license or state identification number.

- The student's and parents' W-2 forms, or other records of money earned

- The student's and parent's prior year income tax return. If you don't have your taxes done or haven't received your tax W-2 forms yet, don't worry. You can always use estimates and file a FAFSA correction later.

- Records of any untaxed income: social security, welfare, veteran's benefits, etc.

- The student's and parents' bank statements.

- Records for the student's and parents' mortgage payments, stock dividends, farm or other business activities, and other investments.

- Student's list of potential colleges.

Now that you know what materials you'll need, let's get started.

FAFSA Overview

With your copy of the FAFSA form and all your supporting materials at hand, we're ready to start.

The FAFSA is 6 pages long, asks 109 questions, and is organized into the following eight sections:

1. Questions 1–32: Student's identification information *(all students must answer these questions)*

2. Questions 33–47: Student's financial information *(all students must answer these questions)*

3. Questions 48–60: Determining student dependence/independence *(all students must answer these questions)*

4. Questions 61–81: Parents' identification information *(all parents must answer these questions)*

5. Questions 82–95 Parents' financial information *(only parents of dependent students answer these questions)*

6. Questions 96–103: Independent students' information *(dependent students do not answer these questions)*

7. Question 104: Colleges you want to receive your FAFSA information (up to four schools can be listed)

8. Questions 105–109: Read, sign, and date (student, parent and, if you used one, adviser who helped you fill out the form)

> **FAFSA Tips** *(continued)*
>
> - If you're filling out the form manually: use black ink, fill in circles completely, and print in capital letters.
> - The best way to reduce the amount of time it takes to do the FAFSA is to have completed your prior year's tax returns before filling out the form.
> - If the parents are divorced, information should relate to the parent with whom the student has lived the majority of time during the prior year.
> - Don't forget to list the FAFSA-provided codes for the colleges you plan on attending. Also, be sure to sign and date the form.
> - If you or your family have unusual circumstances (such as the loss of a job), it is best to fill out the FAFSA completely, following the instructions on the form, and then contact the financial aid offices at the college you plan to attend about your situation.

As you can see, not all sections must be filled out by all students or parents. There is a separate section just for independent students (section 6) and one just for the parents of dependent students (section 5). So, while there are 109 questions on the form, the maximum number any family will answer will be less than 100.

Now it's time for our tutorial to begin. We'll go through the FAFSA, section by section and question by question, to show you what you need to know to fill out the form.

Questions 1–32: Student's Identification Information

For this set of questions, the student is permitted to skip any questions that do not apply. For example, question 11 asks for the student's driver's license and license state; these questions can be skipped if the student does not have a driver's license.

Questions 1–3. Student's name (last, first, and middle initial): The name must be exactly as it appears on the student's social security card. So, don't enter a nickname here.

Questions 4–7. Student's permanent address (not a school address): Don't use a school or office address. If the student is in transition or is homeless, then use the address where mail can be received.

Question 8. Student's Social Security number: Make sure this number is entered correctly; your form will not be processed if this number does not match the student's name. If you don't have a Social Security number, or you can't remember what it is, contact the Social Security office at (800) 772–1213.

Question 9. Student's date of birth: Month, day, and year.

Question 10. Student's permanent telephone number: Students can list a land line or a cell phone number where they can be contacted. Just don't use a forwarded number.

Questions 11–12. Driver's license information: If the student has a driver's license number or state ID, enter it here. If the student has neither, just leave this blank.

Question 13. E-mail: if the student provides an e-mail address, all correspondence will happen electronically (for example, the notice when the student's FAFSA has been processed will be sent to the student's e-mail).

Questions 14–15. Citizenship status: If the student is not a U.S. citizen but is an "eligible noncitizen," his or her eight or nine-digit alien registration number must be provided. To be an "eligible noncitizen," students must fall into at least one of these categories:

1. A permanent U.S. resident with a Permanent Resident Card (I-551)
2. A conditional permanent resident (I-551C)
3. The holder of an Arrival-Departure Record (I–94) from the Department of Homeland Security showing any of the following designations: "Refugee," "Asylum Granted," "Parolee," "Victim of human trafficking," "T-Visa" holder, or "Cuban-Haitian Entrant"

Students who are not citizens or eligible noncitizens are ineligible for federal aid. However, they should still complete the form, because they may qualify for state or college funding.

Questions 16–17. Student's marital status as of the date of application: As you will see later, married students are usually considered "independent students" by the federal government and are required to fill out a separate section in the form.

Questions 18–20. State residency: Enter here where the student permanently resides, not place of birth or college location. Generally, students' state residency is the same state as where their driver's license was issued.

Questions 21–22. Selective service status: These two questions ask first about gender and then about Selective Service registration. Male students over 18 must have registered in order to receive financial aid. If you need to register and haven't done so yet, you can take care of that now at *www.sss.gov.*

Question 23. Drug convictions: This question must be answered. Students must indicate if they have ever been convicted for the possession or sale of illegal drugs. If they have, they cannot qualify for federal aid. That's a pretty stiff penalty. Keep that in mind if you are ever tempted...

Questions 24–25. Family's level of education: Students mark here the highest level of education their mother and father received. This information is requested because some states and colleges offer aid on the basis of parents' level of education (for example, if the student is the first in his or her family to attend college).

Questions 26–27. Student's level of education: These questions are asked because undergraduate students must have completed high school or its equivalent but generally not one or more undergraduate degrees to be considered for full federal aid.

Questions 28–32. Type of aid requested: These questions are asked to determine which federal aid programs students might qualify for. In question 31, when you're asked if you would accept loans and/or work-study funds or not, we suggest you answer that you are interested in "Both." This does not obligate you to apply for or accept these types of funds, but it does keep your options open. Note: students who enroll less than half time (generally that's less than six credit hours) will not qualify for any federal aid.

Questions 33–47. Student's Finances

We're on to the second section of the form. For this set of questions, regarding income and assets, only information related to the student (and, if applicable, the student's spouse) should be supplied here. Parents' financial information is collected later, in questions 61–95i.

FAFSA Warning

The following warning is printed on every FAFSA form: "Be wary of organizations that charge a fee to submit your application or to find you money for college. In general, the help you pay for can be obtained for free from your college or from Federal Student Aid."

Questions 33–35. Student's income tax forms: These questions deal with income tax returns filed for the prior year: If the student didn't file an income tax return, skip to question 39. But, if the student did file or will be filing, the form used must be specified and questions 36 through 38 must be answered. Important: if the student filed a return and therefore is answering questions 36 through 38, do not leave any blanks. If the answer is zero, always enter "0."

Question 36. Student's (and spouse's) adjusted gross income (AGI): This figure is the amount earned by the student and, if applicable, the student's spouse during the prior year, minus the deductions the federal government allows to be taken against that income (for example, tuition and fees, student loan interest). If the student has already completed the tax return for the previous year, take the amount entered on line 37 on the IRS 1040 form, on line 21 on the 1040A, or on line 4 on the 1040EZ. If not, enter your best estimate and submit a correction later, if necessary.

Question 37. Student's (and spouse's) income tax: Enter here the amount of income tax owed for the prior tax year. That amount can be found on line 56 of the IRS 1040 form, on line 35 of the 1040A, or on line 11 of the 1040EZ. If the student did not or will not pay any income tax, enter "0."

Question 38. Student's (and spouse's) exemptions: Enter here the number of exemptions claimed on line 6d on the IRS 1040 form or the 1040A form or line 5 on the 1040EZ.

Questions 39–40. Student's (and spouse's) wages: Students will need to answer these questions whether or not they filed or will file an income tax return for the prior year. This information is on their W-2 forms or pay stubs. Or, if they already completed their tax return, they can take the information from lines 7 + 12 + 18 + Box 14 of the K-1 (Form 1065), or from line 7 of the 1040A, or from line 1 of the 1040EZ. Note: students must supply information for these 2 questions. If the answer is zero, then enter "0."

Questions 41–43. Student's assets: Enter here the student's (and spouse's) bank balances, personal net worth (minus any home equity), and net worth of businesses/farms with more than 99 employees. For the purposes of this question, "net worth" means current value minus debt. Note: if net worth is $1 million or more, enter $999,999; if net worth is negative, enter "0." The amounts reported here must be as of the date the FAFSA is filed. Keep that requirement in mind when making deposits and withdrawals from your bank accounts, etc. Important: information must be supplied for these 3 questions. If the answer is zero, then enter "0."

Questions 44–45. Student's (and spouse's) veteran's benefits: These two questions relate to the amount and type of veteran's educational benefits received between July 1 of last year and June of the current year by the student (and student's spouse). If no benefits will be received, answer "No" and skip to question 46. If student or spouse is receiving benefits, the following code must be used to record which benefits these are:

- enter **1** for Montgomery GI Bill-Active Duty (chapter 30)
- enter **2** for Post-9/11 GI Bill (chapter 33)
- enter **3** for Montgomery GI Bill-Selected Reserve (chapter 16060)
- enter **4** for Reserve Educational Assistance Program (chapter 1607)
- enter **5** for Vocational Rehabilitation and Employment (chapter 31)
- enter **6** for Dependents' Educational Assistance (chapter 35)
- enter **7** for any other type of veterans education benefit

Questions 46a–e: Student's (and spouse's) additional financial information: These five questions relate to specific sources of money the student (and student's spouse) might have received during the prior year:

- education tax credits (from line 50 on the IRS form 1040 or line 31 on the 1040A)
- child support paid
- taxable earnings from need-based employment programs (for example, Work-Study) or employment portions of fellowships or assistantships
- student grant and scholarship aid reported to the IRS in the student's adjusted gross income (for example, from AmeriCorps)
- taxable combat pay

Important: information must be supplied for these five questions. If the answer is zero, then enter "0."

Question 47a–j. Student's (and spouse's) untaxed income: This question is made up of 10 categories of untaxed income, list in the form as a–j:

- payments to tax-deferred pension and savings plans (take the information from the student's W-2)
- IRA deductions and payments to self-employment plans (take from line 28 and line 32 of the IRS form 1040 or line 17 of the 1040A)
- child support received
- tax exempt interest income (from line 8B on the IRS Form 1040 or line 8b from the 1040A)
- untaxed portions of IRA distributions, excluding rollovers (lines 15a minus 15b on the IRS Form 1040 or lines 11a minus 11 b on the 1040A)
- untaxed portions of pensions (from lines 16a minus 16b on the IRS form 1040 or lines 12a minus 12b from the 1040A)

- housing, food, and other living expenses paid to the military or clergy (including cash benefits and the cash value of benefits)
- noneducational benefits provided to the military (such as disability death pensions, or VA Educational Work-Study allowances)
- other untaxed income reported (for example, workers' compensation and disability payments) but excluding student aid, earned income credit, welfare payments, untaxed social security benefits, combat pay, benefits from flexible spending arrangements, etc.
- money received or paid on the student's behalf that isn't reported elsewhere (for example, if the student's grandparents paid for any college expenses)

Important: information must be supplied for each of these 10 categories. If the amount is zero, then enter "0."

Questions 48–60: Determining Dependence/Independence

The questions in this section are designed to determine if the student meets the federal definition of an "independent" student or a "dependent" student. If a student answers "Yes" to at least one of the following 13 questions, that means the student is considered an independent student by the federal government for the purposes of financial aid and is instructed to skip to question 96; that student's parents will not be asked to supply any financial information. If a student answers "No" to all of the questions, that means the student meets the definition of a dependent student—even if the student doesn't live at home or receive any parental financial support—and that student's parents will be asked to supply information for questions 61–95.

The questions the student has to answer in this section are:

- Are you 24 years or older?
- Are you married?
- Are you pursuing an advanced degree (a master's or doctoral degree)?
- Are you active-duty military or a veteran?
- Are you a parent and provide at least half of the support for your children?
- Do you have a dependent (for example, an elderly grandparent), besides your spouse or your children, who lives with you and receives more than half their support from you?
- At any time since you turned 13, were you a foster child, a dependent or ward of the court, or an orphan?
- Are you a legally emancipated minor as a result of a court judgment?
- Are you in legal guardianship as determine by a court?
- Do you meet any of the three definitions provided in the form for being homeless or self-supporting and at the risk of being homeless?

Remember: if you answer "Yes" to any of these questions, you are by definition an "independent" student. If you answer "No" to all of these questions, the federal government classifies you as a dependent student. For information about the definitions used and the implications of being defined as an independent versus dependent student, see chapter 9.

Questions 61–81: Parents of Dependent Students Identification Information

This section is to be filled out **only** by the parents of "dependent" children. If your student answered "Yes" to any of questions 48–60, you as the parent are instructed to skip this section. If your student answered "No" to all of those questions (that is to say, your student meets the definition of a "dependent" student), then information must be provided about you (whether your student lives with you or not) in questions 61–85.

Before we go through these questions, it is important to establish who is the "parent" (or parents) required to supply information for this section of the FAFSA. Here are the instructions provided by FAFSA:

- If the student's parents (biological or adoptive) are married to each other, information is to be provided about both of them.
- If the student's parent is widowed or single, information is provided about that person only.
- If the student's parent is widowed but remarried as of the date the form is filled out, information must be provided about both the parent and the stepparent.
- If the student's parent is divorced or separated, information must be provided about the parent the student lived with more during the past 12 months; if that parent has remarried, information must also be provided about the spouse. If the student did not live with one parent more than the other, then information should be given about the parent who provides the most financial support and/or claims the student as a dependent on the IRS tax return (and, if that parent has remarried, about the new spouse as well).
- Grandparents, foster parents, legal guardians, or aunts and uncles are not considered parents on this form unless they have legally adopted the student.

Unlike the previous three sections, this one is about the dependent student's parents, not about the student. It is best filled out by the parent or with the parent's help.

Questions 61–62. Parents' marital status: The status reported should be as of the date the form is filled in.

Questions 63–70. Parents' identification information: Social security number, legal name (exactly as it appears on the social security card), and date of birth for each of the parents filling out the form.

Question 71. Parent's e-mail: If an e-mail is entered here, it will be used by FAFSA (to let the parent know when the form has been processed) and by the student's legal state of residence and list of potential colleges (to communicate with the parent).

Questions 72–74. State residency: Enter here the parents' state of legal residence and when the parents became legal residents of that state.

Questions 75–81. Parents' household: These questions collect information on the parents' household, in order to determine the amount of allowance that will be available in the EFC calculation to protect a portion of the parents' reported income. Here is a list of the people who can be included as part of the household:

- the dependent student (whether the student is living with the parents or not)
- the parents
- the parents' other children, but only 1) if the parents will provide more than half of the support of those children between July 1 and June 30 of the award year or 2) if the children could answer "No" to questions 48 through 60
- other people who live with the parents, but only if the parents will provide more than half of their support between July 1 and June 30 of the award year

In questions 75–81, information is collected on the parents' household size, number of people in the parents' household who will be college students (at least half time) between July 1 and June 30 of the award year, and whether or not anyone in the parents' household received benefits in the previous two years from the Supplemental Security Income Program, Food Stamp Program, Free or Reduced Price Lunch Program, Temporary Assistance for Needy Families (TANF), or Special Supplemental Nutrition Program for Women, Infants, and Children (WIC).

Questions 82–95: Parents' Finances

For this set of questions, regarding income and assets, only information related to the dependent student's parents should be supplied here. Financial information about the student was already provided, in questions 33–47.

Questions 82–84. Income tax return for the prior year: If the parents didn't file an income tax return, they can skip to question 89. But, if they did file or will be filing, they will need to specify here the form they used and then answer questions 85 through 88.

Question 85. Dislocated worker: For the purposes of this question, and question 103, a person is considered a "dislocated worker" if any of the following apply: is receiving unemployment benefits due to being laid off or losing a job and is unlikely to return to a previous occupation; has been laid off or received a lay-off notice from a job; was self-employed but is now unemployed; or is a displaced homemaker. Parents who quit work are generally not considered a dislocated worker, even if they are receiving unemployment benefits. Note: the financial aid officers at the student's list of colleges may require documentation from any parents who indicate they are "dislocated."

Question 86. Parents' adjusted gross income (AGI): This figure is the amount earned by the parents during the prior year (wages, interest, dividends, alimony, etc.), minus the deductions the federal government allows to be taken against that income. If the parents already completed their tax return, they can take this amount from line 37 on IRS form 1040, line 21 on the 1040A, or line 4 on the 1040EZ.

Question 87. Parents' income tax: Enter here the amount of income tax owed for the prior tax year. Parents can find that amount on line 56 of the IRS form 1040, line 35 of the 1040A, or line 11 of the 1040EZ. Parents who did not or will not pay any income tax should enter "0."

Verification

Just as tax forms can be audited, so can FAFSAs. Each year, the Department of Education selects a group of forms for verification. Some of these are chosen at random; others are selected because there is inconsistent information on the form. If you are asked to verify your information, do so promptly. Otherwise, there will be a delay in processing your FAFSA.

Question 88. Parents' exemptions: Enter here the number of exemptions claimed on line 6d on the IRS 1040 form or the 1040A form, or line 5 on the 1040EZ.

Questions 89–90. Parents' income: These questions ask about the earnings (wages, salaries, tips, etc.) in the prior year for the father/stepfather and for the mother/stepmother. These questions must be answered whether or not the parents filed or will file an income tax return for the prior year. This information can be taken from W-2 forms or from line 7 and 12 and 18 and box 14 of schedule K-1 (form 1065) on the IRS form 1040, or from line 7 on the 1040A, or from line 1 on the 1040EZ.

Questions 91–93. Parents' assets: Parents need to record here their bank balances, real estate (minus the value of their house), trust funds, stocks and stock options, bonds and other securities, educational savings accounts (such as Coverdell and 529 plans), and net worth of businesses/farms with more than 99 employees. Other assets do not need to be reported and are not counted in the financial aid calculations. These include the principal place of residence or family farm, a small business or farm with less than 100 employees, personal possessions (cars, cloths, furniture, etc.), and pensions and whole-life insurance. For the purposes of this question, "net worth" means current value minus debt. Note: if net worth is $1 million or more, enter $999,999; if net worth is negative, enter "0." The amounts reported here must be as of the date the FAFSA is filed.

Question 94. Parents' additional financial information: These five questions relate to specific sources of money the parents might have received during the prior year:

- education tax credits (from line 50 on the IRS form 1040 or line 31 on the 1040A)
- child support paid
- taxable earnings from need-based employment programs (for example, Work-Study) or employment portions of fellowships or assistantships
- student grant and scholarship aid reported to the IRS in the student's adjusted gross income (for example, from AmeriCorps)
- taxable combat pay

Important: information must be supplied for these five questions. If the answer is zero, then enter "0."

Question 95. Parents' untaxed income: This question is made up of nine categories of untaxed income:

- payments to tax-deferred pension and savings plans (take the information from the parents' W-2)
- IRA deductions and payments to self-employment plans (take from line 28 and line 32 of the IRS form 1040 or line 17 of the 1040A)
- child support received
- tax exempt interest income (from line 8B on the IRS form 1040 or line 8b from the 1040A)
- untaxed portions of IRA distributions, excluding rollovers (lines 15a minus 15b on the IRS form 1040 or lines 11a minus 11 b on the 1040A)
- untaxed portions of pensions (from lines 16a minus 16b on the IRS form 1040 or lines 12a minus 12b from the 1040A)
- housing, food, and other living expenses paid to the military or clergy (including cash benefits and the cash value of benefits)
- non-educational benefits provided to the military (such as disability death pensions, or VA Educational Work-Study allowances)
- other untaxed income reported (for example, workers' compensation and disability payments) but excluding student aid, earned income credit, welfare payments, untaxed social security benefits, combat pay, benefits from flexible spending arrangements, etc.

Important: information must be supplied for each of these 9 categories. If the amount is zero, then enter "0."

Questions 96–103: Independent Student's Information

This section is filled out **only** by students who answered "Yes" to at least one of questions 48 through 60. These students, by definition, are classified as "independent" students.

Questions 96–102. Independent students' households: The purpose of these questions is to collect information on an independent student's household, in order to determine the amount of allowance that will be available in the EFC calculation to protect a portion of the independent student's reported income. Here is a list of the people who can be included as part of the household:

- the independent student
- the independent student's spouse
- the independent student's children, if he or she provides more than half of the children's support between July 1 and June 30 of the award year
- other people who live with the independent student, but only if the independent student provides more than half of their support between July 1 and June 30 of the award year

Specifically, information is collected on the independent student's household size, number of people in the independent student's household who will be college students (at least half time) between July 1 and June 30 of the award year, and whether or not anyone in the independent student's household received benefits in the previous two years from the Supplemental Security Income Program, Food Stamp Program, Free or Reduced Price Lunch Program, Temporary Assistance for Needy Families (TANF), or Special Supplemental Nutrition Program for Women, Infants, and Children (WIC).

Question 103. Dislocated worker: For the purposes of this question, an independent student is considered a "dislocated worker" if any of the following apply: is receiving unemployment benefits due to being laid off or losing a job and is unlikely to return to a previous occupation; has been laid off or received a lay-off notice from a job; was self-employed but is now unemployed; or is a displaced homemaker. Independent students who quit work are generally not considered a dislocated worker, even if they are receiving unemployment benefits. Note: the financial aid officers at the student's list of colleges may require verification that the independent student is indeed a "dislocated worker."

The Tutorial Is Nearly Done!

We're impressed. You and your student stuck it out and completed the tutorial. Now, your student won't be one of the more than 8 million who could have qualified for financial aid but never submitted the FAFSA. Only two more steps to go to and then you'll be done.

First, you need to enter the six-digit federal code of the colleges your student wants to receive the FAFSA information. You can find the school codes at *www.fafsa.ed.gov* or by calling (800) 4-FED-AID. Or, you can simply write in the complete name, address, city, and state of the college on the form instead. FAFSA recommends that if your student wants to be considered for state aid, the preferred colleges should be listed first.

Finally, both you and your student need to sign and date the form. And, if you or your family paid a fee for someone to fill out the form or to advise you on how to fill it out, that person must also sign and date the form, provide an address, and supply a social security or employer's ID number.

Filing the Official Form

Now that you understand how to answer the questions, you're ready to fill out the official FAFSA form. You can do this by filling out a paper copy of the form or by answering the questions online. There are several important advantages to filling out the form electronically: you can get online help for each question, your answers are checked automatically for possible errors, electronic calculators can help you figure out the amounts to enter, and you will get your results faster (generally in five days or less). Plus, you'll be able to check the status of your application, make corrections to a processed FAFSA, add or delete a school code, and print out your Student Aid Report (SAR). If you or your student has access to a computer, online filing is definitely the way to go.

MOVING ON

To review: in this chapter we discussed the importance of filing the FAFSA (even if you don't think you can qualify for federal aid), gave an overview of the categories of questions asked in the FAFSA, identified the materials you'll need to assemble before you start, provided some tips to help you in the process, and then launched into a line-by-line tutorial on filling out the FAFSA.

We identified which sections must be filled out by all students, by dependent students only, by independent students only, and by the parents of dependent students only. For each of the questions in these sections, we gave you background information, explanations, and instructions. We recommended that you file the FAFSA electronically and then gave you our reasons why. Finally, we reminded you of the important FAFSA deadlines.

In the next chapter, you'll learn how the government and colleges determine the amount of financial aid you'll receive. We'll give you an in-depth look at how applicants are evaluated and what formulas are used by the federal government and colleges in this process. Before you move on, take a look at the checklist for this chapter.

✔ **CHECKLIST:**

1. Whether or not you think your student can qualify for federal aid, make the commitment to file the FAFSA. That way, you'll keep your options open.
2. Pull together all the materials and forms you will need to fill out the FAFSA.
3. Learn how to fill out the FAFSA by taking the tutorial we offered in this chapter.
4. Be sure you understand the federal definitions of "independent" and "dependent" student, so you can fill out the parts of the FAFSA that relate to your student and your family.
5. If you have access to a computer, file the FAFSA online (rather than filling out a paper copy).
6. Don't procrastinate. Keep the FAFSA deadlines in mind (no earlier than January 1 and no later than June 30). Remember: earlier is better.

CHAPTER NINE

Calculating Your Need

Now that you've completed your applications for student aid, you may be wondering just how the federal government and colleges determine the amount of aid you'll receive. If so, this chapter is for you. We'll explain the process here and take you step by step through a sample case. While calculating your need is not a mandatory part of applying for financial aid, you will have a much better understanding of EFC and financial aid calculations by going through this exercise. "If you're starting early, this can be helpful in understanding the process," says Barry Simmons at Virginia Tech. "Just hearing about EFC and calculations may not do much good, but doing it yourself step by step can be beneficial."

As you've already learned, financial aid programs and offices take your information and conduct a need analysis, which is designed to determine the amount of money your son or daughter will need to afford college. Before we get into the specifics of how this works, it helps to know the four basic principles on which all need analysis is based.

1. Parents are expected to shoulder as much of the financial responsibility for their student's education as they can afford.
2. Students are expected to contribute to the cost of their education.
3. Families are evaluated based upon their current financial situation—not on the future or past.
4. Families are treated in a consistent and equal manner, while recognizing that special circumstances may exist in some situations.

THE TWO METHODOLOGIES

When it comes to calculating need analysis, there are two methods that can be used: the Federal Methodology and the Institutional Methodology.

Federal Methodology

Federal Methodology (FM) is the formula used to calculate your need analysis for the FAFSA. This method was developed by congress to determine eligibility for federally funded financial aid programs.

Institutional Methodology

Institutional Methodology (IM) is an alternative formula for calculating need analysis and is used for the CSS/PROFILE. IM is also used by some colleges for determining institutional aid.

When it comes to calculating the Institutional Methodology, there's no one way to go about it. "As many schools use the Institutional Methodology, there are different types of IM," says Ellen Frishberg of Johns Hopkins University. Regardless, she notes that practically all IM calculations use the same factors. "Five things are really key to any IM calculation," she explains. "First, who's counted in college? Some Institutional Methodology calculations may not count a sibling or parent who is a grad school student. Second, the treatment of assets is different from the FAFSA. Third, medical expenses are also treated differently. Fourth, home equity is important to an IM calculation. And fifth, Institutional Methodology has regional tables for calculations, but not every school can afford to use them."

You'll find that while the FM and IM formulas overlap a bit, the Federal Methodology is generally more lenient for families and students.

YOUR EXPECTED FAMILY CONTRIBUTION (EFC)

The expected family contribution, EFC for short, is the amount your family is expected to pay for your student's education. We've discussed how this EFC is almost always quite different from how much a family can truly afford to pay out-of-pocket for college. Because of this, your "need" analysis may not accurately represent how much money you and your student realistically need to be able to pay for college.

It's important to remember that financial aid programs and colleges define "need" very differently than you do. As you learned earlier, your need is determined by subtracting the amount you are expected to contribute to your student's education from the total cost of college. In other words,

Cost of Attending College (COA)
– Your Expected Family Contribution (EFC)
Your "Need" / Eligibility for Need-Based Aid

The bottom line is that you are expected to contribute at least a portion of your income to your student's education. Regardless of what your need is determined to be, you are responsible for meeting your EFC, whether you have that money or not.

HOW YOUR ASSETS AND INCOME ARE ASSESSED

In order to determine just how much your family is expected to contribute, it's necessary to assess your family's assets and income. Because it's believed that people with more assets and income can afford to pay more for their student's college education, this assessment is essential to calculating need analysis.

In this assessment, your income includes not only your salary and wages from your job, but your interest from bank accounts, dividends from stocks, profits from the sale of investments, and any other sources of income your family receives. Your assets are defined as anything of value that you own: your home, stocks, bonds, savings accounts, CDs, and other investments that are not considered to be cash.

It is very important to remember that the more assets and investments your student has, the less financial aid he or she may qualify for. When schools determine a family's expected contribution (EFC) for college, they expect 20 percent of a student's assets to be used for college, while as little as 5.6 percent is expected to come from the parent's assets. Because of this huge difference, it's wise to hold assets, whenever you can, in your name rather than your student's name.

Protection Allowances

The good news is that a need analysis attempts to be fair, so a protection allowance is built into the calculations. The process takes into account that you've probably been saving for other things instead of, or in addition to, your student's education. Because people save for things like retirement, or the down payment on a house, certain allowances are factored into the calculations. This means that you're able to deduct a certain amount of your assets for these purposes, and the amount that's left after this deduction is used to determine your EFC. The following chart gives the amount of allowances for the 2009–10 school year. You will note that the allowance increases as the age of the older parent increases. This is because the older the parent is, the more he or she needs to save for retirement.

EDUCATION SAVINGS AND ASSET PROTECTION ALLOWANCE FOR FEDERAL EFC FORMULA		
Age of older parent (as of 12/31/2009)	Allowance if there are two parents	Allowance if there is only one parent
25 or less	0	0
26	2,900	1,200
27	5,800	2,400
28	8,700	3,600
29	11,600	4,800
30	14,500	6,000
31	17,400	7,200
32	20,300	8,400
33	23,100	9,500
34	26,000	10,700
35	28,900	11,900
36	31,800	13,100
37	34,700	14,300
38	37,600	15,500
39	40,500	16,700
40	43,400	17,900
41	44,200	18,200
42	45,300	18,600
43	46,400	19,100
44	47,600	19,500
45	48,700	19,900
46	49,900	20,400
47	51,200	20,900
48	52,400	21,400
49	53,700	21,900
50	55,300	22,400
51	56,700	22,900
52	58,000	23,500
53	59,800	24,000
54	61,200	24,600
55	63,000	25,300
56	64,900	25,900
57	66,400	26,500
58	68,300	27,200
59	70,300	27,900
60	72,300	28,700
61	74,400	29,500
62	76,600	30,300
63	79,100	31,100
64	81,300	32,000
65	84,000	32,800

Discretionary Net Worth

This term refers to the amount of your assets after subtracting your protection allowance. Based on the chart, if you are a single parent age 45, you have $57,000 in savings, and your protection allowance is $19,900, then $57,000 minus $19,900 equals $37,100, the amount of your discretionary net worth.

THE FORMULAS

Because both Federal Methodology and Institutional Methodology use slightly different formulas, let's look at each individually. For the Federal Methodology, we will also look at a sample family and calculate their need. At the end of this chapter, you'll also find worksheets and tables that you can use to calculate your own EFC. In addition to the worksheets we've provided, you can also find forms like this online at *www.fsa4counselors.ed.gov/clcf/attachments/1114EFCFormulaGuide0910Attach.pdf.*

These worksheets are not meant to be submitted to any financial aid program, but are offered solely for the benefit of parents and families who wish to calculate their EFC for their own purposes. If you prefer not to fill out worksheets, online sites such as *www.salliemae.com* provide calculators that can estimate your EFC without the detailed paperwork.

Regardless of which method you choose (our worksheets or the online calculators) to figure out your EFC, you'll need your tax documents and records of your assets.

Federal Methodology

A Federal Methodology need analysis takes several things into consideration, including:

- The parent's and student's income from the previous year
- Total income tax paid by the family
- Number of people in the family
- Number of people in the family attending college
- The family's assets (excluding equity in their house)
- The parents' ages
- The cost of living, based on the state in which the family lives

Take a look at the sample calculations we've prepared for the hypothetical Smith family, for a step-by-step example of how FM is done.

Calculating the FM—A Case History

Calculating your Federal Methodology is basically a matter of determining your EFC through the same process the government uses when if analyzes your FAFSA. To make the process easier to understand, let's go through a sample case.

Jane Smith is a high school senior who is about to start her first year of college. She is an only child and lives with her parents in New York. Jane works part time, and last year she made $5,000. She also has $300 in a savings account. Her father is 42 and earns $40,000 a year. Her mother is 41, works part time, and earns $26,136 per year. The Smiths have $10,000 in investments and $3,000 in savings, and Mr. Smith invests $200 each month into his 401(k).

Because the Smith have already filed a FAFSA (we used the 2009–2010 for this example), they had a completed copy handy when determining their EFC.

Satrting on the next page, we'll go through The Smith's FM line by line.

THE SMITHS' FM: LINE BY LINE

Line 1:

The **Parents' Adjusted Gross Income** for last year was $60,290. Using his FAFSA form, Mr. Smith was able to copy this number from line 86 of the FAFSA.

Line 2a:

Mr. Smith's **income from work** was $40,000. This was copied from line 89 of the completed FAFSA.

Line 2b:

Mrs. Smith's **income from work** was $26,136. This was copied from line 90 of the completed FAFSA. By adding these two incomes together, the **total parents' income** earned from work was $66,136.

Line 3:

As tax filers, the Smiths used the amount listed on line 1, making their **Parents' Taxable Income** $60,290.

Line 4:

Using the FAFSA Worksheets A and B, the Smiths did not have any dollar amount to report from Worksheet A. However, because Mr. Smith contributed $200 each month to his 401(k), the total dollar amount for Worksheet B was $2,400. This made their **total untaxed income and benefits** $2,400.

Line 5:

By adding lines 3 and 4, the Smiths determined their **taxable and untaxed income.** $60,290 (Line 3) + $2,400 (Line 4) = $62,690

Line 6:

The Smiths did not have any dollar amount from FAFSA Worksheet C, so this line was $0.

Line 7:

By subtracting line 6 from line 5, the Smiths' **Total Income** was $62,690.

Line 8:

The Smiths' **income tax paid** for last year was $10,020. This amount was copied from line 87 of the completed FAFSA.

Line 9:

Look at Table A1 at the end of this chapter. Because New York gives a tax allowance of 9 percent for anyone earning less than $15,000, and 8 percent for anyone earning more than $15,000, the Smiths qualified for the 8 percent allowance.

According to the instructions at the bottom of the table, the Smiths multiplied their Total Income (line 7) by this percentage.

$62,690 × 8% = $5,015

Therefore, the Smiths **state tax allowance** is $5,015.

THE SMITHS' FM: LINE BY LINE

Line 10:

Looking at Table A2, Mr. Smith's social security tax allowance was 7.65 percent, because he earns less than $102,000 per year. Therefore, multiplying this percentage by the total income, Mr. Smith's **social security tax allowance** was determined to be $3,060.

$40,000 × 7.65% = $3,060

Line 11:

Mrs. Smith's social security tax allowance was also 7.65 percent because she earns less than $102,000 per year. Multiplying this percentage by her income of $26,136, her **social security tax allowance** was determined to be $1,999.

$26,136 × 7.65% = $1,999

Line 12:

Looking at Table A3, the Smiths' **income protection allowance** was $19,730. This is because there is one college student in the household (Jane), and there are a total of three individuals in the household.

Line 13:

Because both parents work, the Smiths' employment expense allowance is either 35 percent of the lesser of their incomes, or $3,200, whichever is less. Mrs. Smith earns less than her husband, so her income was used.

$26,136 × 35% = $9,147

Because 35 percent of Mrs. Smith's income is over $9,000, the Smiths' **employment expense allowance** was $3,200.

Line 14:

Adding lines 8 through 13, the Smiths' **Total Allowances** were $42,054.

Line 15:

To determine the **Available Income (AI),** the Smiths subtracted line 14 from line 7.

$62,690 − $42,054 = $20,636

The Smiths' AI was $20,636.

Line 16:

Because the Smiths have $3,000 in **savings,** this amount was copied from line 91 of the FAFSA.

Line 17:

Because the Smiths have $10,000 in **investments,** this amount was copied from line 92 of the FAFSA.

Lines 18 and 19:

The Smiths do not have a business and/or investment farm, so these lines were left blank.

THE SMITHS' FM: LINE BY LINE

Line 20:

To determine their net worth, the Smiths added lines 16 and 17.

$10,000 + $3,000 = $13,000

This makes their **net worth** $13,000.

Line 21:

Looking at Table A5, the Smiths used Mr. Smith's age of 42, because he is the older of the two parents. Because Mr. Smith is 42 and married, the education savings and asset protection allowance was $45,300.

Line 22:

Subtracting line 21 from line 20, the Smiths got a negative number.

$13,000 − $45,300 = −$32,300

Line 24:

Multiplying line 22 (−$32,311) by 0.12, the Smiths got a negative number again.

−$32,300 × 0.12 = −$4,276

Because the instructions indicate that if this number is negative, enter zero, the Smiths' **contribution from assets** is $0.

Line 25:

Subtracting the zero dollar amount contributed from assets from their AI on line 15, the Smiths' **Adjusted Available Income (AAI)** is the same as their AI.

$20,636 − $0 = $20,636

Line 26:

Using Table A6, the Smiths determined their contribution from AAI. Because their AAI is between $17,801 and $21,400, their contribution is $4,024, plus 29 percent of their income over $17,801.

By subtracting the $17,801 from their AAI of $20,636, the Smiths learn how much income they will have to calculate at 29 percent.

$20,737 − $17, 801 = $2,936

Therefore, $2,936 of their AAI will be assessed at 29 percent.

$2,936 × 29% = $851

This means that in addition to the flat $4,024 the Smiths need to add $851 to that amount

$4,024 + $851 = $4,875

This makes the **total parent's contribution from AAI** $4,875.

Line 27:

The Smiths have **one child in college,** so this line is 1.

THE SMITHS' FM: LINE BY LINE

Line 28:

Dividing line 26 by the 1 in line 27, the Smiths' **Parent Contribution** is the same as their AAI, $4,875. Next comes the income and information for Jane herself.

Line 29:

Copied from Line 36 of the completed FAFSA, **Jane's adjusted gross income** was $5,000.

Line 31:

As a tax filer, her **taxable income** was the same as line 29, $5,000.

Line 32:

Because Jane did not have any additional income, she had a zero on both FAFSA Worksheets A and B. This made her **untaxed income** $0, as well.

Line 33:

As the sum of line 31 plus line 32 is $5,000, Jane's **income** remained at $5,000.

Line 34:

Jane had a zero on the FAFSA Worksheet C, so this line was $0 as well.

Line 35:

This makes Jane's **Total Income** $5,000.

Line 36:

To qualify for tax liability, a person's income must be more than $5,150. Because her income was less than this amount, Jane was **exempt from withholding.** This means her 2008 income tax paid was $0.

Line 37:

Using Table A7, Jane's **state tax allowance** is 6 percent, because she lives in New York. Therefore, multiplying this percentage by her income, Jane's state tax allowance is $300.

$5,000 × 6% = $300

Line 38:

Like her parents, Jane's social security tax allowance is 7.65 percent, according to Table A2.

$5000 × 7.65% = $383

This makes her **social security tax allowance** $383.

Line 40:

According to the instructions, because line 25 is a positive number, this line is zero.

Line 41:

Adding lines 36 through 40 (including line 39, which is the standard income protection allowance of $3,750), Jane's **Total Allowances** are $4,433.

THE SMITHS' FM: LINE BY LINE

Line 42:

Subtracting Line 41 from Line 35, Jane's **Available Income (AI)** is $567.

$5,000 − $4,433 = $567

Line 44:

By multiplying Line 42 by 0.50, Jane's contribution from her AI is $284.

$567 × 0.50 = $284

Line 47:

Because Jane has $300 in **savings,** this amount is copied from line 43 of the FAFSA.

Line 48:

Because Jane has no other **investments,** the sum of lines 45 through 47 is $300.

Line 50:

Multiplying the $300 in line 48 by the 0.20 in line 49, Jane's **Contribution From Assets** is $60.

$300 × 0.20 = $60

Line 51:

To determine the **expected family contribution,** the Smiths added line 28 (the parents' contribution of $4,875), line 44 (Jane's contribution from AI of $284), and line 50 (Jane's contribution from assets of $60).

$4,875 + $284 + $60 = $5,219

THIS MEANS THE SMITHS' EFC IS $5,219.

See the worksheets for "Calculating Your EFC," at the end of this chapter to find charts A1–A7.

Institutional Methodology

Just as the CSS/PROFILE form is more detailed than the FAFSA, you can expect the information involved in calculating your EFC using IM to be more detailed than when using FM. This is true because IM is used in the CSS/PROFILE, as well as other types of institutional aid, where more detailed financial information about a family is desired.

For example, rather than one protection allowance, IM involves several allowances. The Emergency Reserve Allowance (ERA) is one of them. This allowance is designed to protect a family's assets for use in unexpected emergencies, such as medical emergencies, unemployment, or other urgent and expensive situations a family may face.

Other kinds of allowances involved in IM include the Cumulative Education Savings Allowance (CESA), which is designed to protect a family's savings that are designated for their son or daughter's college expenses, and the Low Income Asset Allowance, which acknowledges that low-income families need additional protection for their income because basic living expenses often take the majority of their income. In addition to these allowances, medical and dental expenses, elementary and secondary school tuitions, and home equity are also factored into the equations.

One important factor needed for an IM calculation that is not part of an FM calculation is home equity, so if you are filling out the PROFILE you will need to know how much equity you have in your home. "One of the things that impacted us," admits Karon Ray, parent of three, "is that because we live in military quarters, in a house on base, our housing situation is different from most families. If we chose to buy a house off base, we'd probably qualify for financial aid because of the mortgage. But because that's not the case; the money is in financial assets instead."

In addition, whereas the FM calculations combine the parents and the dependent student into one worksheet, The College Board uses two different worksheets for parents and dependent students. Calculating your Institutional Methodology EFC can be different from college to college. To make it easier to do the calculations of your EFC based on IM, you can use the online calculator at *apps.collegeboard.com/fincalc/efc_welcome.jsp* on The College Board's website.

Not every school requires applicants to fill out the PROFILE. For a list of colleges that do, go to *profileonline.collegeboard.com/index.isp* on The College Board's website. It is interesting to note that some private colleges no longer request the CSS/PROFILE; instead, they have developed their own institutional aid form that uses a variation of the Institutional Method. If your student is applying to a private college that requires its own institutional financial aid form, rather than the PROFILE, that means one more form you'll have to fill out.

HOW COLLEGES USE YOUR EFC

Naturally, calculating your EFC is one thing, but determining how prospective colleges will use your need analysis is another. Once a college knows how much your student's need is going to be, it has to decide how it will meet that need. By deciding this, the college is creating your student's financial aid package.

A college may decide to meet your student's need by offering grants, work-study opportunities, or other types of institutional aid. Colleges have different kinds and amounts of aid available, which is why (as you'll see in the next chapter) your student's financial aid packages will differ from school to school.

In addition, because the costs of your prospective colleges differ, those colleges are going to have calculated different amounts of need in order for your student to attend. Ideally, this would mean that the more expensive colleges and universities your student applies to would offer more financial aid. Unfortunately, this is not always true.

Most colleges insist that they follow your EFC strictly as it is provided by the FAFSA or their own calculations. Your EFC is used to determine your student's need-based aid, but financial aid administrators use their professional judgment to decide how much and what types of financial aid are offered to accepted students. More often than not, this is where a student's grades, background, achievements, and potential come in. In these situations, these factors may translate into offers of merit-based aid in addition to need-based aid.

Depending on the college, need-based aid is not always calculated first. "We actually consider students for merit-based aid first, before we calculate a student's need-based aid," explains Jade Kolb, manager of financial aid at New York University. "If they have a merit scholarship, the need-based aid would complement that."

You're probably well aware that the more a college wants your son or daughter to attend, the more financial aid they are willing to offer. So, while your EFC reflects the FM or IM calculation of the need-based aid your student is eligible for, your final award could be much larger—if the school decides to award merit-based aid to your student.

INDEPENDENT STUDENTS

As we mentioned at the beginning of this chapter, the amount of financial aid awarded is usually based on EFC—a calculation that considers both the parents' and the students' income and assets. Most students entering college for the first time are considered dependent students. Some parents believe that if their student does not live at home and/or does not receive money from them, then he or she "becomes" independent and, because of that, should receive a larger financial aid package. It is true that independent students may be awarded more financial aid than dependent students, but in the eyes of the federal government students do not become independent just because they are paying their own way. Instead, to be declared independent, students must meet one or more of the requirements set up by the federal government for the purposes of financial aid (for a list of these requirements, see chapter 8).

Since most of the students entering college for the first time are considered dependent students, all of the calculations done in this chapter and elsewhere in the book are based on the assumption that your student is a dependent (as defined by the federal government). But even if you are an independent student, most of what we've discussed throughout the book still applies.

Exceptions

The federal government does allow for exceptions, so if you do not meet the published criteria, but have a unique situation that should qualify you as an independent student, talk to your college's financial aid office. These types of situations are considered on a case-by-case basis, and the college's decision is final. Because of this, a student with a unique situation could be considered independent by one college, but not by another.

"We follow federal guidelines when it comes to independent students," says Ellen Frishberg of Johns Hopkins University, "unless there is an exception, such as an orphan or other unique circumstance. For example, one student rejected their parent's Amish background, and currently supports themselves without financial assistance. But such exceptions are rare."

Need Analysis for Independent Students

If you are an independent student, you'll find that colleges will calculate your need analysis slightly differently than we've discussed in this book. Just how a college will calculate your need analysis depends on whether or not you have dependents that rely on you financially, or if you are responsible only for yourself. Therefore, when a single mother is going back to school, the college will also consider the financial impact this has on her child, while an independent student without children will have different financial needs. To better understand your differences in need analysis, contact your college for assistance.

Anything Else?

For the most part, the financial aid process for independent students does not differ that much from dependent students. Financial aid packages are created the same way, and are given the same consideration. However, the one real difference involved is that independent students usually receive more self-help aid than other students do. This is because independent students have greater financial needs than dependent students, and this extra aid is necessary for them to be able to afford college. Because of this, independent students are automatically eligible for additional federal loan funds, particularly from the Stafford loan program.

As you can tell, being an independent student means more than moving away from home, paying some or all of your college costs, and/or filing your own taxes. For those who are truly independent and do not have financial support from parents or a family, however, additional financial aid is available.

MOVING ON

This chapter began by discussing the basic beliefs on which all need analysis is based. We then looked at the differences between Federal and Institutional Methodologies, briefly describing each. After recapping the definition of an EFC and how it is calculated, we then covered how your assets and income are viewed in this process. We looked at allowances and discretionary net worth before comparing FM and IM in more detail.

We calculated a sample family's EFC using the Federal Methodology. Afterward, we discussed institutional formulas and how colleges use your EFC in determining financial aid. Finally, we looked at the definition of an independent student, and how the government and colleges evaluate them for aid.

In the next chapter, you'll get a better understanding of what goes into a college's financial aid offer, and learn more about the various elements involved in a financial aid package. You'll also learn how to compare and negotiate these packages. Before you move on, take a look at the checklist for this chapter.

✓ **CHECKLIST:**

1. Gather your family's federal tax and W-2 forms for calculating your EFC.
2. Request the necessary forms for calculating Federal Methodology, either in paper or online.
3. Complete the Federal Methodology worksheet.
4. Access the forms for calculating Institutional Methodology (if applicable) online.
5. Complete the Institutional Methodology worksheet (if applicable).
6. Save your calculations for comparison to your student's financial aid packages.

Table A1: State and Other Tax Allowance
for EFC Formula Worksheet A (parents only)

STATE	PERCENT OF TOTAL INCOME		STATE	PERCENT OF TOTAL INCOME	
	$0-$14,999	$15,000 or more		$0-$14,999	$15,000 or more
Alabama	3%	2%	Missouri	5%	4%
Alaska	2%	1%	Montana	5%	4%
American Samoa	3%	2%	Nebraska	5%	4%
Arizona	4%	3%	Nevada	3%	2%
Arkansas	4%	3%	New Hampshire	5%	4%
California	8%	7%	New Jersey	9%	8%
Canada and Canadian			New Mexico	3%	2%
Provinces	3%	2%	New York	9%	8%
Colorado	5%	4%	North Carolina	6%	5%
Connecticut	8%	7%	North Dakota	3%	2%
Delaware	4%	3%	Northern Mariana		
District of Columbia	7%	6%	Islands	3%	2%
Federated States			Ohio	6%	5%
of Micronesia	3%	2%	Oklahoma	4%	3%
Florida	3%	2%	Oregon	7%	6%
Georgia	5%	4%	Palau	3%	2%
Guam	3%	2%	Pennsylvania	6%	5%
Hawaii	5%	4%	Puerto Rico	3%	2%
Idaho	5%	4%	Rhode Island	7%	6%
Illinois	5%	4%	South Carolina	5%	4%
Indiana	4%	3%	South Dakota	2%	1%
Iowa	5%	4%	Tennessee	2%	1%
Kansas	5%	4%	Texas	3%	2%
Kentucky	5%	4%	Utah	5%	4%
Louisiana	3%	2%	Vermont	5%	4%
Maine	6%	5%	Virgin Islands	3%	2%
Marshall Islands	3%	2%	Virginia	6%	5%
Maryland	8%	7%	Washington	4%	3%
Massachusetts	7%	6%	West Virginia	3%	2%
Mexico	3%	2%	Wisconsin	7%	6%
Michigan	5%	4%	Wyoming	2%	1%
Minnesota	6%	5%	Blank or Invalid		
Mississippi	3%	2%	State	3%	2%
			OTHER	3%	2%

Multiply Parents' Total Income (EFC Formula Worksheet A, line 7) by the appropriate rate from the table above to get the "State and Other Tax Allowance" (EFC Formula Worksheet A, line 9). Use the parents' State of Legal Residence (FAFSA/SAR #72). If this item is blank or invalid, use the student's State of Legal Residence (FAFSA/SAR #18). If both items are blank or invalid, use the State in the Student's Mailing Address (FAFSA/SAR #6). If all three items are blank or invalid, use the rate for a blank or invalid state above.

Table A2: Social Security Tax

Calculate separately the Social Security tax of father, mother, and student.

Income Earned from Work*	Social Security Tax
$0 - $102,000	7.65% of income
$102,001 or greater	$7,803.00 + 1.45% of amount over $102,000

*Father's/stepfather's 2008 income earned from work is FAFSA/SAR #89.
Mother's/stepmother's 2008 income earned from work is FAFSA/SAR #90.
Student's 2008 income earned from work is FAFSA/SAR #39.
Social Security tax will never be less than zero.

Table A3: Income Protection Allowance

Number in parents' household, including student (FAFSA/SAR #75)	Number of college students in household (FAFSA/SAR #76)				
	1	2	3	4	5
2	$15,840	$13,130	———	———	———
3	19,730	17,030	$14,320	———	———
4	24,370	21,660	18,960	$16,250	———
5	28,750	26,040	23,340	20,630	$17,940
6	33,630	30,920	28,220	25,510	22,820

Note: For each additional family member, add $3,800.
For each additional college student (except parents), subtract $2,700.

Table A4: Business/Farm Net Worth Adjustment
for EFC Formula Worksheet A (parents only)

If the net worth of a business or farm is—	Then the adjusted net worth is—			
Less than $1	$0			
$1 to $115,000	40% of net worth of business/farm			
$115,001 to $340,000	$ 46,000	+	50%	of net worth over $115,000
$340,001 to $565,000	$158,500	+	60%	of net worth over $340,000
$565,001 or more	$293,500	+	100%	of net worth over $565,000

Table A5: Education Savings and Asset Protection Allowance
for EFC Formula Worksheet A (parents only)

Age of older parent as of 12/31/2009*	Allowance if there are two parents	Allowance if there is only one parent	Age of older parent as of 12/31/2009*	Allowance if there are two parents	Allowance if there is only one parent
25 or less ...	$0	$0	45	$48,700	$19,900
26	2,900	1,200	46	49,900	20,400
27	5,800	2,400	47	51,200	20,900
28	8,700	3,600	48	52,400	21,400
29	11,600	4,800	49	53,700	21,900
30	14,500	6,000	50	55,300	22,400
31	17,400	7,200	51	56,700	22,900
32	20,300	8,400	52	58,000	23,500
33	23,100	9,500	53	59,800	24,000
34	26,000	10,700	54	61,200	24,600
35	28,900	11,900	55	63,000	25,300
36	31,800	13,100	56	64,900	25,900
37	34,700	14,300	57	66,400	26,500
38	37,600	15,500	58	68,300	27,200
39	40,500	16,700	59	70,300	27,900
40	43,400	17,900	60	72,300	28,700
41	44,200	18,200	61	74,400	29,500
42	45,300	18,600	62	76,600	30,300
43	46,400	19,100	63	79,100	31,100
44	47,600	19,500	64	81,300	32,000
			65 or over ..	84,000	32,800

*Determine the age of the older parent listed in FAFSA/SAR #66 and #70 as of 12/31/09.
If no parent date of birth is provided, use age 45.

Table A6: Parents' Contribution from AAI

If parents' AAI is—		The parents' contribution from AAI is—		
Less than -$3,409		-$750		
-$3,409 to	$14,200	22% of AAI		
$14,201 to	$17,800	$3,124 + 25% of AAI over	$14,200	
$17,801 to	$21,400	$4,024 + 29% of AAI over	$17,800	
$21,401 to	$25,000	$5,068 + 34% of AAI over	$21,400	
$25,001 to	$28,600	$6,292 + 40% of AAI over	$25,000	
$28,601 or more		$7,732 + 47% of AAI over	$28,600	

Table A7: State and Other Tax Allowance
for EFC Formula Worksheet A (student only)

Alabama	2%	Missouri	3%
Alaska	0%	Montana	3%
American Samoa	2%	Nebraska	3%
Arizona	3%	Nevada	1%
Arkansas	3%	New Hampshire	1%
California	5%	New Jersey	4%
Canada and Canadian Provinces	2%	New Mexico	3%
Colorado	3%	New York	6%
Connecticut	4%	North Carolina	4%
Delaware	3%	North Dakota	1%
District of Columbia	6%	Northern Mariana Islands	2%
Federated States of Micronesia	2%	Ohio	4%
Florida	1%	Oklahoma	3%
Georgia	4%	Oregon	5%
Guam	2%	Palau	2%
Hawaii	4%	Pennsylvania	3%
Idaho	3%	Puerto Rico	2%
Illinois	2%	Rhode Island	4%
Indiana	3%	South Carolina	3%
Iowa	3%	South Dakota	1%
Kansas	3%	Tennessee	1%
Kentucky	4%	Texas	1%
Louisiana	2%	Utah	4%
Maine	4%	Vermont	3%
Marshall Islands	2%	Virgin Islands	2%
Maryland	5%	Virginia	4%
Massachusetts	4%	Washington	1%
Mexico	2%	West Virginia	2%
Michigan	3%	Wisconsin	4%
Minnesota	4%	Wyoming	1%
Mississippi	2%	Blank or Invalid State	2%
		OTHER	2%

Multiply the student's total income (EFC Formula Worksheet A, line 35) by the appropriate rate from the table above to get the "state and other tax allowance" (EFC Formula Worksheet A, line 37). Use the student's state of legal residence (FAFSA/SAR #18). If this item is blank or invalid, use the state in the student's mailing address (FAFSA/SAR #6). If both items are blank or invalid, use the parents' state of legal residence (FAFSA/SAR #72). If all three items are blank or invalid, use the rate for a blank or invalid state above.

CHAPTER TEN

Evaluating Aid Packages

As we've discussed, colleges and universities use the results of your need analysis to create a financial aid package for your student. These packages vary from student to student and from school to school. In this chapter you'll learn about the various elements of a financial aid package, as well as how you can negotiate for more financial aid.

If you used chapter 9 to calculate your EFC, some of this information may be a review for you. However, in order to bring others up to speed, let's backtrack for a moment and begin with a discussion of what you can expect in a financial aid package.

UNDERSTANDING A COLLEGE'S OFFER

Unless your student applied for an early decision, you probably won't start getting those much anticipated letters from the colleges until April, which we affectionately call "Accepted Student Month." Hopefully, you'll find many thick envelopes in the mail. And, when you do, you might be tempted to breathe a sigh of relief and think your work is over. But, it's not. If your student has been accepted at more than one school, you and your son or daughter are going to need to make a decision. Which one to choose? We suspect that the financial aid package offered by each of the colleges is going to play a major role in your selection.

You've already learned that a financial aid package generally provides a combination of gift aid, self-help aid, and work aid, and that this represents the total amount of financial aid your student will receive from the college. When colleges create these packages, they use your need analysis to decide how much financial aid to offer your student. Part of that process involves deciding which types of aid the college will offer to meet that need.

In addition, because your prospective colleges cost different amounts, these schools will have calculated different amounts of need in order for your student to attend. Because of this, you might assume that private and out-of-state colleges are going to provide your student with more financial aid than a local public school. However, that's not always the case. Let's examine why.

Look at the Whole Picture

"When comparing aid packages at schools, always look at the bottom line," says Carly T. Connors, director of admissions at Albany College of Pharmacy. "Many students think that just because they received a large scholarship at one school they are getting a better deal than at another school. Remember that you always need to look at the whole picture—tuition minus scholarships and financial aid."

While your EFC is used to determine need-based aid, financial aid administrators at colleges use their professional judgment to decide if additional aid will be offered. Your student's academic record, achievements, and potential will influence this. If you're fortunate, some merit-based aid will be included in your student's aid packages.

Most families understand the competitiveness involved in getting merit-based aid. The more a college wants a certain student to attend, the greater the amount of financial aid that is offered to the student. Because private schools tend to have more institutional aid than public colleges, intense competition is more common at those schools.

LOOKING AT THE GAP

The first thing you'll probably do when you receive each financial aid package is review the big picture—in other words, you'll immediately look to see if the amount of financial aid being offered is going to be enough to cover your student's costs. If it's not, then this is what colleges call your "unmet need" (the amount, after aid is awarded, that your family is expected to contribute toward the cost of your student's education).

Gapping is another term for "unmet need," and it too refers to the difference between your need (as calculated by the college) and the amount of financial aid offered to your student. If a college determines your need to be $8,000 a year, but your student's package only offers $5,000 in financial aid, then your unmet need, or "gap," is $3,000.

Remember that colleges determine your "need" by subtracting your EFC from the cost of attending that college, so different amounts of unmet need are not going to necessarily reflect the dollar amount of your aid package. For example, let's say your student applies to both a dream school and a safety school. The dream school may offer a $12,000 aid package, while the safety school offers only a $4,000 aid package. At first, the dream school may look like the better choice, but what if that dream school is going to cost $20,000 a year, while your son or daughter could attend the safety school for only $6,000 a year? In that case, the unmet need for your student's dream school would be $8,000 a year ($20,000 in college costs minus $12,000 in financial aid), while the unmet need for the safety school would be just $2,000 a year ($6,000 in college costs minus $4,000 in aid).

This difference in unmet need, alone, shouldn't be the deciding factor in selecting which college your student will attend, but it will tell you how much you'd actually pay for your student to attend various colleges. Deciding the impact of those differences will be up to you.

PACKAGE ELEMENTS

Now that you've got an overall sense of what unmet need means, let's take a look at what makes up a financial aid package. In general, any package you receive will consist of up to three types of aid: need-based aid, merit-based aid, and other sources of aid. We already described these aid categories in chapter 6, but we'll take a closer look at them now, to see how they impact your student's cost of college.

> **College Funds and Gapping**
>
> Don't assume that all gapping is intentionally done by colleges. "For the most part, there is some unmet need with our students," admits Barry Simmons, director of financial aid at Virginia Tech, "but we don't necessarily gap. When the funds for that student run out, there's not much else we can do."

Need-Based Aid

As you're aware, need-based aid can be self-help aid, work aid, or gift aid. Many colleges and universities attempt to balance these three areas, so that no one student is unfairly overburdened with loans. Because of this, most need-based aid is spread out among students fairly equally. It's unlikely in most situations that one low-income student would receive a need-based grant that covered most costs while another student with a similar economic situation would not receive any gift aid. When colleges award need-based aid, their processes are usually standardized, with little room for interpretation.

However, it's important to understand that the amount of need-based aid your student receives will not necessarily be consistent throughout the time they attend college. In an effort to attract students, many colleges change the amount of aid offered to students after they attend the school for a year or two. Not surprisingly, this means incoming freshmen may receive more aid than other students. This is done because once a student begins to attend a college, that school no longer feels it has to attract the person to keep them there. The student is already attending the college and is generally committed to continuing there. In addition, some schools find it unfair to burden freshmen with high loans, because not all of these students will complete college. But, as students get closer to completing their degrees, they are more likely to be able to afford the burden of those higher loans, and the loans offered might increase.

Merit-Based Aid

This is the most flexible area of aid available to colleges, and merit-based aid is used to attract particularly gifted students who excel in particular areas. Academically gifted students may receive grants to tempt them to attend a school, just as talented athletes may be offered a significant scholarship in hopes that they will play for the college's team. Merit-based aid can be anything from grants given to students with high SAT scores to a scholarship for a well-known teenager who may be musically gifted. Merit-based aid also can be used to diversify a campus by attracting minorities or other populations.

Keep that Scholarship!

"If your student receives a scholarship as part of his or her package, always be sure to confirm with the college that it is renewable during the whole time he or she is in school," recommends Carly T. Connors, director of admissions at Albany College of Pharmacy. "You should also find out what GPA is required to keep the scholarship. You don't want your student to lose out because you didn't have all the necessary information."

Colleges that are well known for a particular major, area of study, or athletic team can expect a high number of applicants for those areas. For example, if a school has a particularly good basketball team, that school will likely get a large number of applications from high school basketball players. Because of this, some colleges are placed into a "highly competitive" category, be it for a sport or a specific major. Competition to get into those schools can be fierce. "I frequently have to explain to parents that no matter what a student's achievements, they're compared to the whole applicant pool for that year," explains Jade Kolb, manager of financial aid for New York University. "A student could have a 3.5 GPA, but if our applicant pool for that year has an average of 3.7, they'll have a tough time. It can change from year to year."

Even when a student receives merit-based aid, it may not be as much as was hoped. "A lot of people whose children excel at sports think this will turn into lots of financial aid," explains Joe Sanseverino, whose daughter was offered a lacrosse scholarship. "Parents think there's a good chance their child will get a free ride. That may be true if your child plays football or basketball, but for other sports I don't think it's true. I've had coaches tell me that there's not enough money in lesser-known sports to do that."

Multitask

Even if your student has a good chance of getting an athletic scholarship, encourage them to apply for academic ones. "That's the best situation to be in," says Sanseverino (parent of a student who was awarded a sports scholarship), "because coaches will set aside money for the student's scholarship, then go the admission office and say, 'I want this person to play for us, and here's what I can give them. What can you offer to help?' If the student has good grades, they're likely to get more aid because of academics."

Due to the flexibility involved in merit-based aid, these types of awards continue to be the most controversial type of financial awards. Some consider merit-based aid to be unfair, saying that colleges do not have enough money to offer such high awards to a handful of students. Supporters of merit-based aid insist that high achievements and accomplishments should be rewarded and encouraged to continue. As we've stated earlier, some schools are reducing the amount of merit-based aid that they award each year. You should be aware of this potential trend and keep it in mind as you are looking at financial aid packages.

Private and Outside Scholarships

As we'll discuss in chapter 12, your son or daughter may apply for and receive other types of aid, including scholarships or grants from corporations, local organizations, and private foundations. Because those funding opportunities are not offered through the college itself, they may not be included in your aid package. However, this depends on the source of the outside aid. The scholarship sponsor may choose to notify the college directly, or it may be your responsibility.

> **Look for Local Scholarships**
> "To maximize their chances of receiving a scholarship, students should seek out local scholarships, such as those offered by rotary clubs and junior leagues, and they should start looking for these opportunities as early as ninth grade," says Bill Sliwa, vice president of enrollment management, Lees-McRae College.

If your son or daughter is awarded one of these scholarships or grants, this may impact your aid package. Your student's financial aid package cannot exceed the cost of that college, so if a private scholarship causes this to happen, your other sources of aid may be reduced. We'll explore this further in chapter 12.

COMPARING AID PACKAGES

It's very exciting when your student starts receiving college acceptance letters. But, your next reaction will probably be one of concern: just how will all the costs be paid? You'll only have to wait a week or so to answer that question. By then, you'll have received all of the financial aid packages, and you'll be able to compare the aid offered and find out just how much each school will actually cost you.

Each of these schools will probably offer your student a different combination of gift aid, self-help aid, and work aid. Your next step will be to compare the packages side by side. Only by carefully reviewing the advantages and disadvantages of the offers will you and your student be able to pick the best one.

We've already discussed the idea of unmet need and how you should look at this difference instead of the precise dollar amounts offered by each package. Calculating this gap at each of the schools is a basic way of comparing packages, but here are a number of other things you and your student should consider:

- Don't just look at the bottom line. There are other factors that should also be compared. What type of money is being offered? How much is in aid that does not need to be repaid (grants, scholarships, work-study) and how much is in loans? "How a school meets need is important," says Ellen Frishberg, director of student financial services at Johns Hopkins University. "Regardless of the dollar amount, a package that is 70 percent grants and 30 percent loans is better than a package with 30 percent grants and 70 percent loans."

- Don't assume that the school offering the most gift aid automatically has the best financial aid package. Instead, add up the self-help and work aid. It's possible that your student could attend an expensive college and end up with less debt than if they attended a cheaper school; it all depends what's being offered. "For us, private colleges turned out to be cheaper in the long-term than public schools," admits Connie Gores, a parent and an academic vice president. "My daughter was offered grants by a private school to study abroad, which significantly impacts one year of her education, while public schools didn't have such a program."

- Keep things in perspective when comparing your unmet need from each college. An expensive college may offer more gift aid than other schools, but if that school sets your EFC higher, it may be less attractive. Students who borrow heavily in order to cover a higher EFC will graduate with more debt. Here's a rule of thumb suggested by Mark Kantrowitz, publisher of FinAid.org, that you might want to follow: "Do not borrow more than your expected starting salary for your entire undergraduate education," he recommends. "If your starting salary is going to be $40,000, then you should borrow no more than $10,000 a year for a four-year degree.

Reducing Debt

Many education leaders are looking for ways to reduce the student debt caused by heavy borrowing. Recently, Davidson College decided it will no longer use student loans in its need-based financial aid packages. Instead, students will be offered more grants and work opportunities. Other private colleges, including Princeton and Columbia, have also significantly reduced the amount of aid given in the form of loans.

- Consider the budget you've created for each college (use the COA worksheets you prepared in chapter 4). Expenses that are not taken into consideration by the college, such as personal expenses and travel, may have a large impact on your actual needs. If these amounts are significant, will you need to borrow more? Or, can these expenses be reduced?

- If you receive a scholarship or grant from an outside or private source, check to see if it will have an impact on your aid package. An adjusted aid package may make a college more (or less) attractive than before.

- If a financial aid package includes loans, compare the terms of the various loans to determine which is best suited for you. Here are some factors to consider: Is the yearly interest paid by the government? What is the interest rate? When does repayment start? How much will be owed by the time your student graduates? What will the monthly payments be? Will the loan interest increase after the first year? Be careful about borrowing from several lenders, because this can end up costing more. If you're considering consolidating these loans, be sure to compare the rates and terms.

- Be aware that not all schools send out loan paperwork with financial aid packages. "We wait for students to accept the loans in their financial aid package," explains University of Texas at Arlington's financial aid director Karen Krause, "then we send out the forms for them to start the loan process."

- Did your student receive a work-study award? If so, then you might want to ask the college these questions. Is the job assigned to your student, or will he or she have to find one? How many hours will your student be expected to work each week? What is the pay per hour? How often will your student be paid? Will that payment be sent directly to your student or will the college credit your student's account? Once you know those answers, then determine if your student is prepared to take on the responsibilities of working while going to school.

- Find out if the awards your son or daughter is offered will remain consistent in future years. Although a college may offer more financial aid initially than your other prospective schools, that school may decrease its aid the following year—sometimes to less than what the other colleges offer.

- Are there any caveats attached to the award? Does your student have to carry a certain number of units or maintain a minimum grade point average in order to continue receiving funds?

- Finally, keep this in mind. You are not required to accept every provision in an award package. Certainly, you wouldn't want to turn down any gift aid offered. But, you may not want to accept an unsubsidized loan. Or, you and your student may have decided that work aid is not a good idea. You are permitted to reject any part of a package and still accept the rest of the aid offered.

Above all, remember that there's more to picking the best school for your student than just the cost. Your student may only have to pay $1,000 a year to go to his or her safety school, but what if he or she gets accepted to an Ivy League university and would only have to pay a few thousand dollars more to attend? Would the long-term benefits of an Ivy League degree outweigh the short-term debt? As we've stated, college debt is an investment in your student's future, and sometimes that investment can turn out to be a bargain.

You're probably going to find that there are advantages and disadvantages to each financial aid package you receive, and sometimes the benefits and differences between them are difficult to figure out. When this happens, you may want to make a list of the pros and cons of each offer. If you're having trouble keeping track, go through everything in the aid package. Jot down the costs (including tuition, fees, room and board, transportation, and other expenses) at each school and compare that to the type and amount of aid you've been awarded. The differences between the offers should then become much clearer. Or, if you want to do this online, you can find award comparison calculators at a number of sites, including:

- *www.finaid.org/calculators/awardletter.phtml*
- *www.petersons.com/finaid/code/award_analyzer.asp?sponsor=2859*
- *www.collegeanswer.com/deciding/award_comparison/ac_index.jsp*

NEGOTIATING YOUR FINANCIAL AID PACKAGE

Weighing the Pros and Cons

When you are comparing aid packages, consider making a list of pros and cons for each element in the packages offered to your student. This will help you identify the best total package, not just the package with the best bottom line. For example, one school might offer your student a nonrenewable grant or scholarship for the first year. How will you make up that money in subsequent years?

You Can Negotiate

An interesting straw poll on *www. rspfunding.com/poll.html* revealed that nearly half the respondents who received a financial aid package did not know that they might be able to negotiate a better award. Don't make this mistake yourself. Parents and students can always request a review of their award, particularly if their personal or financial situations have changed.

As you and your son or daughter compare the various financial aid packages, you may notice a significant difference between colleges. Let's say that one school offers your student a need-based grant for low-income families, and that this grant will pay for most of the cost of that college, but the college your student really wants to attend didn't offer any kind of grant at all.

Not too long ago, families were stuck with what they were offered. "Take it or leave it," pretty much summed up financial aid packages, but that's no longer true. Today, it's becoming more common for families to be able to negotiate their financial aid. Many parents argue that if schools want to compete for students, they should be willing to reconsider a financial aid package if another college has made a significantly better offer. You'll find that some colleges, in fact, actually encourage parents to provide them with offers from competing colleges so they can attempt to improve a student's aid. And, if your financial situation has changed since you filed the FAFSA or PROFILE, almost any school is willing to take another look at your awards package.

"Negotiating for additional financial aid is certainly not a problem for us," says Jack Toney, director of financial aid at Marshall University. "I think students should feel welcome to communicate their needs, and we try to work with families to help students attend." However, Toney emphasizes that there are limits when it comes to negotiating. "There's not much we can do with need-based aid," he says. "Institutional aid is really where we can be the most flexible."

When it comes to negotiating, Johns Hopkins is typical of the approach most schools take. "We call it reconsideration, rather than a negotiation," explains Ellen Frishberg. "We will take things into consideration, but we won't pay for your daughter's wedding."

The bottom line is: you should not hesitate to contact a college to discuss the aid offered, especially if there are significant differences between the various financial aid packages you received or if you have new information to report about your financial or personal situation. While no school is going to guarantee that it will change their offer, you should take advantage of their willingness to listen to you. What have you got to lose?

> **Using Professional Judgment**
>
> In 2009, the Department of Education issued an advisory to college financial aid officers, urging them to use their "professional judgment" to help students in financial distress. The letter reminds these officers that they "have the authority under law to make adjustments, especially during these challenging economic times." In particular, the advisory asks colleges to contract parents who might have lost their jobs and remind them that they have the right to appeal for more financial aid because of "special circumstances."

HOW TO NEGOTIATE

If you decide to try to negotiate your financial aid package, you'll need to prepare before contacting the school. First of all, make sure you have a legitimate reason for asking a college to reconsider their financial aid package. Treat the process as if you're making a request, because really, that's what you're doing. Having a negative, angry attitude and insisting that a college increase their aid will destroy any chance of being successful. Be polite.

If you decide to request a reassessment of your award package, take these steps before you start the process:

- Review your budget. Focus on the past 90 days or so. Label your expenses as either fixed or discretionary, and then separate them into individual categories (like housing, utilities, etc.). Compare your current budget against the award letters your student received. Does your EFC in the award package exceed your discretionary expenses? If so, you may have a strong negotiation point, even if your financial situation has not changed since filing the FAFSA.

- Gather together all relevant documents (pay stubs, tax returns, termination notices, etc.) if you plan to negotiate for an increase in aid based on a change in your family's situation (for example, a layoff, a costly medical situation, a foreclosure, a divorce).

- Decide exactly what increase you are going to request. It won't be enough just to ask for more money. You need to be specific about the amount needed. And, you have to be able to present the budget and the documents to justify your request.

Now you're ready to contact the financial aid office or write a letter making your request. Since you don't receive award letters until April and you generally have to pick your student's college by the beginning of May, you probably will want to call or email.

Whatever method you chose, be sure to do the following:

- Remind the school that your student is interested in attending (if not, you wouldn't be asking them to do this). If the school is your student's first choice, state this as well.

- Ask if there is a possibility that you and your student can receive more help with expenses (preferably a grant).

- Give a reason for your request (maybe another college offered a low-income grant, or you are being forced to take a pay cut at your job, or you have incurred large medical expenses). Be specific and show, with documentation and numbers, what extenuating situations have occurred and how they will affect your family finances. If you mention another school's offer, be up front and honest. Explain how your student qualified for that particular aid and ask if this college had considered your student for something similar.

- Acknowledge that you appreciate the person's time and consideration, and that they are welcome to contact you if they have questions.

The Flexibility Factor

"One of the best things you can do is factor in how amenable a college is in unique situations when you're considering schools," says financial aid officer Connie Gores. "If a college tells you they strictly go by the FAFSA and seems reluctant to consider other information, then you won't get far if you have financial troubles later on."

Negotiating by Phone.

Here's how a phone negotiation, based on a change in circumstances as well as a competing offers from other colleges, might go:

PARENT: My daughter is very interested in attending your college. In fact, it's probably her number-one choice. But I have some questions about her financial aid.

FINANCIAL AID OFFICER: What would you like to know?

PARENT: There are a couple of things, actually. First, I'm a bit concerned about the family contribution that was calculated. I don't know how I can possibly come up with that amount. As it is, our income barely meets our expenses. Is there anything you can do to lower that expected contribution?

FINANCIAL AID OFFICER: First, why don't you review the numbers you reported on your application. If there are any errors, let us know and we'll recalculate. Second, if there are any unusually high expenses that aren't reflected in these numbers—high medical bills, for example—let us know. We may have some flexibility there. Third, as you know, you can always take out a PLUS loan to meet your family share.

PARENT: OK, thanks. My husband has been downsized at work and his salary is somewhat less this year than it was when we filled out the FAFSA. I'll send you some documentation on that. But there's something else that bothers us. As I said, your school is probably my daughter's first choice, but frankly the financial aid award isn't as attractive as some others she's received. She's going to have to borrow an awful lot to make it through. Is there any possibility of increased scholarships or grants?

FINANCIAL AID OFFICER: Well, you know, we spend a great deal of time working up packaging guidelines for students. I'll be happy to review hers to make sure we didn't make any errors. Also, if there are any special expenses that she'll have that are not usually considered in our budgets, let me know so we can consider whether the budget we used for her is appropriate.

PARENT: We don't have any unusual expenses. We're just concerned that the two other colleges that have accepted her have made significantly better offers in terms of how much she'll have to borrow or work. If it were just a few dollars difference, I wouldn't say anything. But these are pretty big differences. Big enough that we may have to recommend that she go to one of those other schools. Are you sure you can't do something?

FINANCIAL AID OFFICER: Tell you what. Why don't you send me a copy of your husband's current pay stubs and the offer letters from those other schools. I'll look at them and see what I can do. No guarantees, you understand. But we'd very much like your daughter to come here so I promise I'll give her every possible consideration.

PARENT: Thanks. That's all I can ask.

Negotiating on Writing.

If you are going to write (by mail or email), the content of the letter would be similar to the phone conversation detailed above. When composing your letter, use the following points as a guide:

- Paragraph 1: Thank them for the award, mention your student's interest in attending, and list out some ways your student might contribute to the school (for example, by trying out for a sport, the campus newspaper, or another campus activity). Then, write one or more of the next paragraphs, as appropriate.

- Paragraph 2: Describe any change in your economic or personal circumstances, detail how that affects your ability to come up with the money to pay your unmet need, and ask for an increase in aid based on that; and/or

- Paragraph 3: Ask for additional aid based on your student's recent accomplishments (for example, in sports, in extracurricular activities, in academics, in the community, in your church); and/or

- Paragraph 4: Request an increase based on competing offers. Name the specific schools and the amounts/types of aid awarded. Then, close your letter with paragraph 5.

- Paragraph 5: Thank them for using the information you are providing to review the offer the school made to your student and let them know you are looking forward to hearing back from them soon.

After you make your request, be sure to follow up with the college aid office. Keep your eye on the calendar. Remember, you only have a couple of weeks between the time your student receives the award packages and when you must pick the college your student will attend.

Most of all, be realistic. "When it comes to negotiation, two car payments and a mortgage is not a special circumstance," notes Karen Krause. "Neither is significant credit card debt."

Still, it never hurts to ask. But, as Texas Christian University's financial aid director Mike Scott reminds us, "Just be careful how you do it."

IT'S DECISION TIME

Most colleges expect to find out, by May 1 or so, whether or not your student will be attending in the fall. It's time to make a decision. You should be ready. Your student has received, reviewed, and compared each of the colleges' award packages. You may have even tried to negotiate a better deal from one or more of the schools. We know that financial aid is only one of the factors that you'll use in making your final choice. But, by using what you've learned up to now, we're confident you'll make a well-informed decision.

MOVING ON

To wrap up, we began by discussing how a college creates a financial aid package and by looking at the decisions financial aid administrators make. We defined gapping (unmet need) as an important factor in comparing aid packages.

We then looked at the different types of aid that could be included in a financial aid package: gift aid (grants and scholarships), self-help aid (loans), and work aid. We listed out factors that should be considered when comparing packages. We also discussed private and other kinds of scholarships, addressing the impact they might have on an aid package.

Finally, we talked about how, when, and why families should ask for a reassessment of their financial aid package and how they should go about doing that.

In the next chapter, we'll take a look at another way you might be able to get additional aid to reduce college costs for you and your student. You'll learn about the type of aid your state offers and how to get information about this assistance. Before you move on, though, take a look at the checklist for this chapter.

✓ CHECKLIST:

After receiving your financial aid packages, determine your unmet need for each school.

1. If your student has received any outside or private aid, notify your colleges and find out if it will impact their aid packages.

2. Compare your financial aid packages. Try to get a sense of the pros and cons of what each school offers.

3. If necessary, negotiate your financial aid packages.

4. Once you've made a decision, respectfully decline the awards packages from the other schools that made offers to your student. That way, the awards that were set aside for your student can be offered to others.

CHAPTER ELEVEN

Checking with Your State

While the federal government hands out the lion share of financial aid, individual states (along with the District of Columbia and the U.S. territories and possessions) are close behind. Each year, states award billions in funding to their residents who are interested in working on a college or graduate degree. You don't want to miss out on a chance to get your share of these funds.

STATE AID

Your state can help you pay for college in three important ways. First, as we discussed in chapter 3, state-supported colleges and universities offer low-cost tuition to in-state residents. Just by taking advantage of that in-state benefit, you can save up to $15,000 each year compared to what out-of-state students will have to pay to attend the same school. A second way that states provide assistance is through their prepaid savings and tuition plans; the former helps you grow your money tax free and the later can freeze tuition over time at bargain levels (see chapter 5 for more information). In this chapter, we'll focus on the third way your state can help you pay for college: by awarding state-based financial aid.

Did you know that every state offers a wide variety of need- and/or merit-based scholarships, fellowships, grants, and loans to residents who want a college education? In addition, a majority of the states sponsor forgiveness programs for selected professions (such as education or health care) to recipients who agree to work in specific types of jobs or areas of the state after graduation. And a number of states even offer work-study programs, tuition equalization programs, assistance to students attending private schools within the state, guaranteed free-tuition plans to qualified and needy students, or financial assistance to residents with certain characteristics (minority group members, persons with disabilities, military families, etc.).

While your student is automatically considered for some state-supported funding when you file the FAFSA, most of the financial aid offered by a state to its residents must be applied for separately. To get an idea of the diversity of these individual state programs, take a look at just some of the opportunities that are sponsored by a typical state: Delaware. Even a small state like this offers big rewards to its residents!

- **Diamond State Scholarship:** Up to $1,250 per year, for up to four years in college, to high school seniors in Delaware with outstanding academic records.
- **Delaware Scholarship Incentive Program:** From $700 to $2,200 a year, depending on GPA, for Delaware residents who are enrolled full-time in college in Delaware or Pennsylvania and can demonstrate financial need.
- **Agenda for Delaware Women Trailblazer Scholarship:** $2,500 each year for female residents planning to attend a public or private nonprofit college in the state (selection is based half on financial need and half on extracurricular activities and leadership).
- **Delaware Educational Benefits for Children of Deceased Veterans and Others:** Full tuition at colleges and universities in Delaware for dependents of deceased Delaware veterans, state policy officers, and Department of Transportation employees.
- **Delaware Legislative Essay Scholarship:** Up to $10,000 to Delaware high school seniors who submit essays on a topic of historical significance (topic changes annually).
- **Delaware Open Cross Country Championship Scholarships:** $1,500 for college-bound high school seniors in Delaware who participate in cross country racing.
- **First State Manufactured Housing Association Scholarship:** $2,000 for college to Delaware residents who have lived for at least a year in a manufactured home.
- **John P. "Pat" Healy Scholarship:** $2,000 for up to four years to high school seniors and college students in Delaware who will major in engineering or environmental sciences at an in-state school.
- **Michael C. Ferguson Achievement Awards:** At least $1,000 for college to eighth and tenth grade students who achieve high sores on the Delaware Student Testing Program.
- **Delaware Nursing Incentive Program:** Up to the cost of tuition, fees, and other direct educational expenses to Delaware residents with outstanding academic records who plan to be an R.N. or L.P.N.

Similar programs may be available in your state. How can you get up-to-date information on the state funding opportunities that might apply to your student? The best way is to check with your state's office of higher education. To help you with this, we have compiled a directory listing each of those agencies. With the information provided here, you'll be able to write, call, e-mail, or even check your state's financial aid website.

STATE AGENCY DIRECTORY

Use this listing as the first step in your search for the financial aid offered by your state. We've provided, state-by-state, the name, address, telephone numbers, email, and website for the agency that administers higher education and financial aid for the residents of that state.

Of course, telephone numbers, addresses, and even websites change frequently. So, if you need to update any of the information here, check the state agency's website or go to the U.S. Department of Education's online database of state offices of education at: *www.ed.gov/Programs/bastmp/SHEA.htm.*

Reside in One State, Get Paid to Study in Another

While most state-funded programs are open only to their own residents, many of those programs also allow their residents to attend school in another state. So, even if your student does not plan on attending an in-state school, be sure to see what aid might be available from your state. Likewise, check the funding opportunities offered by the state where your student's school is located; there may be money available for nonresidents. Finally, be sure to find out if your state participates in a regional exchange program (See chapter 13 for more information); you may be able to get help in paying for college that way, too.

Alabama

Alabama Commission on Higher Education
100 N. Union Street
P.O. Box 302000
Montgomery, AL 36130-2000
(334) 242-1998
(800) 960-7773
Fax: (334) 242-0268
Email: deborah.nettles@ache.alabama.gov
Website: *www.ache.alabama.gov*

Alaska

Alaska Commission on Postsecondary
  Education
P.O. Box 110505
Juneau, AK 99811-0505
(907) 465-2962
(800) 441-2962
Fax: (907) 465-5316
Email: customer_service@acpe.state.ak.us
Website: *www.acpe.state.ak.us*

Arizona

Arizona Commission for Postsecondary
  Education
2020 N. Central Avenue, Suite 650
Phoenix, AZ 85004-4503
(602) 258-2435
Fax: (602) 258-2483
Email: acpe@azhighered.gov
Website: *www.azhighered.gov*

Arkansas

Arkansas Department of Higher Education
Financial Aid Division
114 E. Capitol Avenue
Little Rock, AR 72201-3818
(501) 371-2000
(800) 54-STUDY
Fax: (501) 371-2001
Email: ADHE_Info@adhe.edu
Website: *www.adhe.edu*

California

California Student Aid Commission
P.O. Box 419026
Rancho Cordova, CA 95741-9026
(888) CA-GRANT or (888) 224-7268
Fax: (916) 526-8002
Email: studentsupport@csac.ca.gov
Website: *www.csac.ca.gov*

Colorado

Colorado Department of Higher Education
1560 Broadway, Suite 1600
Denver, CO 80202
(303) 866-2723
Fax: (303) 866-4266
Email: executivedirector@dhe.state.co.us
Website: *www.highered.colorado.gov*

Connecticut

Connecticut Department of Higher Education
Student Financial Assistance
61 Woodland Street
Hartford, CT 06105-2326
(860) 947-1800
(860) 947-1855
Fax: (860) 947-1310
Email: info@ctdhe.org
Website: *www.ctdhe.org*

Delaware

Delaware Higher Education Commission
Carvel State Office Building
820 N. French Street, 5th Floor
Wilmington, DE 19801-3509
(302) 577-5240
(800) 292-7935
Fax: (302) 577-6765
Email: dhec@doe.K12.de.us
Website: *www.doe.k12.de.us/programs/dhec*

District of Columbia

Office of the State Superintendent of
    Education
Government of the District of Columbia
One Judiciary Square
441 4th Street NW, Suite 350N
Washington, DC 20001
(202) 727-6436
(877) 485-6751
Email: osse@dc.gov
Website: *www.seo.dc.gov*

Florida

Florida Department of Education
Office of Student Financial Assistance
1940 N. Monroe Street, Suite 70
Tallahassee, FL 32303-4759
(888) 827-2004
Fax: (850) 487-6244
Email: osfa@fldoe.org
Website: *www.floridastudentfinancialaid.org*

Georgia

Georgia Student Finance Commission
Scholarship and Grant Division
2082 E. Exchange Place
Tucker, GA 30084-5305
(770) 724-9000
(800) 505-GSFC
Fax: (770) 724-9089
Email: gsfcinfo@gsfc.org
Website: *www.gsfc.org/gsfcnew/index.cfm*

Hawaii

Hawaii State Postsecondary Education
    Commission
Bachman Hall, Room 209
University of Hawaii
2444 Dole Street
Honolulu, HI 96822-2302
(808) 956-8213
Fax: (808) 956-5156
Email: bor@hawaii.edu
Website: *www.hawaii.edu/academics/admissions/
aid.html*

Idaho

Idaho State Board of Education
P.O. Box 83720
Boise, ID 83720-0037
(208) 334-2270
Fax: (208) 334-2632
Email: Stuart.Tennant@osbe.idaho.gov
Website: *www.boardofed.idaho.gov*

Assets Don't Count

Your student can apply for state
money even if you were not awarded
any federal aid. This is true even for
need-based aid. That's because the
states frequently look only at income
earned and not assets, while the
federal government looks at both in
the need analysis. For parents with
investments and assets but only
modest incomes, the state's approach
is a real plus.

Illinois

Illinois Student Assistance Commission
Scholarship and Grant Services
1755 Lake Cook Road
Deerfield, IL 60015-5209
(847) 948-8500
(800) 899-4722
Email: collegezone@isac.org
Website: *www.collegezone.com*

Indiana

State Student Assistance Commission
    of Indiana
ISTA Center Building
150 W. Market Street, Suite 500
Indianapolis, IN 46204-2811
(317) 232-2350
(888) 528-4719
Fax: (317) 232-3260
Email: grants@ssaci.in.gov
Website: *www.in.gov/ssaci*

Iowa

Iowa College Student Aid Commission
200 10th Street, 4th Floor
Des Moines, IA 50309-3609
(515) 242-3344
(800) 383-4222
Fax: (515) 725-3401
Email: info@iowacollegeaid.org
Website: *www.iowacollegeaid.org*

Kansas

Kansas Board of Regents
Student Financial Aid
1000 SW Jackson Street, Suite 520
Topeka, KS 66612-1368
(785) 296-3421
Fax: (785) 296-0983
Website: *www.kansasregents.org*

Kentucky

Kentucky Higher Education Assistance
    Authority
Student Aid Programs
P.O. Box 798
Frankfort, KY 40602-0798
(502) 696-72000
(800) 928-8926
Fax: (502) 696-7496
Email: studentaid@kheaa.com
Website: *www.kheaa.com*

Louisiana

Louisiana Office of Student Financial
    Assistance
P.O. Box 91202
Baton Rouge, LA 70821-9202
(225) 922-1012
(800) 259-5626, ext. 1012
Fax: (225) 922-0790
Email: custserv@osfa.la.gov
Website: *www.osfa.la.gov*

Maine

Finance Authority of Maine
P.O. Box 949
Augusta, ME 04332-0949
(207) 623-3263
(800) 228-3734
Fax: (207) 623-0095
Email: info@famemaine.com
Website: *www.famemaine.com*

Maryland

Maryland Higher Education Commission
Office of Student Financial Assistance
839 Bestgate Road, Suite 400
Annapolis, MD 21401-3013
(410) 260-4565
(800) 974-1024
Email: osfamail@mhec.state.md.us
Website: *www.mhec.state.md.us*

Massachusetts

Massachusetts Office of Student Financial
    Assistance
454 Broadway, Suite 200
Revere, MA 02151
(617) 727-9420
Fax: (617) 727-0667
Email: osfa@ofsa.mass.edu
Website: *www.osfa.mass.edu*

Michigan

Office of Scholarships and Grants
P.O. Box 30462
Lansing, MI 48909-7962
(888) 4-GRANTS
Email: osg@michigan.gov
Website: *www.michigan.gov/mistudentaid*

Minnesota

Minnesota Office of Higher Education
1450 Energy Park Drive, Suite 350
St. Paul, MN 55108-5227
(651) 642-0567
(800) 657-3866
Fax: (651) 642-0675
Email: info@heso.state.mn.us
Website: *www.ohe.state.mn.us*

Mississippi

Mississippi Institutions of Higher Learning
Office of Student Financial Aid
3825 Ridgewood Road
Jackson, MS 39221
(601) 432-6947
(800) 327-2980
Email: sfa@ihl.state.ms.us
Website: *www.mississippi.edu/riseupms*

Missouri

Missouri Department of Higher Education
3515 Amazonas Drive
Jefferson City, MO 65109-5717
(573) 751-2361
(800) 473-6757
Fax: (573) 751-6635
Email: info@dhe.mo.gov
Website: *www.dhe.mo.gov*

Montana

Montana University System
P.O. Box 203201
Helena, MT 59620-3201
(406) 444-6570
Fax: (406) 444-1469
Website: *www.mus.edu*

Nebraska

Coordinating Commission for Postsecondary
    Education
P.O. Box 95005
Lincoln, NE 68509-5005
(402) 471-2847
Fax: (402) 471-2886
Email: sarah.willnerd@nebraska.gov
Website: *www.ccpe.state.ne.us*

Nevada

Nevada State Department of Education
700 E. 5th Street
Carson City, NV 89701
(775) 687-9200
Fax: (775) 687-9101
Website: *www.nde.doe.nv.gov*

New Hampshire

New Hampshire Postsecondary Education
    Commission
3 Barrell Court, Suite 300
Concord, NH 03301-8543
(603) 271-2555
Fax: (603) 271-2696
Website: *www.state.nh.us/postsecondary*

New Jersey

Higher Education Student Assistance Authority
P.O. Box 540
Trenton, NJ 08625-0540
(800) 792-8670
Email: ClientServices@hesaa.org
Website: *www.hesaa.org*

New Mexico

New Mexico Higher Education Department
2048 Galisteo Street
Santa Fe, NM 87505-2100
(505) 476-8400
(800) 279-9777
Fax: (505) 476-6511
Website: *www.hed.state.nm.us*

New York

New York State Higher Education Services
    Corporation
Grants and Scholarships
99 Washington Avenue
Albany, NY 12255
(518) 473-0410
(888) NYS-HESC
Website: *www.hesc.com*

North Carolina

North Carolina State Education Assistance
  Authority
P.O. Box 14103
Research Triangle Park, NC 27709
(919) 549-8614
(800) 700-1775
Fax: (919) 549-8481
Email: information@ncseaa.edu
Website: *www.ncseaa.edu*

North Dakota

North Dakota University System
Student Financial Assistance Program
State Capitol, 10th Floor
600 E. Boulevard Avenue
Dept 215
Bismarck, ND 58505-0230
(701) 328-2960
Fax: (701) 328-2961
Email: ndus.office@ndus.nodak.edu
Website: *www.ndus.edu*

Northern Marianas

Northern Marianas College
P.O. Box 501250
Saipan, MP 96950-1250
(670) 234-5498, x1000
Fax: (670) 234-1270
Email: financialaid@nmcnet.edu
Website: *www.nmcnet.edu*

Ohio

Ohio Board of Regents
State Grants and Scholarships
P.O. Box 182452
Columbus, OH 43218-2452
(614) 466-7420
(888) 833-1133
Fax: (614) 752-5903
Email: regents@regents.state.oh.us
Website: *www.regents.ohio.gov/sgs*

Oklahoma

Oklahoma State Regents for Higher Education
655 Research Parkway, Suite 200
Oklahoma City, OK 73104
(405) 225-9100
(800) 858-1840
Fax: (405) 255-9230
Email: studentinfo@osrhe.edu
Website: *www.okhighered.org*

Oregon

Oregon Student Assistance Commission
1500 Valley River Drive, Suite 100
Eugene, OR 97401-2130
(541) 687-7400
(800) 452-8807
Fax: (541) 687-7414
Email: awardinfo@mercury.osac.state.or.us
Website: *www.osac.state.or.us*

State Deadlines

Most state programs have their own deadlines, which can range anywhere from September of the year before college to April or later. Even the deadlines for the state programs awarded on the basis of FAFSA information do not necessarily coincide with the FAFSA deadline; frequently, they are earlier than the June 30 federal deadline. When you contact your state agency for information on funding available to residents in your state, be sure to confirm the deadlines for each of the programs.

Pennsylvania

Pennsylvania Higher Education Assistance
  Agency
1200 N. 7th Street
Harrisburg, PA 17102-1444
(717) 720-2800
(800) 233-0557
Fax: (717) 720-3914
Email: info@pheaa.org
Website: *www.pheaa.org*

Puerto Rico

Puerto Rico Council on Higher Education
P.O. Box 19900
San Juan, PR 00910-1900
(787) 641-7100
Fax: (787) 641-2573
Website: *www.ces.gobierno.pr*

Rhode Island

Rhode Island Higher Education Assistance
  Authority
560 Jefferson Boulevard, Suite 100
Warwick, RI 02886
(401) 736-1170
(800) 922-9855
Fax: (401) 732-3541
Email: grants@riheaa.org
Website: *www.riheaa.org*

South Carolina

South Carolina Commission on Higher
  Education
1333 Main Street, Suite 200
Columbia, SC 29201
(803) 737-2260
(877) 349-7183
Fax: (803) 737-2297
Email: cbrown@che.sc.gov
Website: *www.che.sc.gov*

South Dakota

South Dakota Board of Regents
306 E. Capitol Avenue, Suite 200
Pierre, SD 57501-2545
(605) 773-3455
Fax: (605) 773-5320
Email: info@sdbor.edu
Website: *www.sdbor.edu*

Tennessee

Tennessee Student Assistant Corporation
404 James Robertson Parkway
Parkway Towers, Suite 1510
Nashville, TN 37243-0820
(615) 741-1346
(800) 342-1663
Fax: (615) 741-6101
Email: TSAC.AidInfo@tn.gov
Website: *www.state.tn.us/tsac*

Texas

Texas Higher Education Coordinating Board
Student Services
P.O. Box 12788
Austin, TX 78711-2788
(512) 427-6101
(800) 242-3062
Fax: (512) 427-6127
Website: *www.thecb.state.tx.us*

Utah

Utah System of Higher Education Assistance
  Authority
Board of Regents Building, The Gateway
60 S. 400 West
Salt Lake City, UT 84101-1284
(801) 321-7294
(877) 336-7378
Fax: (801) 321-7299
Email: uheaa@utahsbr.edu
Website: *www.uheaar.edu*

Vermont

Vermont Student Assistance Corporation
P.O. Box 2000
Winooski, VT 05404
(802) 654-3798
(888) 253-4819
Fax: (802) 654-3765
Email: info@vsac.org
Website: *www.vsac.org*

Virginia

State Council of Higher Education for Virginia
Financial Aid Office
James Monroe Building
101 N. 14th Street, 9th Floor
Richmond, VA 23219-3659
(804) 225-2600
Fax: (804) 225-2604
Email: communications@schev.edu
Website: *www.schev.edu*

Virgin Islands

Virgin Islands Department of Education
1834 Kongens Gade
Charlotte Amalie
St. Thomas, VI 00801
(340) 774-0100
Fax: (340) 779-7153
Email: education@usvi.org
Website: *www.doe.vi*

Washington

Washington State Higher Education
   Coordinating Board
P.O. Box 43430
Olympia, WA 98504-3430
(360) 753-7800
Fax: (360) 753-7808
Email: info@hecb.wa.gov
Website: *www.hecb.wa.gov*

West Virginia

West Virginia Higher Education Policy
   Commission
Office of Financial Aid and Outreach Services
1018 Kanawha Boulevard E., Suite 700
Charleston, WV 25301-2800
(304) 558-4614
Fax: (304) 558-5719
Email: financialaiddirector@hepc.wvnet.edu
Website: *www.hepc.wvnet.edu*

Wisconsin

Wisconsin Higher Educational Aids Board
P.O. Box 7885
Madison, WI 53707-7885
(608) 267-2206
Fax: (608) 267-2808
Email: HEABmail@wisconsin.gov
Website: *www.heab.wisconsin.gov*

Wyoming

Wyoming Community College Commission
2020 Carey Avenue, 8th Floor
Cheyenne, WY 82002
(307) 777-7763
Fax: (307) 777-6567
Email: khosseini@commission.wcc.edu
Website: *communitycolleges.wy.edu/business/
Index.htm*

MOVING ON

To summarize, in this chapter we discussed the importance of state aid, the diversity of state funding available, and the best ways to get information about money from your state. We reminded you to look at both your state of residency and the state where your student will be going to college (if they are different), to check for funding leads in both locations. Then, we provided, state by state, information for the agencies you should contact about the scholarships, fellowships, grants, loans, and other funding opportunities available to state residents.

In the next chapter, we'll focus on money that's available from private sources, including clubs, organizations, companies, foundations, and even individuals. We'll take a look at common scholarship myths, the best ways to search for funding, the best strategies to use in your search for scholarships, and how to spot scholarship scams. Before you move on, though, let's take a look at the checklist for this chapter.

✔ **CHECKLIST:**

1. Check into the various ways that your state can help you pay for college. Make sure you find out:
   - What you will save by attending an in-state public college or university versus an out-of-state or private school.
   - What specific financial aid programs are offered to the residents of your state.
   - What financial aid programs might be offered by the state where you will be attending school.
   - What prepaid savings and tuition plans are offered by your state.

2. Use the state directory we've compiled to contact (by phone, mail, email, or online) the agency in your state that administers or coordinates scholarships, fellowships, grants, and loans for residents. Don't forget about the agency in the state your student will be going to college (if it is different).

3. Pay particular attention to the deadlines for each of the state programs. Remember: state aid deadlines are frequently very different than federal deadlines.

CHAPTER TWELVE

Searching for Private Scholarships

Nearly $150 billion in financial aid is awarded to students every year. Most of these funds come from the federal government, states, colleges, and private lenders. That's why we've focused on how to apply for funding from these sources in chapters 5 through 11. But, now that you know the hows and whys of filling out the FAFSA, the PROFILE, and aid applications from your student's potential colleges, it's time to discuss one more major source of funding for your student: financial aid offered by private sources (foundations, organizations, clubs, companies, and even individuals). This type of funding is often referred to as "private" (because much of it comes from private sources) or "outside" (because these scholarships are funded by sources outside the federal government or a college).

Each year, students receive $6 billion or more from these private or outside sources. Your student could be one of them! But, you may be thinking, searching for these individual scholarships is not going to be worth the effort. You may think that your student won't qualify, or the process is too time consuming, or the awards won't be big enough to make a difference. Let's take a look at some of these concerns, to see which are based in fact and which turn out to be just myths.

COMMON CONCERNS ABOUT APPLYING FOR SCHOLARSHIPS

Concern #1: Middle class families can't qualify for private scholarships.
While there are financial aid programs set aside just for students with documented need, there are just as many, or more, that never consider income in the selection process. Since middle class families can have trouble qualifying for "free" money from the federal government or the student's school, private scholarships offer an excellent opportunity to level the playing field and let students at any income level compete equally for scholarships.

Concern #2: Only "A" students get these scholarships.
Again, there are programs that are awarded solely on the basis of academic excellence or class rank. It always helps if students have a strong academic record. But, there are thousands of other programs that don't ask about GPA or that set the minimum requirement at 3.0, or 2.5, or even 2.0. In fact, there are even some scholarships that are open only to students with "B" or "C" grades.

Concern #3: U.S. citizenship is required.

Generally, this is correct. But, not always. Noncitizens who possess a green card or have permanent residency status also qualify for most financial aid. And, there are many scholarships that do not ask about citizenship, at all, on their application forms. Finally, there is a small portion of scholarships set aside specifically for foreign students or students in the United States who cannot document U.S. citizenship.

Concern #4: You have to be a woman or a minority to be selected.

It's true that there is aid set aside just for women or minorities. But, then again, there are scholarships open only to students who are Italian, or chemistry majors, or residents of St. Louis, or cheerleaders, or talented singers, or hearing impaired, or from a military family, or interested in attending a career college, or members of a specific organization—or practically anything else you can imagine. To illustrate: take a look at this abbreviated list of diverse scholarships posted on *www.FinancialAidFinder.com*:

- **Duck Brand Duct Tape Stuck at Prom Contest** ($3,000) for high school students whose prom attire is made from duct tape
- **TCI Scholarships** ($1,000) for college students who are tall (at least 5' 10' for a woman and 6' 2" for a man)
- **Fountainhead Essay Contest** ($10,000) for the best student essay based on the philosophy of Ayn Rand's *The Fountainhead*
- **Patrick Kerr Skateboard Scholarship** ($5,000) for high school seniors who are skateboard activists

Well, you get the point. The variety is amazing. There are scholarships for practically any characteristic your student might have.

Concern #5: Private scholarships will reduce the federal or college aid awarded.

This can be an issue. Students are not permitted to "profit" from financial aid. So, if the total amount of aid received by your student (including the private scholarships) exceeds your student's actual Cost of Attendance (COA), then an equal amount of aid your student received in the financial aid package may be cut back. Should you and your student end up in that "fortunate" situation, work with the college financial aid office to see that it is the loans component (rather than any free money source) that is reduced. Even if your student's financial aid package did not cover the entire COA, private scholarships can be viewed as a personal financial resource and might reduce the amount awarded in the financial aid package. Again, should that happen, try to arrange for self-help aid to be reduced before any other component. The rule to follow is: a grant that doesn't have to be paid back, whatever its source, is always worth more than a loan of the same amount.

Concern #6: Scholarship applications are too much work.

Scholarship applications are work. But, if your student has already filled out college applications or applications for college/state aid, most of that work (for example, the essays and resumes) can probably be repurposed for the scholarship application. Here's another way to look at this issue. Think of the process not as "work" but as a "job." Let's say your student spent 50 hours searching and applying for private scholarships. And, after all that time and effort, only two or three scholarships, totaling about $3,000, were awarded. That works out to $60 per hour, which is many times more than most students can expect to get paid for doing pretty much any other activity. Now, does the process begin to sound like a good use of time?

Concern #7: You have to write a great essay to be selected.
There are a number of writing competitions and yes, for them, you do have to be an excellent writer. For the other types of scholarships, however, it's more about what you write than how you write it. And, you'll be glad to know, many scholarship sponsors ask students to fill out an application and, maybe, submit a resume, but do not require an essay at all.

Concern #8: Most scholarship awards are too small to make a real difference.
Scholarship awards can run from $50 all the way up to $30,000 or more, or the full cost of college. It all depends on the scholarship. But, don't write off the smaller awards. After all, if you win four $500 scholarships, you've paid for your annual community college costs in most cases. Win four $1,000 scholarship and you are well on your way to paying off the tuition for a year at a public four-year scholarship. Even if you win just one $1,000 award, that is $1,000 less that doesn't have to be borrowed or paid for out of family funds.

Concern #9: There's too much competition for these scholarships.
You're right and wrong on this one. When it comes to the general national and well-publicized scholarships, there are huge numbers of students who are eligible and can apply; so it is hard to be chosen for those. On the other hand, when it comes to the smaller, more focused, more local, and/or less publicized scholarships, fewer students compete and it is much easier to be successful. How do you find out about these less "competitive" scholarships? We'll cover that later in this chapter.

Concern #10: There's no guarantee you'll get a scholarship.
This is not a myth; this is true. Searching for scholarships can be difficult and time consuming. There are no guarantees. And, if a financial consultant, a search service, or an Internet site promises you a scholarship, keep that fact in mind. But there are things that you and your student can do to increase significantly the chances of winning a scholarship. The rest of this chapter describes the best strategies you can use to find and, hopefully, win a scholarship.

WHERE TO LOOK

While there has been a decline in the number of scholarships and other "free" money that colleges are able to offer (as a result of state funding cuts, increased institutional costs, and dwindling endowment funds), it is good to know that private scholarships are alive and well. The money is there. But, you have to know how to find it.

When you fill out the FAFSA and the PROFILE, you are automatically considered for basic federal and some state and college-based aid. Unfortunately, when it comes to private scholarship aid, there's no one central registry. So, looking for financial aid takes determination and a certain amount of creativity. You and your student will need to develop a plan for the financial aid search, just the way you would develop a strategy for a job search.

To be sure you don't miss any programs that might be available, you will need to check a wide variety of sources in the community, at your student's high school or college, from your state, in books from the library or bookstore, on Internet sites, or (possibly) from a commercial search firm.

Community Resources

Be sure to check out the resources in your community. Contact organizations (particularly service and professional groups) and businesses in your area, because these groups regularly sponsor funding programs. Some of the most likely community prospects are: Rotary, Elks Club, American Legion, 4-H or FFA, Boy and Girl Scouts, Urban League, Masonic clubs, American Association of University Women, and the PTA.

If you are not sure which agencies are best to approach, check with your town's chamber of commerce. Don't overlook labor unions. Do this even if you aren't in a union; many of the programs sponsored by unions are open to nonunion applicants. Read the newspaper; funding programs offered by local groups are frequently described there. Contact the trust department of banks in your community; they often administer scholarship programs for local students. Does your community have a community foundation? That would be an excellent place to check, because these foundations administered financial aid programs aimed principally at students in your area.

While you're thinking about community resources, don't forget to check with the personnel office at the company you and/or your student works for. As we'll discuss in the next chapter, many companies pay for part or all of their employees' college tuition costs and some of them extend similar benefits to their employees' dependents.

Campus Resources

It is wise for you and/or your student to tap into the resources that are available at your student's campus. Check the bulletin boards (for example, in the high school guidance office, the college financial aid office, various academic departments at the college, the guidance department's website) for announcements of school-based or outside (private) scholarships. Try to attend any financial aid workshops offered sponsored by the school.

Of course, you or your student will want to talk to the financial aid officers and deans or department heads at the colleges your student is considering about the funding programs offered by or through the school (particularly those that are not automatically awarded through the school's financial aid package). Here are some questions you should ask:

- Is there a printed or online list of funding opportunities available at that school?
- Does the school have a limit on the amount of aid it will provide to student applicants?
- Do applicants have to be able to demonstrate financial need to receive scholarship aid from the school?
- What are the college's financial aid application deadlines?
- If students don't qualify currently for college scholarships, will they be considered seriously if they apply for aid in subsequent years?
- What is the practice the school follows when it comes to private (outside) scholarships?
- Will outside scholarships reduce the financial aid offered by the school?

State Resources

You will be automatically considered for some state-based funding when you fill out the FAFSA. But, there are hundreds of other state-funded financial aid programs that must be applied for individually. Some of these scholarships and grants target students with specific personal characteristics (ethnicity, disability, gender, academic record, income level, etc.) and others focus on critical workforce needs or specific segments of the population (for example, military families or senior citizens). Most states give their own residents a break on tuition, and some even offer funding to nonresident students who are going to study in that state.

The best way to find out the special opportunities your state is offering is to check with your state's agency for higher education or financial aid. To make it easy for you to do this, we have provided a comprehensive list of these agencies, including their telephone numbers and websites, in chapter 11.

Printed Sources

In this Internet age, you might be tempted to bypass books and go directly online to search for scholarships. That would be a mistake. You would miss out on the incredible convenience, comprehensiveness, vetted information, and serendipity that only books can offer you.

Printed financial aid directories fall into two categories: general listings and targeted listings. If you're just starting to look for private scholarships, or you're not sure where your student will go to school or what he or she will major in, your best bet is to start with a general directory. That way, you get the broadest listings (thousands of scholarships are described) and the greatest amount of information in one place. While there are a number of general directories available, the most popular and current ones are:

- *Kaplan Scholarships: Billions of Dollars in Free Money for College* (published by Kaplan)
- *Scholarship Handbook* (published by The College Board)
- *The Scholarship Book: The Complete Guide to Private-Sector Scholarships, Fellowships, Grants, and Loans* (published by Prentice Hall)
- *Scholarships, Grants and Prizes* (published by Peterson's)
- *The Ultimate Scholarship Book: Billions of Dollars in Scholarships, Grants and Prizes* (published by Supercollege)

If your student knows what he or she wants to study or if your student has unique personal characteristics, then your next step is to see what targeted directories are available. You'll probably be surprised to see how focused these listings can be. For example, there are directories published just for women, specific minority groups, military families, persons with disabilities, students majoring in specific subject fields (nursing, business, engineering, and education, etc.), middle-class students, and students with particular religious affiliations. For an example of the diverse coverage offered by these targeted directories, check out *www.rspfunding.com/prod_prodalpha.html*.

Whether you purchase a financial aid directory or use one at the library, always make sure you are working with an up-to-date edition. Contact information, eligibility requirements, and deadline dates for financial aid programs change frequently, and you don't want to miss out on any opportunities just because you used outdated information.

Internet Sources

Enter the term "scholarships" in a search engine like Google, and you'll get 27 million hits. Obviously, you can't find scholarship opportunities online by searching yourself. Fortunately, you don't have to. There are scores of scholarship search sites available to you on the Internet. For a rather comprehensive list of these, go to the list of links at: *www.college-scholarships.com/free_scholarship_searches.htm*.

These free search sites make it easy to look for money for college. You enter a site, spend 20 minutes or less filling out a personal information form, and a list of scholarships (hopefully matching your characteristics) is displayed almost instantly. But while a number of these sites can be very helpful (and the price is certainly right!), others are more concerned with capturing your personal information to resell to marketers than they are in providing quality, comprehensive, or current information. On the surface, it's hard to tell which is which. They all look attractive and professional, and almost none of them tell you exactly when the information was last updated (there are generally no "publication" dates for online databases the way there are in printed directories), or what is specifically included and excluded in their listings (information that you usually find in a print directory's preface or introduction), or truly how many separate programs are in their database (forget the claims of 1 million or more records; that number of separate scholarship programs simply does not exist).

So, how do you know which search sites are worth your time? The best way is to check with your student's guidance counselor or financial aid officer for recommendations or consult with other parents and students to find out what worked for them. If you're still not sure or you can't wait and want to start searching today, then the best approach is to stick with the sites that have been around the longest. These include (but are certainly not limited to):

- College Board's Scholarship Search
  www.apps.collegeboard.com/cbsearch_ss/welcome.jsp
- FastWeb's Scholarship Money
  www.fastweb.com
- Peterson's Scholarship Central
  www.petersons.com/finaid/landing.asp?id=806&path=ug.pfs.scholarships
- SallieMae Fund's Scholarship Searches
  www.thesalliemaefund.org/smfnew/sections/search.html
- Scholarships.com
  www.scholarships.com
- Scholarship Experts
  www.scholarshipexperts.com
- The U.S. Department of Education's Scholarship Wizard
  www.studentaid2.ed.gov/getmoney/scholarship/v3browse.asp

Even though these online scholarship search sites are relatively quick and easy to use, students and parents frequently leave them not completely satisfied. That's because they only get to see program descriptions for the scholarships the sites identify as matches (and some of these end up not being matches at all), they almost never get to browse through the listings to see if there are other appropriate programs, a number of the programs that end up in their search results are either single school based (and not ones they want to attend) or don't have enough detail to determine if the student qualifies, and many of the programs showing up in their results are the same ones that untold thousands of other students who searched on that database are also seeing. For those reasons, if you're really serious about looking for scholarships that can help you pay for college, you'll want to search for funding both ways, in print and online. That way, you'll get the best of both worlds.

Commercial Sources

Sometimes, families are so overwhelmed by all the information out there that they decide to use a consultant or commercial service—one that will match a student with available scholarships. After all, if Match.com can make successful matches, maybe a scholarship search service can do so as well. And, undoubtedly, there are services that can. But, be very careful. Before you spend money for searches that you can do yourself, read our scholarship scam section at the end of this chapter.

SEARCH TIPS

Now that you are ready to do your scholarship search, using print and/or online sources, here are some tips for you to help in the process.

Learn the Language

One of the first steps you can take, as you begin your search for scholarships, is to become familiar with the language. What does it take for a student to be classified as "independent," what exactly defines "financial need," what is the difference between FAFSA and PROFILE, how does EFC differs from COA?

Like all other specialized areas, financial aid has its own vocabulary and set of abbreviations. If you are going to maneuver successfully through the field, you'll need to know how to speak this special language. To help you in the process, we've compiled a Financial Aid Dictionary, which brings together definitions for all of the important financial aid terms. You'll find that resource near the starting on page 193.

Think Positively, But Be Realistic

As we discussed earlier in this chapter, never assume that your family makes too much money or your student's grades aren't high enough to compete successfully for a scholarship. There are thousands of programs that are less concerned with income level or test scores than with you or your student's personal, organizational, or educational background. Keep this in mind when you design your search strategy. Don't forget to look for financial aid that is based on factors like these:

- residency in a particular geographic area
- participation in sports and hobbies
- involvement in school, community, or church projects

- work at a particular company
- membership in a labor or trade union
- affiliation with a particular church or religion
- membership in a specific organization or social group
- ties to the military
- ethnic or national background
- physical condition
- career goals

Get Organized

Before your student begins the application process, take time to gather up all the documentation and materials that are going to need. These include school transcripts, standardized test scores, financial aid forms (FAFSA, PROFILE), income tax forms and other financial information, and proof of eligibility (if your student is going to apply for membership-based funding). Make sure your student lines up references and has a couple of core essays on hand that can be customized.

Don't Apply If You Don't Qualify

Sometimes, when applicants begin a search for financial aid, they are tempted to apply for all the programs they see listed on a scholarship bulletin board, or on the Internet, or in the financial aid directories they have checked. A blanket approach like this wastes the applicant's time and puts an unnecessary burden on the program's selection committee. Some program sponsors have found, in fact, that this wholesale shopping approach has driven the costs of administering an award beyond the total amount of the award itself.

So, students should read the eligibility information in each program description carefully and think if they can package themselves to meet the requirements. If they can, they should go ahead and apply. But, if they really don't meet the requirements, they should just go on with their search. It's true that you can't win a scholarship if you don't apply. On the other hand, you can't compete if you don't qualify. Be sensible and courteous. Follow this rule: don't apply if you don't qualify.

Always File the FAFSA

Some parents and students think that because of their income level, they probably won't qualify for need-based financial aid and, consequently, don't fill out the FAFSA. This is a mistake. Many privately-sponsored scholarships (even those based on merit) require applicants to have submitted the FAFSA. So, keep your options open and fill out the form. And do it every year.

Limit Your Competition

Design your search strategy to focus on programs that limit your competition. Rather than look for just the major and well-publicized programs, try to locate programs with very specific eligibility requirements. Look for funding opportunities that restrict applicants by specific residency, gender, nationality or ethnicity, religion, organizational memberships, subject specialty, avocational interests, career goals, life experiences, etc. Never forget: the smaller the number of eligible applicants, the greater your chance to stand out. That means more scholarships that you can win. And here's another bonus. Scholarship sponsors like to go with a winner. The more extensive your list of awards is, the more impressive you'll look, and the easier it will be to get that next (and maybe even larger) award.

Set up a Scholarship Alert

Some scholarship search sites, like *fastweb.com,* will send you notices when scholarship deadlines are approaching or new scholarships have just been added to their database. But, another way that you can find out when new scholarships become available is to sign up for Google Alerts. Go to *www.google.com/alerts* and sign up to receive email updates based on your choice of topic. You can have these alerts set as they happen, once a day, or once a week. So, for example, let's say you are interested in engineering scholarships. You would put in your search terms (for example: engineering scholarships deadline) and your email address and receive notices every time Google finds a match.

Don't Be Late

Ideally, you and your student should start to think about scholarships as early as the 10th or 11th grade in high school. That way, you can learn about what's available and perhaps even tailor your student's activities to meet some of the requirements of the programs that look most promising to you. But, even if haven't done that, it's still not too late to begin the process. Don't delay. Start today.

Definitely don't wait until your student is accepted to college before you begin your search. If you do, you'll miss out on most private scholarships. While there are some scholarships that accept applications at any time, the deadlines for most private aid applications are the same as, or even precede, college admission deadlines. So, start looking for scholarships during the summer (or even earlier) and begin to submit your applications in the fall. After March or April, there are few scholarship programs still accepting applications.

> **Searching is a Year-Round Activity**
>
> "Parents usually do scholarship searches once, and then forget it," says Virginia Tech's director of financial aid Barry Simmons. "But searches should be done quarterly, because new scholarships pop up every few months."

One last tip: don't stop once your student goes off to college. Students should definitely continue to look for funding opportunities even after starting school. Did you know that there are even more scholarships available to students once they are in college than there are for college-bound high school seniors? Make scholarship searching a year-round activity for you and your student. Your return on this "investment" could be big!

DON'T GET SCAMMED

When you're searching for financial aid, you need to be careful. While most scholarships are legitimate and most scholarship search services/websites are reliable, there are exceptions. The key, of course, is to be able to distinguish between the two. That's not always easy. Most scams sound official. They frequently use impressive names, like "National," and "Federation," and "Foundation." They have professional looking websites and informative looking promotional materials. To make sure you don't get taken, the next

> **Knowledge Is Your Best Scam Defense**
>
> As Bob Williams, former president and CEO of the Better Business Bureau, explains, "Fraudulent scholarship and loan companies are counting on families in desperate need of financial resources to not thoroughly investigate their company."

section will given you the information you need to spot a scam, the questions you need to ask before you sign with a commercial financial aid service, and the action you should take if you suspect a scam.

How to Spot a Scam

According to the Federal Trade Commission (FTC), each year a number of unscrupulous companies promise or guarantee lucrative financial aid packages or large scholarship awards. Many use high pressure sales pitches at seminars, where attendees are required to pay immediately or risk losing out on the "opportunity." Most of these companies offer a "money back guarantee," but when you read the fine print, you'll see that they have set up conditions that make it impossible for a client to get a refund. Sometimes, the companies take an upfront fee, but never deliver any service, not even a list of potential sources. Other companies inform students they have been selected as scholarship "finalists," but to get the award they need to pay an up-front fee. Another approach commonly used by these companies is to get a student's checking account number, to "confirm eligibility," and then debit that account without the student's consent. As a variation on this approach, some companies will ask for authorization to charge a small monthly or weekly fee to a client's checking account but then use that authorization to debit the account on an ongoing basis. How can you spot these unscrupulous companies? The FTC says to watch for these tell-tale lines:

- "We'll do all the work for you."
- "The scholarship will cost you some money."

- "You've been selected" by a "national foundation" to receive a scholarship you never applied for.
- "You're a finalist" in a contest you never entered.
- "The scholarship is guaranteed or your money back."
- "You can't get this information anywhere else."
- "We just need your credit card or bank account number to hold this scholarship"
- Skeptical at Seminars.

Many parents and students find it helpful to attend financial aid seminars. Most of these meetings (especially the ones sponsored by the student's school) are educational in nature and worth attending. Some free seminars, however, are conducted with the sole purpose of separating you from your money. To be sure you don't get taken, follow these six rules:

1. Take your time. Don't rush to pay for anything at the seminar. Above all, don't yield to high pressure sales tactics. You're not going to miss out on any "opportunities" if you don't sign right then.
2. Check out the organization before you sign with them. You can do this by talking to your student's financial aid adviser or guidance counselor. You might find out that they can provide the same kind information and service—and for free!
3. Don't be swayed by success stories or testimonials; these might be presented by "shills" who are paid to describe inspiring results. Instead, get the names of a couple of local families who have used these services in the past year and check with them about their level of satisfaction with the service.

> **Don't Be Pressured**
>
> "Many of the less-legitimate companies apply high-pressure tactics," says Gregory A. Ashe of the FTC's Bureau of Consumer Protection. "Legitimate companies don't use nerve-wracking tactics to pressure you to do something quick."

4. Be concerned if the seminar leaders are reluctant to answer questions or give evasive answers.
5. Get information on exactly what the service will cost, what services you will get for the money, and what is covered in the company's refund policy.
6. And never, ever, give out your credit card or bank account number until you have followed all the steps above.

Choose an Adviser Carefully

With four-year college education costs rising faster than the rate of inflation, many parents are understandably concerned about how to pay those costs without saddling themselves or their children with heavy debt. Some of them turn to private financial aid consultants for advice. This advice comes at a price. If you decide to go this route, you'll want to be sure that your adviser can provide more information and service than you could get on your own. Most of all, make sure that your adviser is experienced and knowledgeable. Be cautious if the consultant suggests tricks or procedures to reduce income, transfer assets, or represent you to negotiate financial aid packages. The first two of these approaches have serious financial implications and the last one may be institutional unacceptable. You'll want to make sure that your adviser is experienced and knowledgeable. Be sure to check out credentials and request references.

What to Do If You Suspect a Scam

Many times, parents and students who suspect a scam don't take any action because they don't know what to do. Here is a list of agencies that you should contact 1) to determine if a company and/or offer is legitimate or not; or 2) to report a suspected scam.

School Officials. Inform the appropriate school representative (a counselor, if the student is in high school; a financial aid office, if the student is in college). Show them any literature, application forms, correspondence, or other documentation received. They may be able to determine if the operation is legitimate or not. Even if they can't, they can give advice on how to proceed.

State Consumer Protection Office. You can also check with this office (in your state or the company's state) to see if complaints have been filed against the company. For information on how to contact the office in your state, go to *www.consumeraction.gov/state.shtml*.

Better Business Bureau. Another way to check on the reliability of a company is to see if any complaints have been lodged with the Better Business Bureau. An easy way to find that out, no matter where the company is located, is at *www.bbb.org/us/Find-Business-Reviews*. You can view a report of past complaints or file one yourself there.

> ### If It Sounds too Good...
>
> To protect yourself from scholarship scams, keep two things in mind. First, if the offer seems too good to be true, then it probably is. Second, if you have to pay money to apply or receive further information—even a nominal fee—then it is probably a scam. Most legitimate scholarship offers are competitive and free. Ernie Shepelsky, vice president of enrollment services at Vaughn College of Aeronautics and Technology can't stress this point enough. "Never, under any circumstance, should a family pay even five dollars to someone who says they will help them find a scholarship," says Shepelsky. "If anyone asks for money—even one dollar, even one time—it is absolutely a scam!"

State Attorney General Office. If a firm claims to be incorporated, you can check with the Attorney General's office in the state where the company is located. All states require corporations to file their articles of incorporation and many states require corporations to file a copy of their annual report, as well. In addition, the office will be able to provide a telephone number where you can call to find out the company's incorporation date, address, type of incorporation (nonprofit or for-profit), directors and other principals, and registered agent. Finally, the office can tell you if the company has up-to-date business licenses and if any complaints are on file there. To get contact information for the Attorney General in your state, go to *www.naag.org.*

Federal Trade Commission. You can register a complaint with them, but be aware that the FTC does not take action on individual cases; they will respond only when it sees a pattern of possible fraudulent activity. If you want to alert them to a problem, fill out the form at their website: *www.ftccomplaintassistant.gov.*

National Fraud Information Center. Any information you give this center is passed along to the Federal Trade Commission and the appropriate state Attorney General's office (thus, skipping two of the steps listed above). To file your complaint, go to *www.fraud.org.*

U.S. Postal Service. If the problem involves mail fraud, you can file a complaint *https:// postalinspectors.uspis.gov/contactUs/filecomplaint.aspx.*

MOVING ON

In this chapter we examined some common financial aid myths, looked at the ways you and your student could find private scholarships, identified the best strategies to use when searching for scholarships, and discussed how to spot a scholarship scam (up to 7,500 of these are reported each year) and what actions to take if you think you might be scammed.

Now that you've searched and applied for all the traditional forms of financial aid, we'll take a look, in chapter 14, at some of the creative alternatives to financial aid that are available to help you pay for college. We've grouped those alternatives into school-based and worked-based strategies, and we'll identify which ones your student can use before or even after starting college. But, before we do that, let's take a look at the checklist for this chapter.

✓ CHECKLIST:

1. Make a decision to search for private scholarships. Even if your son or daughter isn't a star athlete or a top student, you can still find scholarships on the basis of personal characteristics (gender, ethnicity, religion, disability, talents), hobbies, club activities, extracurricular activities, ties to the military, or career plans.

2. Searching for scholarships is very similar to applying for college. Set up your plan:

   a. Look for leads in your community, at your student's school, from your state, in print resources, and online.

   b. Start early (remember: most private scholarship deadlines fall between September and April).

   c. Don't just look for national scholarships; try to find programs with specific eligibility requirements that are a good match for your student and will limit the competition.

   d. Keep a record of what you've done and plan to do

   e. Line up references.

   f. Develop a couple of core essays that can be modified.

   g. Have your student continually update a résumé and customize it each time it's going to be sent out.

   h. Set up a Google Alert, so you can be notified anytime new information is posted about scholarships that could be a match for your student.

3. Check with your student's potential schools about any possible financial implications of winning a scholarship. Make sure, if there could be a reduction of your student's award package, that it will come out of loans rather than gift aid.

4. Spend some time with the Financial Aid Dictionary at the end of this book. To communicate well, you need to be able to speak the language.

5. Pay particular attention to the deadlines for each of the scholarships. Set up a program, like Google Calendar, to remind you what applications are due when.

6. Watch out for scholarship scams (refer back to the popular scam pitches we identified) and use the list in this chapter to notify authorities if you suspect a scam.

CHAPTER THIRTEEN

Finding Alternatives to Financial Aid

Up until now, we have discussed financial aid options available from the federal government, your state, individual colleges, private lenders, and scholarship sponsors. There is a reason we covered those first. Each year, billions of dollars in scholarships, fellowships, grants, and loans from those sources are given to college students to help them pay for their education.

As important as financial aid is, though, it is not the only strategy you can use to cut your college costs. There are dozens of other creative approaches that you might try, individually or in combination, to help you pay for college. These alternatives to financial aid are described in this chapter and are grouped into two sections: school-based strategies and work-based strategies.

Parents: if you are the ones reading this book up to now, be sure to share this chapter with your student.

SCHOOL-BASED STRATEGIES

Earn College Credits Before Graduating High School

Depending on the college, students may be able to shave off a sizeable portion of the cost of a four-year college degree by taking courses while in high school or being home schooled and, then, by scoring well on the Advanced Placement (AP) tests. Nearly half a million students take advantage of this strategy each year. While not every college accepts AP credits (check with the schools you are considering), this approach is definitely worth considering. Eliminating just one course by using AP credits could save you $600 or more. Plus, research conducted by Crux Research revealed that taking Advanced Placement courses helps students when they are applying for college scholarships; 31 percent

> **Another AP Advantage**
>
> According to The College Board, students who take Advanced Placement (AP) classes and tests "are more likely to graduate from college in four years" than students who don't.

of colleges look at their applicants' AP record when selecting recipients. For more information on this strategy, go to *www.collegeboard.com/student/testing/ap/about.html*.

Take Other Tests to Earn College Credit

Another effective college cost-cutting strategy is to take a proficiency exam that will measure your knowledge of specific subjects. Although there are several sources of these exams (some even prepared and conducted by a student's own school), the most commonly-accepted of these is the College-Level Examination Program (CLEP). Depending on a college's policy, a satisfactory score on CLEP exams can earn students from 3 to 12 college credits. So, by using what you already know (from independent study, prior course work, on-the-job training, professional development, cultural pursuits, or internships), you may be able to reduce your college requirements and, in that way, cut down on your costs. For more information, go to *www.collegeboard.com/student/testing/clep/about.html*.

Before you arrange to take the CLEP or any other equivalency examinations, the American Council on Education recommends that you follow these three steps:

1. Know what factors affect your college's decision to award credit. Every college has its own rules. It is a student's responsibility to find out these policies before taking an equivalency exam.
2. Find out who at the college makes the decision to award credit for students passing these exams. Sometimes this will be the college admissions officer. Other times, it will be a faculty member, department chair, or dean. Talk to this person. Know what will be expected of you.
3. Understand what options are available if credit requests are rejected. If you are not satisfied with your school's review process, you may want to look for another institution in your area that will accept your credits.

Participate in a Dual Enrollment Program

Get a head start. While you still are in high school, check and see if your school participates in a dual enrollment program with local colleges or universities. Dual enrollment programs allow high school students to earn college credits before they graduate. Many of these programs are free and some schools even loan textbooks.

Look for Schools with Little or No Tuition

It may be true that in most cases you only get what you pay for, but there some notable exceptions. This is one. There are several private schools that, if you are lucky enough to get in, charge little or no tuition at all (although they may charge room and board). For example:

- Alice Lloyd College *(www.alc.edu)* in Kentucky

- Berea College (*www.berea.edu)* in Kentucky
- College of the Ozarks (*www.cofo.edu*) in Missouri
- Cooper Union *(www.cooper.edu)* in New York
- Curtis Institute of Music (*www.curtis.edu*) in Pennsylvania
- Deep Springs College (*www.deepsprings.edu*) in California
- F.W. Olin College of Engineering (*www.olin.edu*) in Massachusetts

Along the same lines, Stanford University has announced that it will no longer charge tuition to students whose families earn less than $100,000 a year and will waive all room and board fees for students whose families earn less than $60,000 a year. MIT has a similar plan; the school offers free tuition for those whose families are earning less than $75, 000 per year.

Some states also offer free tuition, usually for their brightest students. In New Jersey, for example, if you are in the top 20 percent of your graduating class, you may be eligible to attend your local community college at no charge. Washington state exempts students from lower income families from paying some or all of their tuition. And, the military academies charge little or no tuition (although there is a service obligation if you complete a certain number of credits there). More on those military institutions later in this chapter.

Look for Colleges with Affordable Tuition

Get the most for your money. Price does not always reflect quality. There are many schools where you can receive your entire education for less money than a single year would cost at another school. All without sacrificing quality.

The best bargains, by far, can be found at state colleges and universities. These generally have strong academic programs, high quality faculty and—best of all—bargain tuition rates for in-state residents. Many of these schools consistently show up in the "top 100" school listings. But, you can find educational bargains at private schools as well. To see some of the lists available that identify bargain colleges, look here:

- Kiplinger's "Best Values in Public Colleges" (*www.kiplinger.com*)
- U.S. News "Best Values" (*www.consusrankings.com/category/colleges-universities/us-news-colleges-universities*)
- USA Today/Princeton Review "Best Value Colleges" (*www.usatoday.com/news/education/best-value-colleges.htm*)

Pay (Close to) In-State Prices for an Out-Of-State Education

Many states have reciprocal or exchange programs. These programs offer residents of one state the opportunity to attend postsecondary institutions in neighboring states, at little or no extra cost. For example, more than 140 public and private schools in the states of Indiana, Kansas, Michigan, Minnesota, Missouri, Nebraska, North Dakota, and Wisconsin participate in the Midwest Student Exchange Program and charge no more than 150 percent of the in-state resident tuition rate (for specific programs) to students from other states in the exchange program. To find out what reciprocal programs are available to residents in your state, contact the regional exchange program that covers your state (see the sidebar) or check with your state's higher education agency (a list of those can be found in chapter 11).

Ask about Tuition Deals

Colleges have become increasingly creative in developing monetary programs that will attract students. Some of these programs are not widely publicized; information about them is provided only when a student inquires.

No one school will offer all of the innovative and nontraditional tuition assistance programs listed here, but many will have at least one of them. Check with the financial aid officer at your school if see any of these are offered:

- tuition rebates or discounts
- installment plans (especially those without interest charges)
- prepayment discounts (sometimes, prepayment can shave 10 percent or more off the price of tuition)
- tuition price guarantees (for example, tuition will only increase a specified percentage each year)

- family plans (when more than one family member attends the same school)
- bonuses for advanced payment (prepay four years of tuition and some colleges "lock in" the tuition rate for that entire period)

- alumni tuition breaks. (for children of alumni; these are also referred to as legacy programs)
- moral obligation loans (some colleges waive the tuition for selected students who, in turn, agreed to take on the moral obligation of paying the money back after graduation)
- off-hours or summer discounts
- older student tuition reductions
- help for former farmers
- help for students whose parents are unemployed
- help for displaced homemakers

Go to a Community College First

Once a second-class citizen in the educational community, junior and community colleges are now emerging as a wise educational choice for people who want to take a two-step approach to earning a bachelor's degree, re-entering the workforce, learning a special skill, or improving their knowledge in technical areas.

Compared to four-year colleges and universities, community and junior colleges offer many advantages. They are more responsive to part-time students, are more tolerant of open-ended completion dates, have more relaxed admission policies (many automatically admit anyone with a high school diploma or its equivalent), are more sensitive to the needs of working students (many classes are offered in the early morning, late afternoon, evening, or on the weekend), and are in very convenient locations (there's probably a campus or branch near you). That makes it easy for students to live at home and commute to college—another cost saving measure. In fact, according to the U.S. Department of Education, students living at home can save as much as $6,000 per year.

But perhaps the most important advantage is the enormous tuition savings community colleges can offer students. Community colleges have become the bargain of the century. Tuitions there average around $2,000 per year nationally and can cost as little as $480 per year (the going rate in California) for students without a bachelor's degree. Compare that to fees at four-year colleges or universities, where, according to *Forbes,* tuition averages $18,000 per year. At private institutions, tuition can be even higher—up to $35,000 or more annually. That means, if you attend a community college for two years, you could save $69,000 or more in tuition alone. Very few students could ever win a scholarship of that magnitude!

Plus, after you transfer to a four-year school to finish you degree, you'll end up getting all the prestige of that school at just a fraction of the price paid by students who started there as freshmen. Just be sure that before you take any classes you check with the four-year college you plan to attend to make sure the school will accept your community college credits.

There are thousands of community and junior colleges operating in the United States. For a fairly comprehensive list of these (with links to their websites), go to *www.utexas.edu/world/comcol/state.*

Pursue Distance Learning or Online Education

Online Does Not Mean Easy

Online or distance learning classes are not easier than traditional programs. In fact, they may be more difficult, because they require more commitment and self-motivation than regular college work. Pursue this course of study only if you are self-directed and work well in an unstructured environment.

When we think about earning a college degree, we usually think about "attending college." By this, we mean sitting in a classroom being taught by an instructor. While it is true that the majority of students do earn their degrees this way, there are thousands of others each year who are working on a degree without ever or hardly ever spending time in a college classroom.

Online or distance learning offers one of the most flexible ways for you to go school, especially if you are working or taking care of family members. You don't have to commute and you can study when it is convenient for you. Plus, these courses are generally less expensive than classes offered on a traditional college campus. In addition, online or distance education programs frequently give credit for prior learning (both informal and formal), thus reducing what you'll have to pay for tuition even more.

But, be careful. Not all online classes, certificates, or degrees are created equal. You need to find out if the credits you earn from these classes can be transferred, in case you want them to count at a traditional four-year college. And, look into the program's accreditation. There are different types and levels of accreditation. Is the online or distance education program you're considering fully accredited? A good way to check is to go to the Council for Higher Education Accreditation's website (*www.chea.org*) and see if the agency accrediting the program is recognized by the Council.

Take the Maximum Number of College Credits

Many colleges and universities charge by the semester rather than by course credit hours. If that's true at your school, and it's academically possible for you to do so, you should take the maximum number of credits allowed. By doing this, you may be able to reduce the amount of time it takes you to graduate and, therefore, the amount of money you spend on your education.

Become Active in Student Organizations

Some schools give tuition breaks to students who take on leadership roles in student government, student activities programs, student organizations, or student services. So, you not only save on tuition, but you pump up your résumé at the same time.

Take Some Classes at a Less Expensive School

Even students who opt for a traditional four-year college can save money by taking many of their required courses at a community college or a less expensive four-year college or university in the area. Similarly, look into taking summer courses at a less expensive school and transferring the credits to your degree-granting institution. This can result in a savings of thousands of dollars. But, before you sign up for off-campus classes, check with your admissions office to make sure that credit for those courses will be accepted at your school.

Accelerate Your Schooling

There are two main ways you can do this:

- Attend a school that offers a three-year bachelor's degree option. For example, Hartwick College (a liberal arts school in Oneonta, New York) now gives its students the opportunity to complete an undergraduate degree in three years, which would save one full year of tuition and fees (currently, a year there costs nearly $43,000). To do this, though, you will have to take about 20 credit hours per semester and sign up for summer school as well.

- Attend a school that offers a five-year bachelor's/master's degree option. If you have been planning to go to graduate school after college, this may be an effective cost-cutting strategy for you. Hundreds of schools throughout the country offer combined bachelor's and master's degrees in selected subject areas that can be completed in five years. Even better, some of those schools (for example, Clark University in Worcester, Massachusetts) charge only four-year tuition rates for these five-year programs.

Reduce Expenses

Make a list of the nonschooling expenses you will have during your college years. Generally, these could include:

- housing
- food
- utilities

- telephone and Internet
- clothing
- laundry and dry cleaning
- entertainment
- personal expenses
- transportation and travel
- insurance
- medical expenses
- child care
- prior indebtedness

Think creatively about how you might cut your expenses in each of these areas. Each dollar saved is a dollar you don't have to come up with from savings, loans, scholarships, work, or other sources.

And, if you have the discipline to pay off your credit card balances every month, then be sure to charge these expenses on a card that gives you back rewards in cash, gifts, or airline miles. You're going to have lots of expenses, and those "rewards" can really add up.

WORK-RELATED STRATEGIES

While many students routinely get a job during the summer months to earn extra money, there are several other work-related strategies available to them, as well, that can help them pay for college.

Work on Campus

Even students who receive federal aid or private scholarships often need to work while going to school. If you did not receive Federal Work Study and are willing to work while taking classes, be sure to look into the employment opportunities at your school. Not only is this the most convenient place to work, but you may find that your college or university offers their employees a tuition reduction plan or tuition waiver program. That would give you a double benefit: a salary plus a way to cut your college costs. While you're at it, ask if the school has a resident adviser program (where students receive reduced tuition or reduced room/board charges in exchange for working in the residence halls). While some students and parents might worry that working while going to school could negatively impact academic performance, 20 years of research reported in the widely-acclaimed book, *How College Affects Students* (published by Jossey-Bass), concludes otherwise; the research has shown that working can actually enhance academic performance, particularly if that work takes place on campus.

Participate in Cooperative Education

Nearly 1,000 colleges and universities around the country offer cooperative education programs, a highly sophisticated work-for-credit program where students alternate between study and work (more than 80 of the Fortune 500's top 100 employers have signed up for this program). Participants generally earn between $2,500 and $15,000 per year from their work assignments. As a result, many co-op students graduate from college with little or no debt. Plus, they rack up real-world experience, giving them a distinctive advantage over other college students who didn't work while going to school.

The structure of the cooperative education program varies from school to school. In general, though, one or more of these three scheduling options are offered: 1) alternating college cooperative education program: students work full time for 3 to 6 months; 2) parallel college cooperative education program: students work 15 to 20 hours per week and attend classes either part time or full time; 3) summer session program: students work 2 to 3 months during the summer. Typically, because of the work assignments, it takes five year for students in cooperation education programs to complete a "four-year" degree.

Gain a Competitive Edge in the Job Market

The National Association of Colleges and Employers (NACE) reported in its 2009 Job Outlook Survey that 76 percent of employers would prefer to hire new college graduates who have relevant work experience. "For college students, that experience is most typically gained through an internship or co-op assignment," explains Marilyn Mackes, NACE's executive director. She goes on to say: "Our studies show that in a poor economy, when employers do have jobs, they often look first to their own interns and co-op students."

But the extra time investment can pay off big. In addition to providing cash for college for the student during the program, cooperative education has another important benefit: nearly half of all participants are offered a full-time job with their company after graduation. For more information on this option, check out the National Commission for Cooperative Education's website: *www.co-op.edu.*

Try an Internship

Along the same lines, internships offer a way for students to earn money for college (particularly between semesters or during the summer). While some internships are nonpaying (although they may offer academic credit), many can be a source of cash for college, through stipends, subsequent scholarships, or both.

There are many sites you can use on the Internet to find internships. Here are three to get you started:

- *www.vault.com/graddegree/internships/internshipsearchform.jsp*
- *www.rsinternships.com*
- *www.internships.com/students.cfm*

Cash from Your (or Your Parent's) Company

Look into this if you are currently employed, or if your parents are. Many companies pay for part or all of college tuition costs for their employees' or their employees' dependents. In fact, according to E. Faith Ivery, the president of Educational Advisory Services, approximately half of today's major corporations either prepay or reimburse 100 percent of tuition costs, and 75 percent of all companies having a staff of 20 or more participate in some form of tuition reimbursement. If you or your parents happen to be looking for a new job and you have a choice, consider working for an employer with a tuition aid plan.

Let the Military Pay

If you have been thinking about a career in the military (or you are willing to serve in the military), why not let the military help you pay for college? There are four basic ways you can do this: attend a military academy, take ROTC, enroll in armed forces candidate training programs, or enlist in the armed forces.

Attend a Military Academy

Military academies are very competitive. But, if you have excellent grades, have an outstanding record of extracurricular activities, can demonstrate strong leadership skills, are in good health, and are willing to serve in the military after graduation, this approach may be for you. Since most appointments to the academies are made by members of the U.S. Congress, be sure to tell your senator or congressional representative about your interest. Most military academies charge little or no tuition, but you must agree to serve in the armed forces upon graduation for five to eight years. Here is a list of the qualifying military academies and the websites where you can learn more about them:

- U.S. Air Force Academy
  HQ USASA/RRS
  USAF Academy, CO 80840
  (800) 443-9266
  www.academyadmissions.com
- U.S. Coast Guard Academy
  31 Mohegan Avenue
  New London, CT 06320-8103
  (860) 444-8724
  www.admissions.uscga.edu

- U.S. Merchant Marine Academy
  300 Steamboat Road
  Kings Point, NY 11024
  (516) 773-5000
  www.usmma.edu/admissions

- U.S. Military Academy at West Point
  West Point, NY 10996
  (845) 938-4011
  www.admissions.usma.edu

- U.S. Naval Academy
  117 Decatur Road
  Annapolis, MD 21402-5018
  (401) 293-4361
  www.usna.edu/Admissions

Take ROTC

The Reserve Officers' Training Corps (ROTC) is a college-based program that was established to prepare students to become military officers. Except for the U.S. Coast Guard, each branch of the armed services award competitive merit-based scholarships to students who participate in this program. These scholarships offer financial assistance for one year, two years, three years, or four years of the participant's college education. Some are available for students in any subject major, others are for students specializing in a particular field (e.g., health, nursing), and a few are for students with specific ethnic heritage. These scholarships usually pay tuition at the participant's college (up to $16,000 per year) and provide funds for laboratory fees, on-campus education fees, textbooks, classroom supplies, and equipment. Participants also receive up to $500 per month (as an allowance) for the school term. In return, participants must agree to take training courses during college and serve as officers in a branch of the armed services following graduation for two to four years on active duty and four to six years in the National Guard or Reserves, for a total of eight years of military service. Note: Not all colleges have an ROTC program. More information on ROTC can be found on the websites of each of the three main branches of armed services:

- Air Force: *www.afrotc.com*
- Army: *www. armyrotc.com*
- Navy: *www.nrotc.navy.mil*

Enroll in Armed Forces Candidate Training Programs

Like ROTC programs, these are intended for students still in college who are willing to serve as a commissioned officer in the armed forces (in specialized areas) after graduation. Usually, the program is open to college juniors or seniors. Participants generally receive tuition and/or a monthly stipend (up to $500) while in school.

Enlist in the Armed Forces (Including National Guard and Reserves)

There are several different types of assistance offered once you are in the military (including National Guard and Reserves): including paid college classes, federal funds for college after leaving the military (e.g., Montgomery GI Bill), money for college from state or nongovernmental sources after leaving the military, and money for dependents (children and spouses) while in or after leaving the armed forces.

Money from the Military

Each year, millions of dollars in scholarships, loans, and grants are awarded to military families (current military personnel, veterans, and their spouses, children, grandchildren, etc.) to help them pay for college. How can you find out about these opportunities? You can search the scholarship finders at Military.com (*www.aid.military.com/scholarship/search-for-scholarships.do*) or at MOAA's website (*www.moaa.org/scholarshipfinder*). Or, look for this book at your library or in a bookstore: Financial Aid for Veterans, Military Personnel, and Their Dependents.

Anna and Robert Leider spell out an interesting strategy in their frequently updated book, *Don't Miss Out* (published by Octameron Associates), that students could follow if they decide to join the military and take advantage of some of the programs that would be open to them; keep in mind that this is only one of many ways that students can use military service to help pay for college. Their suggestion: "Go on active duty for three or four years. While on active duty, take off-duty courses (for which the military will pay up to 90% of the tuition costs) and make sure the courses add up to an associate degree. At the same time participate in the Montgomery GI Bill. When you are ready for discharge, you will have credit for two years of college" and quite a hefty tuition kitty (could be $24,000 or more) to help you pay for the last two years of college.

Of course, the decision to serve in the military—for whatever reason—cannot be taken lightly. There are very serious pros and cons, and these must be weighed carefully. But if you do decide to join the military, we want to be sure you know that, because of your service to our country, there will be many financial aid options open to you, your dependents, and even your descendants.

MOVING ON

In this chapter we looked at creative alternatives to financial aid that your student can use to help reduce the costs of college. We covered both school-based and work-based options. Your student can put some of these strategies into effect even before graduating from high school. And, it doesn't stop there. We've suggested additional approaches your student can pursue once in college.

But, let's be realistic. Even if your student is able to get financial aid and/or is able to use some of the alternatives we discussed here, there still might not be enough money from these sources to pay your student's entire way through college. So, in our final chapter, we'll take a look at things your family might need to do to cover the remaining costs. You'll learn about various types of loans, what kinds of tax credits you can receive, and what it takes to qualify as an independent student. Before you move on, however, take a look at the checklist for this chapter.

✔ **CHECKLIST:**

1. Share this chapter with your student.

2. Apply for all the federal, state, college, and private-sector sources of financial aid you can.

3. But, at the same time, you and your student should look beyond traditional forms of financial aid to find alternative ways to cut down on college costs.

4. Identify which school-based and work-based strategies your student might be able to pursue before graduating from high school, when choosing a college, and even after enrolling in school.

5. Check with your student's potential schools before pursuing any of the alternatives covered in this chapter, to determine which ones they offer or are willing to accept.

6. Then, get to work on making these alternatives to financial aid pay off for you.

CHAPTER FOURTEEN

Making it Work

Before we go any further, give yourself a pat on the back. By now you've applied for federal, state, college, and private aid, received aid packages from all your student's prospective colleges, compared the pros and cons of each, picked a college, and had your student consider various alternatives to financial aid. At this point, you should feel pretty good about the work you've done and comfortable knowing that nothing has been left to chance.

You're in the home stretch, but there's still one step left. Here's why. Even if you and your student received financial aid from various sources and were creative about coming up with alternative ways to pay for college, you're probably facing a "gap" between the outside money you received and your student's total college costs. So, now you're going to have to make some choices about which family resources to use to pay the remaining amount.

In chapter 5, we discussed the various incomes and investments parents can use to pay for college, but now that the process is nearly over, it's time to start making some hard decisions. Depending upon your situation, you may have enough money in the bank or investments and are willing to use it to cover your share of college expenses; if so, consider yourself lucky. Or, you may have enough to pay for your share of expenses, but you don't want to because that would have a significant impact on your savings. Or, you've looked over your finances and scraping all that money together just isn't possible. When that happens, it usually means a trip to the bank for a loan.

In this chapter, we're going to discuss several topics that will help you make an informed decision about paying for your share of college. To start, let's look at just when you'll be forced to write that check.

WHEN WILL I BE EXPECTED TO PAY?

That's often the big question on parents' minds at this point. "Just exactly when am I going to have to send the school a check?" If your student's college operates by semesters, you generally will need to make a payment when the school year starts (around the beginning of September) and again when the following semester starts (usually in January). If your student's college operates by quarters, you'll be expected to make a payment when each quarter starts. But what about all the other expenses? When do they have to be paid?

It might be helpful to set up a payment schedule for you and your student. To do that, use the list of expenses below and jot down the amounts you calculated on your COA worksheet in chapter 4 for the college your student will be attending.

- **By Fall Registration**
  — One-half of the year's tuition
  — One-half of the year's room and board

- **When Your Student Arrives for the Fall Semester**
  — Travel costs for getting to college
  — Relocation costs for moving your student
  — Personal expenses associated with relocating

- **When Classes Start for the Fall Semester**
  — One-half of the year's books and supplies

- **When Spring Semester Starts**
  — Balance of the year's tuition
  — Balance of the year's room and board
  — Balance of the year's books and supplies

- **As Necessary**
  — Fees for classes, labs, and other activities
  — Phone and utility bills
  — Clothing and laundry expenses
  — Transportation costs
  — Medical and dental expenses
  — Personal and miscellaneous expenses

As you undoubtedly noticed when doing your COA worksheets, these expenses really add up. Every family has a different way of handling expenses; some parents pay for things themselves, some give their students a monthly allowance to cover items, and some set aside a certain amount for each semester without budgeting. Only you'll know what method is going to work best for your son or daughter, depending on your (and your student's) spending habits.

YOU DON'T HAVE TO PAY EVERYTHING UP FRONT

Obviously, the good news about to all these expenses and bills is that you won't have to pay for everything up front. You may have to stick to a budget so you won't come up short, but many parents prefer to have these expenses spread out. After all, how many people walk into a dealership and write a check for the full amount of a new car?

Tuition Payment Plans

Colleges realize that some parents want to make regular monthly payments for school, just as they do for a car or mortgage. Because of this, many colleges offer tuition payment plans. These plans allow you to spread the tuition, room, and board costs out over time, instead of writing a check at the beginning of the semester. Most plans start in May or June before the fall semester and run until February or March, and can include anywhere from nine to 12 monthly payments.

You should realize that these plans are not loans (although some companies that offer tuition payment plans also offer consolidation loans, so don't get confused). Families do not pay interest on tuition payment plans, and they are not need based. There usually are a few fees involved, so be sure you ask before signing up. Colleges that offer these plans might do so themselves, or they may partner with an outside provider who administers (or oversees) the plan.

Share Your Experience with Your Child

If you paid for your college education, worked while enrolled, or contributed in some other significant way to the expense of your own education, share that information with your son or daughter. It could inspire him or her to step up to finance more of his or her education, or even to become more successful. Edmund Luzine, the owner and founder of Adirondack Capital Management, followed in his father's and grandfather's footsteps in paying for college. "I had a full academic scholarship to Syracuse University to study science and/or engineering that funded tuition, fees, books and provided a part-time job (via ROTC).

"My father worked for one full year after high school, in construction, before pursuing a five-year program to earn an architecture degree at Syracuse University. The one year on the job provided a unique, hands-on real-world education, to complement his formal classroom training.

"My grandfather walked many miles each day to attend a better high school, in order to increase his chances of matriculating into Union College. He traded commodities while at Union to pay for his education there and to get into Albany Medical College—fairly rare for most plastic surgeons these days."

Sharing your story could be a way to open a meaningful discussion about responsibility, college costs, and what your child is willing to do to invest in his or her future.

If you intend to budget your share of college expenses, tuition payment plans can be very helpful because they force you to be structured and consistent—something that can be difficult if a bill is not technically due. Before you sign up for any plan, however, be sure you are aware of all your responsibilities and any fees associated with the plan.

HOW MUCH CAN YOU AFFORD TO BORROW?

When buying a car or house, many families begin by determining how much they can afford to pay each month. Doing so gives the family an idea of how expensive a purchase they can make based on what the monthly payments will be. When you start planning monthly payments for college, you should do the same. This is especially true if you intend to take out a loan for college.

Debt-to-Income Ratio

A good way to go about this is to use the same criteria that lenders use when you apply for a loan, which is called a debt-to-income ratio. To do this, compare the amount you make each month with the amount you pay in loan payments. Your total monthly payments for housing (in other words, your rent or mortgage and home equity loans) ideally should be less than 28 percent of your monthly income. Your combined monthly payments for all other loans (including education loans, credit cards, and other installment loans, such as car loans) should be less than 9 percent of your monthly income. If you add up all the monthly payments for these loans, the total amount in this debt-to-income ratio should be less than 37 percent of your monthly income. If it is, then the difference between your amount and 37 percent is how much you would be able to afford to pay each month for a college loan.

For example, let's say your family's income is $4,000 each month, and you currently pay $1,200 each month in loan payments. Start by finding out how much you can, by the definition above, "afford" to make in loan payments:

$$\$4,000 \times 0.37 = \$1,480$$

(Percents are represented by two decimal places, so 37 percent = 0.37.)

This means that of the $4,000 your family makes each month, up to $1,480 of that amount can be used for loans. Next, add up the loan payments you make each month. For example:

Monthly Mortgage or Rent	$900
Monthly Car Payment	$200
+ Monthly Payments on Credit Cards	$100
Total Monthly Payments	$1,200

In this example, your family pays $1,200 each month in housing and existing loans. Now, subtract the difference between these two numbers and you'll know that amount you have available to pay for college loans:

37% of Your Monthly Income	$1,480
− Total Monthly Payments	$1,280
Amount You Can Afford to Pay	$200

In this case, your family could afford to make a $200 loan payment each month for your student's college education.

WHICH LOAN IS BEST FOR YOU?

Now that you know how much your family can afford to pay in student loans each month, let's discuss the types of loans out there and try to determine which type of loan is best suited for you.

Home Equity Loan

These loans allow you to borrow at any time against the equity in your home and are fixed amounts given for a defined term. This means that you take the entire amount of your loan in one lump sum and then make payments for a predetermined number of months. Often, a home equity loan has a lower interest rate and better terms than other loans, making it the least expensive loan available. In some situations, the interest from these loans can be written off for income taxes.

Another option is a home equity line of credit, which is similar to a home equity loan except that you receive a credit card rather than the lump sum. The credit card is used as needed, up until the credit limit has been met. The advantage of this is that you pay interest only on the money you actually borrow.

Borrowing against the equity in your home can be an excellent way to pay for college, but choose this type of loan carefully; you risk losing your home if your family can't make payments. Plus, equity loans can be hard to get if your credit is not excellent or if there is a depressed housing market.

This option is best suited to the following situations:

- When your college doesn't offer a tuition payment plan
- When the monthly payments of a tuition payment would be too high
- When you need to borrow funds to meet smaller costs of your student's education, such as books and supplies, or transportation expenses
- When you need to borrow the entire amount you'll pay the college

Federal PLUS Loan

As you learned in chapter 6, PLUS loans are non-need-based loans for parents of undergraduate students. PLUS loans can be included in financial aid packages, or parents can borrow up to the total unmet need for the college at any time. Borrowers must begin payments 60 days after receiving the funds, and repayment can take up to 10 years, depending on the amount you borrow.

Federal Perkins Loan

If your student is eligible for a Perkins loan, you'll be notified by his or her college, and they'll instruct you on the paperwork and your options. Because these loans are not available to all families, you may find their favorable terms and interest rates better suited to your needs than any other loans.

Federal Stafford Loans

Most colleges participate in the Stafford loan program, so your award letters may notify you if you qualify, and for how much. Remember that even if you don't qualify for a need-based subsidized loan, you can always apply for an unsubsidized Stafford loan because it's not need based. Private lenders, such as banks and credit unions, offer both unsubsidized and subsidized Stafford loans, so you'll need to shop around to compare rates and interest. Although interest rate for a Stafford loan may be more than a PLUS loan, repayment doesn't start until after your son or daughter graduates from college.

Federal Direct Student Loan

If your college does not participate in the Stafford loan program, it probably is part of this program. These loans are similar to Stafford loans, except that they are offered directly by the federal government. You'll need to ask your student's college for information if you're interested.

Many colleges are working to make the loan process easier to complete and understand. "We try to make our instructions as user-friendly as possible," says Karen Krause, director of financial aid at the University of Texas at Arlington. "And we're finding that our website is a good way to do this. It makes things easier to digest than getting pages upon pages of information with your paperwork."

Private Loans

About 25 years ago, private companies began realizing that government-funded financial aid was not keeping up with the rising cost of college. Because of this, private lenders started to offer loans for college. Depending upon your credit, you can borrow up to the full amount of your unmet need. Moreover, because these companies compete for business, you may be able to negotiate lower fees, more time to repay the loan, and somewhat competitive interest rates. Terms for repayment and interest will vary from lender to lender, so be sure to shop around.

To determine if you can qualify for a private loan, lending companies look at three things:

- Your debt-to-income ratio (which we explained earlier in this chapter)
- Your credit history
- Your income (if you're self-employed, you'll need to have been in business for at least a year)

Several factors will influence which kind of loan is best suited for you and your student. Your income, financial situation, credit history, mortgage or rent, cost of your student's college, and how much money you need are all going to impact your choices. As you did with financial aid packages in chapter 10, you may want to compare loans by looking at the pros and cons of each, paying special attention to interest and repayment terms.

WHAT SAVINGS SHOULD I USE?

In addition to or in place of loans, families might consider using their various savings accounts and investments to pay their share of college costs (see chapter 5 for a discussion of various savings vehicles). Some types of savings and investment are better suited to pay for college than others.

Tax Benefits

When it comes to tax benefits, your best choices are 529 plans and education saving accounts. Distributions from both of these types of accounts are tax free and, if you have them, are the first place you should tap to get money for college. Your other types of investments could be used to pay for college, but you'd have to pay taxes on the money you made from them.

Flexibility

If you don't have a 529 or education savings account, your next best bet might be to sell some stocks, mutual funds, or bonds to help pay for your student's education. Unlike 529 plans and educational savings accounts, anytime you sell these investments at a gain, you'll have to pay income tax on them (if you sell them at a loss, you do get to deduct that on your income tax). In either case, you'll only need to sell as many shares as you need to cover the expense. This, combined with the ever-changing price of investments, makes them a good choice in helping to pay for college when flexibility is important.

401(k)s and IRAs

You should try to avoid using your retirement account to pay for college. Although many people don't realize this, you may have tax consequences if you take money out of your 401(k) or IRAs before retirement (although you will not have to pay the 10 percent early withdrawal penalty if the money is used for education). The exact extent of the penalties will depend on your plan but, in almost all cases, you will lose money if you use your retirement accounts to pay for college.

You should also keep in mind that you can't borrow for your retirement, but you can borrow for your child's education. Therefore, whatever you do, try your best to keep your retirement money for your retirement.

Some of the options mentioned above may not be available to you, while others may not be appropriate to use. In fact, in some situations, it might even be a good idea to borrow money for college rather than use savings and investments. There's no easy answer, and if you have significant investments and savings, contact your financial consultant for advice.

Transfer Assets from Student to Adult

As we discussed earlier, the more assets and investments your student has, the less financial aid they may qualify for, now and in the future. Remember that when schools determine a family's expected contribution (EFC) for college each year, they expect 20 percent of a student's assets to be used for college, while as little as 5.6 percent is expected to come from the parent's assets. Because of this huge difference, it's wise to transfer assets in your son or daughter's name to yours—but only if and when this meets federal and state guidelines.

LUCRATIVE TAX BREAKS

We've already discussed (in chapter 5 and above) some of the tax advantages in setting up educational savings accounts. But, there are other lucrative education-related tax breaks offered by the federal government that can translate into money back to you—and that's money you can use to pay, or pay yourself back, for college. These tax breaks come in three forms: credits, deductions, and exclusions.

Tax Credits

Tax credits give the taxpayer dollar-for-dollar reductions of taxes owed. That means that you are able to subtract the credits in full, directly from your federal income tax liability. There are two credits that are available specifically to help offset the costs of higher education: the American Opportunity Tax Credit and the Lifetime Learning Tax Credit.

American Opportunity Tax Credit

Introduced in 2009 as part of Congress' stimulus package, this $2,500 college tax credit replaces (at least temporarily) the Hope Scholarship Tax Credit. Under the new program, many more families (including middle income and above) can qualified. For example, even married couples filing jointly who have modified adjusted gross incomes of $160,000 ($80,000 for single parents) can claim the full American Opportunity tax credit. Above that income level, the credit does gradually phase out. Even if you don't pay income tax, or don't owe $2,500 in income tax, you still can benefit from this program, as long as the student had at least $4,000 in eligible college-related expenses. What are eligible expenses? Those are any tuition and related expenses (for example, fees and books) paid to any accredited academic institution (by the parent, spouse, or dependent) that weren't covered by the tax-free portion of an educational savings account, tax-free scholarships, Pell grants, employer-provided educational assistance, veterans' educational assistance, or other tax-free payments received as educational assistance.

Here's how it works. If you don't owe any income tax and you or your student had at least $4,000 in qualified educational expenses, you will receive $1,000 from the IRS after you file your tax return. If you owe less than $2,500 in taxes, you will have your tax bill wiped out and receive the remainder of the $2,500 tax credit in cash. So, for example, if you would otherwise owe $1,500 in income tax and you qualify for this credit, then you would not have to pay any tax and you would receive a check from the IRS for $1,000. And, here's another benefit that wasn't available in the Hope program: this credit can be claimed for all four years of undergraduate study, as long at the student attends school at least half time.

Lifetime Learning Tax Credit

This tax credit offers up to $2,000 per family. It works this way. The taxpayer (you or your student) can claim this credit for up to 20 percent of the first $10,000 paid in tuition and related expenses. That amount is subtracted directly from the income tax owed to the federal government. Unlike the American Opportunity tax credit, this Lifetime Learning credit is "nonrefundable." That means that if taxpayers owe less tax than the maximum amount ($2,000) of the Lifetime Learning credit, they can only take a credit up to the amount of taxes they actually owe.

A family may claim both a Lifetime Learning credit and the American Opportunity credit at the same time, as long as the same student is not used as the basis for both credits. If a taxpayer is claiming an American Opportunity credit for a particular student, none of that student's expenses can be applied to the Lifetime Learning credit. For married couples filing jointly, eligibility for the Lifetime Learning credit begins to phase out when their adjusted gross income (AGI) exceeds $96,000. For single parents, the phase out begins at $48,000.

Educational Tax Deductions

The federal government also offers tax deductions for education-related expenses. You are permitted to deduct from your taxable income the amount you paid in tuition and fees, up to a maximum of $4,000, as long as your adjusted gross income does not exceed $80,000 for an individual or $160,000 for a couple. While this deduction is not as lucrative as the tax credits (which give you a dollar-for-dollar reduction in the tax you owe), it will reduce the amount of income that's subject to tax.

In addition, the federal government allows three variations on interest deductions for student loans: 1) taxpayers who meet certain requirements may be able to deduct up to $2,500 of the interest paid on student loans (depending on income and filing status); 2) children who are "independent" and take out students loans in their own names are also eligible to deduct the interest; 3) parents who take out a student loan for their child can deduct the interest, as long as the child was a dependent when the loan was received.

Income Exclusions

Like tax deductions, income exclusions reduce the amount of income that's subject to tax. The federal government offers several education-related exclusions, including

1. College savings withdrawals: If you take money out of a 529 savings plan (see chapter 5 for a discussion of this plan) to pay eligible college bills, none of the withdrawal is taxable—no matter how much you withdraw or how much income you made. But, you can't claim an education deduction or the tax credits for expenses paid by the money you took out of your 529 plan.
2. Employer paid expenses: Up to $5,250 paid by your employer for your college tuition, books, or fees is tax free.
3. Scholarships: these funds are tax free if you are a candidate for a degree at an educational institution and the money is spent only on tuition and fees (but not room and board).

Take Advantage of These Tax Breaks

For most of you, these tax breaks can result in money back in your pocket. That means money that you could use to pay for future college expenses. Unfortunately, most Americans know little about these breaks. According to a recent survey of 1,000 taxpayers conducted by CfK Roper and commissioned by CCH, few knew which tax breaks (including higher education tax credits and deductions) were beneficial to them. Don't be one of them.

To learn more about these tax breaks, and to find out if you qualify, talk to a tax adviser or visit the IRS website at *www.irs.gov* and download a copy of Publication 970.

HELP YOUR STUDENT MANAGE COLLEGE EXPENSES

Budgeting: Closing the Communication Gap

As your son or daughter actually begins to attend college, your Cost of Attendance worksheet is facing a reality check. Suddenly, your student "must have" more money. In some cases, there may be new and unforeseen expenses, essential and pressing (at least in the mind of your student).

Now, before college starts, is the time for you and your student to have a serious discussion about a budget. Make it clear that budgeting is a necessity. Whether you choose to give your student a lump sum to last a semester or to make monthly deposits into a checking account depends on the nature and habits of your son or daughter. You know them pretty well by now, so choose the best plan of action.

Money management skills aren't genetically inherited. They're learned and can always be improved. College can be an opportunity for your student to acquire financial habits, knowledge, and skills that can last a prosperous lifetime.

Work

As we've said before, studies show that students who work reasonable part-time hours may actually do better in college. The money earned can help pay for essentials like books as well as the extras, like parking fees on campus or a weekly pizza with everything (although many students might think of that as an essential).

If your son or daughter is eligible for a work-study program, that's great. If not, there are usually jobs on campus and in nearby towns available—catering, library reference desk work, babysitting, even paid research opportunities with professors in some cases. Ask your son or daughter to consider this option, but remember not to overdo it. Part-time work is great, but a full-time job might make grades suffer.

Credit Cards

Most of us have learned the hard way about the dangers of credit cards. Millions of Americans each year rack up debt by using these plastic cards for convenience, then realize they've spent more than they earn. Often, this means paying off debt for years to come, or worse, declaring bankruptcy.

Shared Responsibility

"Even though we consider it our responsibility as parents to pay for college, we realize that it is very important to have your child contribute a portion and have a vested interest," says Erin Devine, a mother of a college student. "Our daughter contributes to each semester's tuition bill and is expected to work summers and on-campus during the school year to earn spending money that gets deposited directly into her checking account."

Mounting Student Debt

In 2009, college seniors graduated with an average credit card balance of $4,100, up from about $2,900 in 2004. They used an average of four credit cards and only 17 percent said they regularly paid off their balances each month.

Source: SLM Corporation.

It used to be that you had to have a job before you could qualify for a credit card, but today teenagers with part-time jobs are offered credit cards with a limit high enough to buy a car. By the time your student starts college, they will be bombarded with credit card offers (even more so if they already have one)! If you've had problems with them yourself, make sure your son or daughter learns from your mistakes!

"We believe that a sixteen-year-old needs to learn about credit, so we let our children get a card with a $500 limit," says parent Karon Ray. "By the time they started college, they were aware of the dangers of credit cards." Karon's husband, Clark, noted that sometimes technology may actually help students be more responsible. "I'd recommend that students get a credit card where they can have their monthly statements and bills emailed to them, and have a monthly payment taken out of their checking account. I know from experience that college students can let mail and bills stack up until its too late, but they always check their email."

Credit cards can be good to have for emergencies and limited use, but your son or daughter will have to be mature and show restraint if he or she wants to stay out of trouble. Your student needs to build a good credit history, and the best way to do that is to limit him or her to one credit card, and make sure it has a reasonable interest rate and credit limit.

When starting out, students should treat their credit cards as a type of insurance—something they'll use only in emergencies where there's not enough cash on hand and they know they'll have the money to pay for the purchase in the near future. As with any insurance, however, the cards should only be used when completely necessary. (Actually, we'd all be a lot better off if everyone thought of credit cards in this way.)

SOLIDIFY YOUR PLAN

You've taken a look at various ways to pay for your share of college, and it's time to put together a plan. Here are a few strategies for you to try out and compare as you make a decision. We've listed these in ranked order, putting the options we consider most desirable first.

- Pay as you go along from your income and assets (savings, investments, etc.).
- Take the money you get from education-related tax breaks and use that to pay at least part of next year's college costs.
- Borrow your share of college costs from the Federal PLUS program.

- Pay your share through a combination of the Federal PLUS program, your income and assets, and other loans.
- Borrow your share of college costs from other loan programs (Stafford loans, private loans, etc.).
- Borrow your share using a home equity loan or line of credit.

"Many people don't seem to realize that it's possible to use a combination of options when paying for college," says Connie Gores, Winona State University's vice president for student life and development. "For example, I know a family that has put half of their student's college costs on loans, and are paying off the other half through tuition payment plans. This way, the monthly payments aren't too much, and the loans aren't overwhelming, either."

Depending upon your income and investments, you may already have a financial planner. If not, you may want to consider getting one. These professionals are often known as stockbrokers, but there are individuals who assist families in everything from planning to retirement, to creating a budget, to (you guessed it) paying for college. If you don't have a financial planner, ask around for recommendations. Check with your lawyer, accountant, or friends.

IN A PINCH, CONSULT A FINANCIAL AID COUNSELOR

For a fee, you and your student can also get help from a financial aid counselor. These individuals can be costly, and if you've understood most of this book, you probably won't need one. However, if you continue to have problems along the way, or can afford to pay an expert for advice, it may be worth the money. Odds are, however, their advice and information will be very similar to whar you're reading in this book.

Be cautious when seeking out an advisor, as scams and fraud in this area are on the rise (see chapter 12). Watch out for advisers who seem overly aggressive, charge hefty fees, or recommend strategies that you

> **Be Alert!**
> "We met with a financial planner who specializes in helping parents pay for college," says Erin Devine, a mother of a college student. "After the two-hour consultation, we decided not to continue as his whole strategy seemed to be finding sneaky ways to shield income or employ your child to almost 'launder' the money."

think are unethical. If you are unsure about the legitimacy of a particular financial aid counselor or adviser, call your student's or a local college's financial aid office for advice.

FINALLY...YOU'RE DONE (FOR NOW)!

As we stated when we began this book, there's no easy, one-size-fits-all answer for financial aid. But, you stuck with us, through 14 chapters, and now you should feel educated and well-prepared to make an informed decision for yourself.

To wrap up this last chapter, we began by discussing just when you can be expected to pay for your son or daughter's college. We then looked at how tuition payment plans can keep you from having to pay everything up front, as well as how to determine the loan payment you can afford.

Next, we reviewed the various loans available to you, and mentioned why credit cards are almost always a bad idea. You learned about the major educational tax credits and deductions that might help you in the future, as well as compared financial strategies to see which are best suited to help you pay for college.

Remember, this book is not meant to be the final word on paying for college. Hopefully, though, it's provided you with a road map to navigate the process, helped you to understand your options, given you the confidence to search for scholarships, shown you how to apply for financial aid, and motivated you to work out ways to lower the cost of higher education for you and your student.

Even though you're done, you're not really finished—not until your student finally graduates from college. So, shelve this book where you can find it easily. You're going to need it again, next year, when you start the process over again. But, with the experience you've acquired and the guidance in this book, you should feel like a pro next time.

Good luck. And, don't hesitate to share your successes with us!

✓ CHECKLIST:

1. Contact the college your student is attending to find out key dates in the payment cycle. Work these dates into your household budget and calendar to help prepare in advance.

2. Ask your college about payment tuition plans. Request information and consider the pros and cons of such a plan.

3. If your college doesn't offer a payment plan, contact a few outside organizations to find out what private loan programs are available.

4. Calculate your debt-to-income ratio before agreeing to a plan. Calculate the amount you can afford for a monthly debt payment.

5. Research various types of loans to determine which is best for you and your son or daughter.

6. Become familiar with and apply for all appropriate tax credits and deductions.

7. Discuss the hazards and benefits of a credit card with your student.

8. Research the advantages and disadvantages of using your savings and investments to help pay for your share of college costs. If you have a financial adviser or attorney, consult them before establishing any savings or loan plan.

Speaking the Language: Your Financial Aid Dictionary

Every field has its own vocabulary. If you are going to maneuver successfully through the financial aid maze, you'll need to know the language. Do you know what exactly defines "financial need?" Under what circumstances can a student be declared "independent?" Is COA the same as COE? What's the difference between the FAFSA and the PROFILE? How much money is a family "expected" to contribute to a student's education? Are scholarships and scholarship/loans the same thing? These words, initials, abbreviations, and phrase—along with hundreds of others that you are likely to encounter as you conduct your financial aid search—are covered here. Soon you'll be speaking the language just like a pro!

— A —

A.A.: Associate of Arts degree. For more information, see *Associate Degree*.

Academic Period: A specified period of enrollment (such as a quarter, semester, trimester, credit hours).

Academic Year: The school year, which generally lasts about nine months (at least 30 weeks of instruction)—typically September through May. The academic year is generally divided into semesters (four to five months) or quarters (three months). Scholarships are usually awarded for one academic year.

Accreditation: Approval given to schools that have met certain requirements established by a state, the federal government, or a recognized accrediting agency. Generally, students who attend a nonaccredited school are ineligible for state or federal aid (and, sometimes, private aid as well).

Accrued Interest: This relates to the cost of a loan. It's the interest that accumulates on loans and must be paid at a later date.

Acknowledgement: Students often receive an acknowledgement letter after they have submitted a supplemental aid application. This is also referred to as a "confirmation report."

ACT: See *American College Testing Program.*

Adjusted Gross Income: The amount of family income that remains after deducting local, state, and federal taxes; medical expenses; living allowances; and other factors that are used in the Federal Methodology system of need analysis.

Admissions Officer: These staff members work in the office that recruits potential students, reads applications, and decides which applicants are admitted.

Adult Learner: Students who are older (generally 25 or older), living away from their parents or self supporting, and/or whose primary role is something other than learner (such as parent, spouse, retiree, worker).

Advanced Placement (AP): Credit and/or advance standing awarded to students who have taken college-level courses in high school and passed certain examinations (e.g., those offered by the College Board).

Aggregate Loan Limit: The maximum allowable unpaid outstanding loan debt throughout the student borrower's academic career.

AGI: See *Adjusted Gross Income.*

Aid to Dependent Children: This program assists low-income parents with children (between the ages of 18 and 22) who are attending a postsecondary school.

American College Testing Program (ACT): The ACT consists of a series of standardized tests given in the United States and abroad throughout the year. The tests measure a student's verbal comprehension, mathematical ability, and problem solving skills. A student's score on this test can be considered by colleges and financial aid sponsors in the selection process.

American Opportunity Tax Credit: Along with the "Lifetime Learning Credit" (described elsewhere in this list), this is part of the federal tax credit system available to students. Under this program, which was introduced in 2009 as part of Congress' stimulus package, you can receive a maximum tax credit of $2,500. This program replaces, at least temporarily, the former Hope Scholarship Tax Credit.

Annual Loan Limit: The maximum federal loan amount that a guarantor may guarantee for a borrower for an academic year.

Annual Percentage Rate: Usually expressed as a percentage, this figure represents the total annual coast of a loan (including all fees and interest).

Anticipated Completion (Graduation) Date: The date the school or lender expects a student to complete the requirements of a degree or other program.

AP: See *Advanced Placement.*

Appeal Procedures: Students may request a college to reevaluate their eligibility or the amount of their award. Some of the reasons a student might wish to appeal: parent lost a job, parent became ill, parent died, need to add information not included in the original application.

Application Essay: This is an important part of college applications and, often, of financial aid applications. The essay can give a more personalized perspective of the applicant, as well as an indication of the applicant's writing ability.

A.S.: Associate of Science Degree. For more information, see *Associate Degree.*

Asset Protection Allowance: An allowance, subtracted from a family's total assets, that is used to determine the Expected Family Contribution.

Assets: Any or all of the following: money in checking, money market, and savings accounts and the value of stocks, bonds, mutual funds, home or business, other real estate, trust funds, etc. Assets are considered in determining Expected Family Contribution (EFC). Generally not considered assets: cars and other personal possessions (like stamp collections and musical instruments).

Associate Degree: Degree earned at some two-year colleges. Generally, the associate of arts (A.A.) and associate of science (A.S.) degrees are granted after students complete a program of study similar to the first two years of a four-year college or university curriculum. The associate in applied arts (A.A.S.) is generally awarded after the student has completed a two-year technical or vocational program.

Award Letter: See *Financial Aid Award Letter.*

Award Year: The period of a given calendar year and the following calendar year for which financial aid is granted.

— B —

B.A.: Bachelor's of Arts degree. For more information, see *Bachelor's Degree.*

Baccalaureate Degree: See *Bachelor's Degree.*

Bachelor's Degree: Degree (B.A., B.S., etc.) awarded for the successful completion of study at a four-year college or university. Also referred to as a "baccalaureate degree."

Bankruptcy: Judicial action that declares a person legally insolvent and causes that person's property to be distributed to creditors. However, federally loans cannot usually be discharged by a bankruptcy.

Base Year: The calendar year (ending on December 31) that precedes the financial aid award year. For example, the calendar year for 2010 is the base year for the 2011–2012 award year.

BIA: Bureau of Indian Affairs.

Borrower: The person who signs and agrees to repay the loan; this can be a student, parent (natural or adoptive), or legal guardian

B.S.: Bachelor of Science degree. For more information, see *Bachelor's Degree*.

Bursar's Office: The office at the student's university that handles the billing and collection of university charges.

— C —

Campus-Based Financial Aid Programs: These financial aid programs (primarily from the federal government) are administered directly by the postsecondary institution. Schools participating in any of the campus-based program (e.g., Federal Perkins loans, Federal Supplemental Educational Opportunity Grants, Federal Work-Study) receive a certain amount of funds for each program. Each school sets its own deadline for applying for these funds. When that money is gone, there are no more awards from that program for that year. You'll probably miss out on aid from the campus-based programs if you don't apply early.

Cancellation (of loan): Some loans have a cancellation provision, which permits part or all of the loan to be forgiven, canceled, or repaid if the recipient meets certain conditions (e.g., teaching in a certain geographic area, designated school, or particular subject). These are often called "scholarship/loans," "forgivable loans," or "loans-for-service." Loans may also be canceled because of disability or death.

Capitalization: When borrowers and lenders agree to defer the interest payments as they come due, then the unpaid interest is added to the principal balance of a loan and, as a result, increases the total outstanding loan balance.

Certificate: Awarded in recognition of successful completion of a particular program or course of study (generally in a junior college, vocational school, community college, or continuing educational program).

Certification: Verification from an academic institution that the student is enrolled at least half time, is making satisfactory academic progress, and is eligible for federal or private loans. This process must be made prior to disbursements of loan funds.

Citizen/Eligible Noncitizen: To be an eligible citizen or noncitizen for federal financial aid purposes, you must be one of the following: a U.S. citizen, a U.S. national (including natives of American Samoa or Swain's Island), or a U.S. permanent resident who has an I-151, I-551, or I-551C (Permanent Resident Card). If you don't fall into one of these categories, you can still qualify, if you have an Arrival-Departure Record (I-94) from the U.S. Immigration and Naturalization Service (INS) showing one of the following designations: refugee, asylum granted, indefinite parole and/or humanitarian parole, Cuban-Haitian entrant with status pending, conditional entrant (valid only if issued before April 1, 1980), or victims of human trafficking (T-visa) Citizens and eligible noncitizens may receive loans from the FFEL and Direct Loan programs at eligible American or participating foreign schools. You are NOT eligible for federal student aid if you have only a Notice of Approval to Apply for Permanent Residence (I-171 or I-464A) or if you are in the U.S. on an F1 or F2 student visa only, or on a J1 or J2 exchange visa only. Also, persons with G series visas (pertaining to international organizations) are not eligible for federal student aid. Citizens of the Federated States of Micronesia, the Republic of the Marshall Islands, and the Republic of Palau are eligible only for Federal Pell Grants, Federal Supplemental Educational Opportunity Grants, and Federal Work-Study.

COA: See *Cost of Attendance*.

Co-Borrower. See *Cosigner*.

COE: Cost of Education. For more information, see *Cost of Attendance*.

Collateral: Property pledged by a borrower to protect the lender and secure the loan. If the borrower defaults, that property can be claimed by the lender.

Collection: Action taken by lenders, guaranty agencies, servicers, and/or collection agencies when a borrower defaults or is delinquent on the interest and/or principal of a loan.

College Work-Study Program: See *Federal Work-Study Program*.

Commercial Lender: See *Lender*.

Conditional Awards: These scholarships, loans, or other awards require additional information or documents (e.g., transcripts, tax statements, verification of enrollment) before the award goes into effect. If the information/documentation is not provided or varies from previously submitted information, the award may be modified or withdrawn.

Confirmation Report: See *Acknowledgment*.

Consolidated Loan: This occurs when an eligible lender pays off one or more existing student loans and creates one new loan. Borrowers must begin repayment (or have entered a grace period) before the loans can be consolidated. All major federal loans are eligible for consolidation. Consolidated loans usually have lower monthly payments, longer repayment periods, and greater interest. Note: consolidation does not increase existing loan limits.

Cooperative Education: When participating in this type of program, which is also called co-op education, college students alternate periods of classroom instruction with periods of related employment. Students are paid for their work at the prevailing wage. It usually takes five years (rather than four) to complete a bachelor's degree under the cooperative plans, but students graduate with a year of practical work experience in addition to their academic studies. This program is separate from the Federal Work-Study program.

Co-Signer: A person who, in addition to the borrower, signs the promissory note for a loan and is responsible for paying the loan back if the borrower does not. Co-signers, also sometimes known as co-makers or co-borrowers, must be creditworthy and U.S. residents.

Cost of Attendance (COA): Sometimes, this is called the "Cost of Education." The phrase refers to the total amount it will cost a student to go to school: tuition and fees, on-campus room and board (or a housing and food allowance for off-campus students), and allowances for books, supplies, transportation, child care, costs related to a disability, and miscellaneous expenses. Also included are reasonable costs for eligible study abroad programs. For students attending less than half time, the COA includes only tuition and fees and an allowance for books, supplies, transportation, and dependent care expenses.

Cost of Education: See *Cost of Attendance*.

Credit Bureau: An agency that collects and maintains credit histories and other financial information about individuals. When a student applies for a loan, the lender contacts credit bureaus to supply this information.

Credit Report: A report credit bureaus prepare and issue that details an individual's assets, debts, delinquencies, and other related financial matters. Lenders use these reports to determine if a loan request will be approved or denied as well as to set the terms of the loan (e.g., interest rate, fees, etc.). The federal government requires that credit-rating agencies provide consumers with one free report on their credit each year.

Credit Score: Based on the information in a credit report, a credit score (from 0 to 850) can be calculated that summaries an individual's credit history (assets, debts, credit inquiries, late payments, etc.). Lenders are interested in this score because they consider it an indicator of how creditworthy a borrower is.

Creditworthiness: An indication that an individual has an acceptable credit history based on the criteria established by the lender.

CSS/Financial Aid PROFILE: Offered by the College Board, this is a financial aid application service (also known as the PROFILE). This form is required by some academic institutions. After students fill out the application, member colleges, universities, graduate and professional schools, and scholarship programs use the information collected on PROFILE to help them award nongovernmental student aid funds.

Custodial Accounts: These are accounts that parents or other family members set up in a child's name, as a way to save for college. Earnings in the account are taxed at the children's marginal tax bracket, rather than at their parent's (or other family member's) level. UGMAs and UTMAs are examples of custodial accounts.

Custodial Parent: This is the parent with whom the dependent student lives. If the student's parents are separate or divorced, this is the parent whose financial information is used in the need analysis.

CWSP: College Work-Study Program. For more information, see *Federal Work-Study Program*.

— **D** —

Data Release Number: Found in the upper-right corner of the first page of the Student Aid Report, this number is used to identify the student's FAFSA data for release to additional schools (beyond the six schools already listed on the student's original FAFSA form).

Debt-Management Counseling: See: *Entrance Interview*.

Default: This occurs when a borrower fails to make a required payment or fails to comply with the other terms spelled out in their loan (or promissory note). Default may also result from failing to submit requests for deferment or cancellation (both terms are defined elsewhere in this list) on time. If you default, your school, the organization that holds your loan, the state, and the federal government can all take action to recover the money you borrowed, including notifying national credit bureaus of your default. This could affect your credit rating for a long time. In addition, the organization holding your loan could ask your employer to deduct payments from your check. If you decide to return to school, you will not be entitled to receive any more student aid. Finally, the Internal Revenue Service may be able to withhold your income tax refund (and apply that amount to the amount you still owe).

Deferment: Under certain circumstances, lenders may allow borrowers to postpone payments that otherwise would be required on a loan. Some loans, like the federal subsidized loans, do not accrue interest during that deferment period. The repayment period is usually extended by the length of the deferment period.

Delinquency: Loans are delinquent as soon as the borrower fails to make payments on the date due. Accounts remain delinquent until borrowers bring their accounts current.

Department of Education (ED): This is the unit of federal government that is responsible for providing and administering a number of major federal aid programs, including the Federal Pell grants, the Federal Supplemental Educational Opportunity grants, the Federal Perkins loans, the Federal PLUS loans, the Federal Stafford loans, the Federal Consolidation Loans, and the Federal Work-Study program.

Dependent Student: Students who have access to parental support are viewed by the federal government as "dependent" students. They do not qualify for "independent" student status. For federal student aid purposes, a dependent student is one who was born within the past 24 years, is not a U.S. armed forces veteran, is not enrolled in a graduate or professional program, is not married, is not an orphan or ward of the court, has no legal dependents or spouse, and does not meet various definitions of homeless.

Direct Lending: Some federal loans, like the William D. Ford Federal Direct Loan Program, are available directly from the government—rather than from a commercial lender.

Disbursement: Payment of loan proceeds by the lender to the school, to be delivered to the borrower. These funds are usually made co-payable to the school and the borrower. During consolidations, this term refers to sending payoffs to the loan holders of the underlying loans being consolidated.

Discharge: See *Cancellation (of Loan)*.

Disclosure Statement: Issued by the lender to detail the amount of the loan, the total cost of the loan (including the interest rate, any additional finance charges, and any additional fees), and the consequences of defaulting of the loan.

Due Diligence: As required by the federal government, lenders or other loan holders/servicers must be able to show diligence in making, servicing, and collecting insured federal student loans. Otherwise, they might lose the insurance (against default claims) of the loans.

DRN: See: *Data Release Number*.

DVA: U.S. Department of Veterans Affairs (formerly the VA: Veterans Administration).

— E —

Early Decision: Also known as early action, early notification, and early evaluation. Some schools offer early decision admission plans, which notify those students who have requested that the college make its admission decision earlier than usual (generally in December of the student's senior year). Students must apply for these plans by mid-November of their senior year. There are two basic types of early decision plans: Students who apply under the First Choice Plan must withdraw their applications from all other colleges as soon as they are notified they are accepted by a first-choice college; students applying under the Single-Choice Plan may apply only to their first-choice college, unless they are rejected by that school. In either case, students applying under "early decision" generally will be expected to commit before they know how much financial aid they will receive.

ED: U.S. Department of Education. For more information, see *Department of Education*.

Education IRAs: These are tax deferred education savings accounts that let parents save up to $2,000 per year per child. Earnings can be withdrawn tax free when they are used for the child's education.

EFC: See *Expected Family Contribution*.

EFN: See *Exceptional Financial Need*.

EFT: Electronic funds transfer.

Eligibility Criteria: Most financial aid programs have specific conditions that students must meet to be considered for that award. Some programs require financial need; others do not. Other factors commonly considered: academic record, ethnic background, gender, extracurricular activities, professional affiliation, citizenship, age, and career interests.

Eligible Program: A course of study that leads to a degree or certificate and meets the U.S. Department of Education's requirements for an eligible program. To get federal aid, you must be enrolled in an eligible program. There are only two exceptions to that rule: 1) if a school has told you that you must take certain courses to qualify for admission into any of its eligible programs, you can get a Direct Loan or an FFEL Program Loan (or your parents can get a PLUS Loan) for up to 12 consecutive months while you are completing the course work—as long as your are enrolled at least half time and meet the usual student aid eligibility requirements; 2) if you are enrolled at least half time in a program to obtain a professional credential or certification required by a state for employment as an elementary or secondary school teacher, you can get a Federal Perkins loan, Federal Work-Study, or a Direct FFEL Stafford loan (or your parents can get a PLUS loan) while you are enrolled in that program.

Emergency Loans: Short-term loans available from colleges or private sources to students who have emergency expenses (e.g., high book costs, expensive equipment requirements, health problems). Many of these loans charge low or no interest.

Enrollment Status: A student's credit hour load at college (e.g., full time, half time, part time).

Entitlement Program: Under this type of program, students who meet the eligibility requirements receive assistance; there is no further selection process. The federal Pell grant program is an example of an entitlement program.

Entrance Counseling/Interview: Federal regulations require that a loan repayment and debt management counseling session (the "entrance" interview) be conducted by a college's financial aid office. The student must attend this session before a federally-guaranteed education loan can be disbursed. Student borrowers must also attend an "Exit Interview" when they graduate or attend school less than half time, where they receive information on their loans and when repayment begins.

ESAR: Electronic Student Aid Report.

ETS: Educational Testing Service (the company that produces and administers the SAT and other educational achievement tests).

Exceptional Financial Need: This is a measure used to determine students with the greatest need. The exact definition of what constitutes this need varies by program.

Exit Counseling/Interview: See *Entrance Counseling*.

Expected Family Contribution: A formula has been established by Congress to determine how much of your family's financial resources should be available to help pay for school. This amount is referred to as the Expected Family Contribution (EFC). In determining this amount, such factors as taxable and nontaxable income, assets (e.g., savings and checking accounts), and benefits (e.g., unemployment, Social Security) are considered. The EFC is subtracted from the COA to determine your eligibility for aid from many of the basic federal student aid programs.

— **F** —

FAF: Financial aid form. For more information, see *Financial Aid PROFILE*.

FAFSA: See *Free Application for Federal Students Aid*.

FAA/FAO: See *Financial Aid Administrator*.

FAT: See *Financial Aid Transcript*.

FC: See *Family Contribution*.

Federal Direct Loan Program (FDLP): This is a college-administered program. It is also known as "Direct Lending." Students at participating colleges can borrow directly from the federal government (rather than commercial lenders), through the subsidized or unsubsidized Federal Stafford Loans Parent PLUS loans, and William D. Ford Federal Direct Loan Program.

Federal Family Education Loan Programs (FFELP): Low-interest federally-supported student loans, including Federal Stafford Loans (subsidized and unsubsidized), Federal Parent Loans for Students (PLUS), and federal consolidated loans. These loans are made by private lenders and guaranteed by the state designated guaranty agencies on behalf of the federal government.

Federal Methodology: See *Federal Need Analysis Methodology*.

Federal Need Analysis Methodology: This is the standardized method used to determine a student's and/or a family's ability to pay for college (EFC). The information used in the formula is taken from the FAFSA. This process is also referred to as the Federal Methodology (FM).

Federal Pell Grant: An award to help undergraduates pay for their education after high school. This is the largest need-based student aid program sponsored by the federal government. To apply, use the Free Application for Federal Student Aid (FAFSA).

Federal Perkins Loans: Formerly called the National Direct Student Loan Program (NDSL), this federal program provides low-interest loans to undergraduate and graduate students who can demonstrate exceptional financial need. Colleges administer the program.

Federal PLUS Loans (FPLUS): Under this program, parents of undergraduate students are permitted to borrow up to the full cost of their child's education (less any other financial aid received). The interest rate charged is variable. Loans are not based on income but on parents' creditworthiness.

Federal Processor: The organization that computes eligibility for federal aid by processing the information submitted on FAFSA forms.

Federal Stafford Loans (FSLS): Formerly known as Guaranteed Student Loans (GSLs), students borrow these funds directly from banks or other lending institutions. There are two types of Stafford Loans: subsidized (which are need based) and unsubsidized (which do not require financial need). The federal government pays the interest on subsidized Stafford loans while the students are in college, but students with unsubsidized loans may be asked to pay interest while in school.

Federal Supplemental Educational Opportunity Grant Program (FSEOG): Grants are made to undergraduate students with exceptional financial need—those with the lowest Expected Family Contribution. Priority is given to federal Pell grant recipients. This is a campus-based program. Funds do not need to be repaid.

Federal Work-Study Program (FWS): This is a form of federal need-based student aid that is open to both undergraduate and graduate students. Participants work at jobs on– or off-campus while attending school. The amount earned cannot exceed the student's established need. This is a campus-based program.

Fellowships: Financial aid programs for graduate and postgraduate students. No payment is necessary. Although the terms are frequently used interchangeably, "fellowships" are different from "scholarships"; scholarships are intended to support undergraduate study.

FFELP: See *Federal Family Education Loan Programs.*

Financial Aid: A general term that describes any type of assistance that comes from a source other than the student or the student's family. There are many different types of financial aid, including scholarships for undergraduate study, fellowship for graduate study, loans, work-study programs (sometimes this includes internships), and emergency aid. The funding programs can be sponsored by the federal, state, or local governments, colleges, or private sources (sororities, fraternities, corporations, foundations, organizations, clubs, etc.).

Financial Aid Administrator: The staff member at a postsecondary school who is responsible for preparing, coordinating, and communicating information about financial aid. Also known as a financial aid officer (FAO).

Financial Aid Award: See *Financial Aid Package.*

Financial Aid Award Letter: This notice is sent from a college or other financial aid sponsor. It describes the terms of the financial aid offer (how much aid is being offered and in what form—a nonrepayable grant or scholarship, student employment, repayable loan, etc.). Students should respond in writing to all award letters, by accepting, rejecting, or requesting additional information on the financial assistance offered.

Financial Aid Form (FAF): See *CSS/Financial Aid PROFILE.*

Financial Aid Package: The total financial aid a student receives, including federal, state, private, and college scholarships, loans, and work-study opportunities. Unsubsidized Stafford loans and PLUS loans are not considered part of the package. According to the federal government, "using available resources to give each student the best possible package of aid is one of the major requirements of a financial aid administrator."

Financial Aid PROFILE: See *CSS/Financial Aid PROFILE.*

Financial Aid Transcript: An official record of all federal aid received by a student at each school attended.

Financial Need: The difference between what it costs to attend an institution (COA) and a student's (and/or a student's family's) ability to pay (i.e., the Expected Family Contribution). Often, this is expressed by this formula: COA – EFC = Need. Each family's financial situation is different. The information you report on your financial aid application is used to calculate your need. The type of needs methodology used can determine the amount of need assessed. Financial need is considered in the selection process of many undergraduate scholarships and most undergraduate loans. Financial need is less of a consideration on the graduate school level.

529 Plans: See *Section 529 Plans*.

Fixed Interest Rate: The interest rate charged on a loan is fixed—i.e., it stays the same (doesn't go up or down) for the life of the loan.

FM: See *Federal Need Analysis Methodology*.

Forbearance: This is an authorized period of time during which the lender agrees to temporarily postpone a borrower's total loan repayment obligation, to allow an extension of time for making loan payments, or to accept smaller loan payments than were previously scheduled. Forbearance does not alter the repayment status of the student's loan, and interest continues to accrue.

FPLUS: See *Federal PLUS Loans*.

Free Application for Federal Student Aid (FAFSA): A free need analysis form published by the federal government (also referred to as the federal form). This form must be used to apply for all federal student aid. In many states, it is also sufficient to establish eligibility for state-sponsored aid programs. It is available from the high schools and from colleges that participate in federal student aid programs as well as from the Department of Education: call (800) 4-FEDAID or visit this website: *www.fafsa.ed.gov*.

Free Money: A popularly-used term to refer to financial aid (for example, scholarships or grants) that does not need to be repaid.

FSEOG: See *Federal Supplemental Educational Opportunity Grants Program*.

FSLS: See *Federal Stafford Loans*.

Full-Time Student: A student who is registered for 12 semester hours or more.

FWS: See *Federal Work-Study Program*.

FY: Fiscal year.

— G —

Gap: See *Unmet Need.*

GED: See *General Education Development.*

General Education Development (GED): The equivalent of a high school degree. The GED is a standardized national examination taken by persons who, for whatever reason, haven't completed the formal requirements for a high school degree. The test measures educational attainment in 5 areas. Students who pass the examination earn the equivalent of a high school diploma.

Gift Aid: This term is used to refer to funding (e.g., a scholarship) that does not have to be repaid. Currently, the popular term for this is "free money."

GPA: See *Grade Point Average.*

Grace Period: A period of time during which loan repayment is not required. Generally, interest does not accrue during this period either.

Grade Point Average (GPA): A system to evaluate overall academic performance. The numerical equivalent of the grade (e.g., A = 4, B = 3) a student earns in a course is multiplied by the number of units assigned to that course; these grade points are then totaled for all courses taken by the student and divided by the total number of units the student has earned. Grade point average is often requested by financial aid sponsors, as one measure of the applicant's academic ability.

Graduate Student: A student enrolled in studies above the baccalaureate level at an institution of higher education. This includes advanced professional students as well (e.g., law).

Graduated Repayment: A scheduled way of repaying a loan, where the initial monthly payments are smaller and become larger as time goes on. This schedule generally cannot exceed 10 years.

Grant: The federal government and many student aid agencies use this term to refer to financial aid that does not have to be repaid. When the term is used in that way, it functions as a synonym for "scholarship." Sometimes, in the literature, this type of aid is termed "free money." Another meaning for this term: funds that are provided to support research, creative activities, or other independent projects.

Gross Income: The amount of income received, before deductions, taxes, and other allowances are subtracted.

GSL: Guaranteed Student Loan. Now known as the Stafford Loan Program.

Guaranteed Student Loan Program: Former name of the Federal Stafford Loan Program.

Guaranty Agency: The state agency or private non-profit organization that administers the Federal Stafford Loan and Federal PLUS loan programs in your state. The federal government sets loan limits and interest rates, but each state is free to set its own additional limitations, within federal guidelines.

— **H** —

HACU: Hispanic Association of Colleges and Universities.

Half-Time Students: There are three different ways to measure half-time status: 1) at least six semester hours or quarter hours per term, at schools measuring academic progress by credit hours and academic terms (semesters, trimesters, or quarters); 2) at least 12 semester hours or 18 quarter hours per year, at schools measuring progress by credit hours but not using academic terms; or 3) at least 12 hours per week at schools measuring progress by clock hours. Schools may choose to set higher minimums than these. Note: The Federal Stafford loan requirements are slightly different. You must be enrolled in school at least half time to receive the Federal Stafford loan, Federal PLUS loan, or Federal Direct Student Loan. Half-time student enrollment is NOT required to receive aid from the Federal Pell grant, Federal Supplemental Educational Opportunity Grant, Federal Work-Study, or Federal Perkins loan programs.

HBCU: Historically Black Colleges and Universities.

Holder: The institution (lender, secondary market) that holds a loan promissory note and has the right to collect from the borrower. Many banks sell loans, so the initial lender and the current holder could be different.

Hope Scholarship Credit: Now replaced (at least temporarily) by the American Opportunity Tax Credit.

— **I, J, K** —

IM: See *Institutional Methodology*.

Income: Money received from any or all of the following: salary, dividends, interest, sale or rental of property or services, business or farm profits, certain welfare programs, some subsistence allowances (e.g., child support, social security).

Income-Based Repayment: Also known as Income-Sensitive Repayment and Income-Contingent Repayment. The amount of the monthly payments for a loan is based on the amount of income earned by the borrower; the amount to be paid monthly is reviewed annually.

Independent Student: You are classified as an "independent" student by the federal government only if you meet 1 of these requirements: You were born more than 24 years ago, you are married, you are a graduate or professional student, you have legal dependents other than a spouse, you are an orphan or ward of the court, you are a veteran, or you meet the definition of homeless. If you do not meet any of these requirements, you are, by definition, a dependent student.

Independent Study: A program of study where students work independently (generally under the guidance of a faculty member) rather than attend structured classes.

Ineligible Noncitizens: Some noncitizens are eligible to apply for federal aid. These are defined under the term "Citizen/Eligible Noncitizen." But, there are noncitizens who are NOT eligible for federal student aid. These include: holders of student visas, exchange visitor visas, or G-series visas, those who have only a Notice of Approval to Apply for Permanent Residence, and those who hold a Form I-688A.

Institutional Methodology (IM): This is used primarily to calculate EFC for private school or privately-sponsored financial aid. For more information, see *Federal Need Analysis Methodology* and *CSS/Financial Aid PROFILE.*

Institutional Student Information Record (ISIR): The record the Department of Education uses to transfer electronically the Information students provided on the FAFSA to the schools selected by them on that form.

Insurance: The protection that guaranty agencies offer to lenders to protect them from losses on student loan claims.

Insurance Fee: The fee charged by guaranty agencies on certain loans; it is deducted from loan proceeds to cover defaults.

Interest: Calculated as a percent of the loan amount, this is a fee charged to borrowers for use of the lender's money. For more information, see *Fixed Interest Rate* and *Variable Interest Rate.*

Interest Capitalization: Unpaid interest is added to the principal balance of a loan; the end result of this is to increase the total outstanding balance due. See also *Capitalization.*

Interest-Only Loans: Payments are set up to cover only the accrued interest owned and not the principal balance. Generally, however, borrowers can make payments toward principal if they wish (but they are not required to do so, or to do so consistently).

Interest Rate: The rate charged a borrower until the loan principal is repaid.

Interest-Subsidy Payments: The interest payments made to lenders by the federal government on behalf of students who receive subsidized federal loans and are in school at least half time (or are in a grace period).

International Student: A student who is not a citizen or resident of the United States but who wishes to attend school in this country.

Internships: Short-term (a semester or academic year) work experience programs that usually relate to the student's major or field of study. The assignment may be on campus or at another location. It may be full or part time. Some internships offer a stipend; others are unpaid (but may provide college credits).

IRS Offset: This is when the Internal Revenue Service (IRS) appropriates the income tax refund from a borrower with a defaulted FFELP loan.

— **L** —

Late Charges: A penalty borrowers may have to pay to the lender if all or part of a requirement installment payment is not made on time.

Leave of Absence: A break in enrollment that is officially approved by the school at a student's request.

Legal Dependents: For dependency determination: a child or other person (but not a spouse) who lives with and receives more than half of his or her support from the student. In general: individuals (including spouses) who receive more than half of their support from someone else.

Legal Guardians: Individuals appointed by the court to use their own finances to support a person placed in their charge.

Legal Resident: A person who has met national, state, or local requirements for being declared a resident of that area. Another meaning for the term: an individual who is not an American citizen but who is still eligible for federal student aid.

Lender: A financial institution (bank, credit union, etc.) or other qualified program that makes Federal Family Education and PLUS loans, as well as other private loans, to students and their parents.

Lifetime Learning Tax Credit: Along with the Hope Scholarship Credit, this is one of two federal tax credit systems available to students. Under the Lifetime Learning Credit, you can receive a maximum tax credit of up to $2,000.

Loan: Money provided to an individual for a specific amount of time; the recipient must promise to repay the funds. Usually, but not always, interest is charged. This is one of the major forms of financial aid available to students. There are many types of loans available, including private loans, federal and state loans, college-based loans, and forgivable loans (also known as scholarship/loans or loans-for-service).

Loan Principal: This is the total amount borrowed and includes the original amount loaned, plus any interest or fee that has been capitalized.

Loan Proceeds: The net amount a borrower receives from a loan (the amount borrower less any fees charged).

Loan Servicer: An organization that administers and collects education loan payments on behalf of the lender.

— M —

M.A.: Master's of Arts. See *Master's Degree.*

Major: Most colleges require students to specialize (major) in a specific subject or discipline—generally during their junior and senior years.

Master's Degree: A graduate degree (M.A., M.S., etc.) granted by universities; usually involves taking at least one full year of classes beyond a bachelor's degree plus writing a thesis or taking a comprehensive examination.

MDE Processor: See *Multiple Data Entry Processor.*

Merit-Based Aid: Financial aid is often referred to as either need-based or merit-based. Programs that consider an applicant's achievements, talents, or other merits, but do not factor in financial need in the selection process, are known as merit-based.

Methodology: There are a number of systems (or methodologies) used to calculate Expected Family Contribution. One of the most important is the Federal Need Analysis Methodology.

Minor: Some colleges require or allow students to develop a secondary area of concentration (minor), in addition to their major. For example, a European history major may have a French minor.

Multiple Data Entry (MDE) Processor: The Department of Education has contracted with a number of organizations to process federal student aid applications (e.g., College Scholarship Service, American College Testing).

— N —

National Student Loan Clearinghouse (NSLDS): A central repository for the collection of postsecondary enrollment status, this non-profit organization is responsible for helping postsecondary institutions meet their reporting responsibilities to their students, the loan industry, and the federal government. Students can use NSLDS' database to find out about the aid they've received, including outstanding balances and the status of their loans and disbursements.

Need: See *Financial Need.*

Need Analysis: A system used to calculate Expected Family Contribution. For information on the need analysis system used by the federal government, see *Federal Need Analysis Methodology.*

Need Analysis Form: There are several forms available. For federal and some state aid, the Free Application for Federal Student Aid (FAFSA) is required. The majority of public colleges also use this form. For many private colleges, the Financial Aid PROFILE may be needed. Some states require their residents to use their own form; e.g., Pennsylvania applicants are required to submit the PHEAA Aid Information Request (PAIR), available from the Pennsylvania Higher Education Assistance Agency.

Need-Based Aid: Financial aid awarded on the basis of the applicant's financial need. Other factors may also be considered.

Net Income: The amount of gross income received minus deductions and allowances.

Noninstitutional Costs: College-related costs that are not charged directly by the student's school (e.g., books, supplies, transportation, off-campus room and board, miscellaneous expenses).

Non-Need Based Aid: Federal aid is often referred to as either need-based or non-need based. Non-need programs do not take into consideration an applicant's level of financial need in the selection process. Other factors, instead, are used (e.g., musical, athletic, or purely academic accomplishments). Merit-based programs are an example of non-need based aid.

Notification: See *Financial Aid Award Letter.*

— O —

Off-Campus: Housing that is either not owned by the school or located on school property.

On-Campus: Housing this is owned by the school or located on school property.

Open Admissions: Particularly common on the junior or community college level, this system admits high school graduates and other adults without regard to their academic qualifications (they need only have a high school diploma or its equivalent).

Origination Fee: This is a processing fee charged by the lender to the student as part of "originating" the loan. Like the insurance fee, this fee is usually subtracted from the loan principal before the funds are disbursed to the borrower.

Out-of-State Student: Students who are not legal residents of a state or local district that is responsible for the supervision of the student's institution. Generally, the tuition charged out-of-state students is much higher than that charged to legal residents.

Overawards: This occurs when the student's Expected Family Contribution, the student's own resources, and the financial aid awarded to the student exceed the student's cost of attendance. Overawards are not allowed if the student is receiving federal aid.

— **P** —

Package: See *Financial Aid Package.*

Packaging: This refers to the particular combination of scholarships, loans, and work opportunities that is put together for each student.

Parent: The natural mother and/or father, or the adoptive mother and/or father, or any legal guardian.

Parent Loans for Undergraduate Students. See *Federal PLUS Loans.*

Parent's Contribution: The amount parents can reasonably be expected to provide toward the cost of postsecondary education for their child, given their particular combination of assets and liabilities. For more information, see *Expected Family Contribution.*

Part-Time Student: A student who is registered for less than 12 hours of credit per semester.

Pell Grant Program. See *Federal Pell grant.*

Perkins Loan Program: See *Federal Perkins Loans.*

PIN: This stands for "personal identification number." You should sign up to get a PIN from the U.S. Department of Education. That PIN can be used each year to electronically apply for federal student aid and to access your federal student aid records online. If you don't already have a PIN, you can request one at *www.pin.ed.gov.*

PLUS: Parent Loans to Undergraduate Students. See *Federal PLUS Loans.*

Portability: Financial aid programs are generally either school-based (can be used at only 1 school or a specified group of schools) or portable (can be used at whatever school the student chooses to attend—within limits). Print and Internet resources that focus on "portable" financial aid programs are more useful than those that include school-based programs. Your best source of information on school-based programs is the school itself.

Postsecondary Education: This includes all education occurring after high school, both undergraduate and graduate.

Preferred Lender List: This is a list of lenders that a college suggests its students consider when taking out federally guaranteed student loans. Keep in mind: the lenders on these lists are not the only ones you can use; you are allowed to borrow from any federally-approved lender.

Prepaid Tuition Plan: A college savings plan guaranteed to rise in value at the same rate as college tuition. Several states and institutions offer such programs.

Prepayment: Borrowers can choose to make a payment that is more than the amount due on their loan. If you are doing this on your federal loan, keep in mind that the excess funds will be applied in this way: first to any outstanding fees and charges, next to outstanding interest, and finally to the principal balance of the loan. There is never a penalty for prepaying principal or interest on a federal student loan.

Principal: See *Loan Principal.*

Private Loans: Students sometimes turn to private loans (not sponsored by governmental agencies) when their personal resources and/or financial aid do not cover all their educational costs. These loans, which are offered by banks and other financial institutions or schools to parents or students often carry a higher interest rate than do federal or state loans.

Professional Judgment; FAAs are frequently able to use their professional judgment to adjust a student's financial aid package, based on extenuating circumstances or additional information.

Promissory Note: A binding legal document that borrowers sign when they get a student loan. The note lists the conditions under which they are borrowing and the terms under which they agree to pay back the loan. It includes information about interest rates and about deferment and cancellation provisions (if any). Be sure to read and save any promissory note you sign; you will need to refer to it later when you begin to repay the loan.

Proprietary Schools: These are privately-owned postsecondary institutions that are legally permitted to make a profit. Most of these schools offer technical and vocational courses. Not all of these schools are accredited and a number of them are not eligible to offer the full array of federal funding. Be sure to check before you enroll.

PSAT/NMSQT (Preliminary SAT/National Merit Scholarship Qualifying Test): Serves as a qualifying test for awards from the National Merit Scholarship Program and some others (including the National Hispanic Scholar Award). The test is administered by high schools nationwide each October. In structure, it is a shortened version of the SAT.

— Q —

Quarter: An academic term, generally 11 weeks in length. While four quarters make up the academic year, most students attend only the first three quarters.

— R —

Rebate: Some loans give student borrowers a rebate upfront. In exchange, students must make their first 12 required monthly payments on time; it they don't, the rebate amount is added back to the principal balance of their loan. If you are interested in this option, check with your lender to see if it available.

Regular Student: A student who is enrolled in an institution to obtain a degree or certificate. Generally, to receive aid from the major federal student aid programs, you will need to be a regular student.

Repayment Incentive: This is a benefit that the Department of Education offers borrowers, to encourage them to repay their loans on time. This is the way it works: if a certain number of payments are made on time, the interest rate charged on the borrower's loan may be reduced.

Repayment Plan: The plan established to repay a loan. It generally spells out the principal and interest due on each installment, the interest rate charged, the frequency of payments, the due date of the first payment, and the total number of installments due. It is possible to change your repayment plan. For example, you can usually lower your monthly payment by changing to another repayment plan with a longer term to repay the loan. There are usually no penalties for changing repayment plans.

Residency Requirements: This term can be used in two different ways: 1) the minimum time a student must spend in a particular geographic location to be considered a resident, or 2) the minimum time a student must spend taking classes on campus to be eligible for graduation.

Rolling Admissions: Applications for admission that are considered as soon as all the required paperwork has been submitted. Generally, there is no specific deadline.

— S —

SAR: See *Student Aid Report*.

SAT Reasoning Test: This is a test that measures a student's ability in math, critical reading, and writing. SATs are offered throughout the year at test sites in the United States and abroad. Students generally take this text during their junior or senior year in high school. Many colleges and financial aid sponsors require students to take and report their scores on this test.

SAT Subject Tests: A companion to the SAT Reasoning Test, this is used to measure a student's ability in specific subject areas, including English, mathematics, sciences, history, and foreign languages. Some colleges, but only few scholarship sponsors, require students to take 1 or more of these tests.

Satisfactory Academic Progress: To be eligible to receive and continue receiving federal student aid, you must be maintaining satisfactory academic progress toward a degree or certificate. You must meet your school's written standard of satisfactory progress. Check with your school to find out its standard. If you are enrolled in a program that's longer than 2 years, the following definition of satisfactory progress also applies to you: you must have a C average by the end of the your second academic year of study or have an academic standing consistent with your school's graduation requirements. You must continue to maintain satisfactory academic progress for the rest of your course of study.

Scholarships: This is a type of financial aid for undergraduates that does not have to be paid back. In popular terms, it is also referred to as grants, gift aid, and free money. Although the terms "scholarships" and "fellowships" are frequently used interchangeably, it is proper to think of scholarships as awards for undergraduate students and fellowships as awards for graduate or postgraduate students.

Scholarship/Loans: This is a form of financial aid that has a service and/or cash repayment obligation as a condition for receiving the funds. A student promise to deliver specific services after graduation or repay all funds, plus interest. Also known as forgivable loans and loans-for-service.

School Year: See *Academic Year*.

Secondary Market: This refers to organizations that purchase student loans from originating lenders, so those lenders can make additional student loans. If an organization buys the loan, that organization then owns and becomes the holder of the loan. Only education loans under the FFEL program are sold in the secondary market.

Section 529 Plans. This is another type of account (like Education IRAs and Custodial Accounts) in which money invested for educational purposes can be grown tax deferred. The plan is named for the section of the IRS code authorizing its existence. The specifics of these plans vary from state to state. For more information, see *www.savingforcollege.com*.

Selective Service Registration: If you are male, at least 18 years of age, a citizen or eligible noncitizen, and not currently on active duty in the armed services, you must register with the Selective Service in order to receive federal student aid. A statement appears on the Student Aid Report (defined below) that allows you to state either that you have registered with the Selective Service or to explain why you are not required to register. Citizens of the Federated States of Micronesia, the Marshall Islands, and Palau are exempt from registering.

Self-Help Aid: A term used to refer to funds that come from loans or student employment.

Semester: An academic term, generally 17 or 18 weeks in length. Usually, schools have two semesters and one or more summer sessions.

SEOG: Supplemental Educational Opportunity Grant. For more information, see *Federal Supplemental Educational Opportunity Grant.*

Service Academies: There are five academies administered by the armed services: U.S. Military Academy (West Point), U.S. Air Force Academy; U.S. Naval Academy (Annapolis); U.S. Coast Guard Academy; and U.S. Merchant Marine Academy.

Servicer. See *Loan Servicer.*

Simplified Needs Test: A way of calculating Expected Family Contribution, when the following situation occurs: parents have an adjusted gross income of less than $50,000 and family members have filed an IRS Form 1040A, 1040TEL, or 1040EZ or are not required to file. Unlike other formulas, this one does not consider assets.

Stafford Loan: See *Federal Stafford Loans.*

Statement of Educational Purpose: Students must sign this document if they are going to receive federal need-based funds. The document states that the student promises to use the money only to pay for educational expenses.

Student Aid Report (SAR): This is the document produced by the U.S. Department of Education that notifies students by email or mail of the results of the processing of their Free Application for Federal Student Aid (FAFSA). The student's eligibility for aid is indicated by the EFC, which is printed on the front of the SAR. In addition to the Information Summary that SARs have, some reports will also have an Information Review or Request Form and a Payment Voucher. The SAR must be submitted to the student's college to certify eligibility for federal student aid.

Student's Contribution: This is the amount that students are expected to pay towards their college costs. It is based on an analysis of their income, assets, and liabilities. The student's contribution, along with the parents' contribution, make up the Expected Family Contribution. The EFC is considered when a student's level of financial need is determined.

Study Abroad: As part of their college education, many students take advantage of study abroad opportunities. Study abroad programs allow students to spend a semester or a year in a foreign country, studying at a university, while receiving credit that will count towards their degree. Generally, students participate in this program during their junior year, but many colleges offer study abroad programs for students at any level.

Subsidized Loans: These are federally guaranteed loans that are awarded on the basis of financial need. The federal government pays interest on the loan while the student is in school and for 6 months after graduation. Subsidized loans include direct subsidized, direct subsidized consolidation loans, federal subsidized stafford loans, and federal subsidized consolidation loans.

— T —

Traditional Student: A full-time college or university student who is between the ages of 18 to 25. Students over the age of 25 are often referred to as "nontraditional" students

Transcript: A list of all classes taken and grades received. Many financial aid sponsors require a copy of an applicant's official transcript as part of the application process.

Transfer Programs: An organized set of classes offered by community and junior colleges for students who plan to continue their education at a four-year college or university.

Transfer Students: These are students who have attended one college for a period of time (ranging from one term to three years) who are or will be attending another institution. Some scholarships are set aside specifically for transfer students.

Trimester: An academic term that generally lasts 15 weeks. There are three trimesters each year. Most students enroll in only two trimesters a year.

Tuition and Fee Waivers: Many colleges will waive tuition and/or fees for certain categories of students (e.g., senior citizens, children of alumni, veterans, persons with disabilities).

Tuition Payment Plan: These plans are short-term (12 months or less) installment plans that split tuition into equal payments. White these plans are generally interest free, they may have a fee or finance charge.

— U —

Undergraduate Student: A student working on a baccalaureate or first professional degree (e.g., a Bachelor of Architecture).

Unmet Need: The difference between a student's cost of attendance and the student's available financial resources (including any financial aid that has already been awarded).

Unsubsidized Loan: Federal loans that are not based on financial need (e.g., Unsubsidized Stafford Loan). Since the loan is not subsidized, students must pay all interest charges that accrue on the loan.

Upper Division: The last two years (junior and senior years) of undergraduate study. There are schools that offer only lower-division classes (e.g., community and junior colleges), both lower-division and upper-division classes (four-year colleges and universities), and only upper-division classes.

— V —

Variable Interest Rate: As opposed to fixed rates, these rates are adjusted at regular intervals (e.g., monthly, quarterly, or yearly). A number of federal loan programs (e.g., federal Stafford loans) carry variable rates that are set annually.

Verification: This is the process your school uses if it needs to confirm the data reported on your FAFSA. Your school has the authority to contact you for documentation to supports any of the information you reported on your form. The federal government randomly selects approximately 1/3 of all financial aid application for verification, but some schools verify 100% of their financial aid recipients.

Verification Form: Sent by a student's college or servicer; the student needs to complete this form and return it to the school.

— W, X, Y, Z —

Work-Study: Work-study assignments are awarded as part of a financial aid package and require the recipient to work to receive any money. Unlike cooperative education or internship programs, which are integrated into an academic program, this approach is meant simply as a way for paying for college (see also *Federal Work-Study Program*).

Going Online for Help

When we sat down to write Kaplan's *Paying for College*, our goal was to identify, verify, summarize, and organize the basic information that parents would need to be able to make informed decisions about how to pay for their student's college education. In gathering this information, we reviewed hundreds of books, articles, expert comments, and online sites. In the process, we were struck by the number of incredibly useful information resources that are just a click away on any computer. We knew you'd be interested in these. So, in this section, we are highlighting some of our favorite places to go online for help. We've grouped these sites into the two dozen or so topics that parents most consistently ask about. These range from accreditation and college bargains to tuition discounts and ways to save both before and during college.

We referred to some of these sites previously in the book; others are new to this section. All of them were verified right before this new edition was published. But, as we are all aware, web pages can and do change over time. If you are ever have a problem linking to one of these sites, just drop us an email and we'll make sure you get an updated link.

Accreditation

Council for Higher Education Accreditation Database
www.chea.org/search/default.asp

Database of Accredited Programs and Institutions
www.ed.gov/admins/finaid/accred/index.html

Regional Accreditation for Online Schools
distancelearn.about.com/od/accreditationinfo/a/regional.htm

Advanced Placement

AP Tests
www.collegeboard.com/student/testing/ap/about.html

Careers and Salaries

Occupational Outlook Handbook
www.bls.gov/oco

College Bargains

FindCollegeCard's Least Expensive Colleges
www.findcollegecards.com/blog

Kiplinger's Best Values in Public Colleges
www.kiplinger.com

U.S. News' Best Values
www.consusrankings.com/category/colleges-universities/us-news-colleges-universities

USA Today/Princeton Review's Best Value Colleges
www.usatoday.com/news/education/best-value-colleges.htm

College-Level Examination Program

CLEP Exams
www.collegeboard.com/student/testing/clep/about.html

Cooperative Education Programs

National Commission for Cooperative Education
www.co-op.edu

Federal Grants

Academic Competitiveness Grant
studentaid.ed.gov/PORTALSWebApp/students/english/AcademicGrants.jsp

National SMART Grant
studentaid.ed.gov/PORTALSWebApp/students/english/SmartGrants.jsp

Pell Grants
www.ed.gov/programs/fpg/index.html

Supplemental Education Opportunity Grant
studentaid.ed.gov/PORTALSWebApp/students/english/FSEOG.jsp

TEACH Grants
studentaid.ed.gov/PORTALSWebApp/students/english/TEACH.jsp

Federal Loans

Loan Consolidation
www.loanconsolidation.ed.gov

Perkins Loans
www.ed.gov/programs/fpl/index.html

PLUS Loans
studentaid.ed.gov/PORTALSWebApp/students/english/parentloans.jsp

Stafford Loans
studentaid.ed.gov/PORTALSWebApp/students/english/studentloans.jsp

Financial Aid Calculators

College Board's College Financing Calculators
www.collegeboard.com/student/pay/add-it-up/401.html

FinAid Calculators
www.finaid.org/calculators

SallieMae's "How to Pay for College" Calculators
www.salliemae.com/content/payforcollege/pfc.html

U.S. Department of Education's Forecaster
www.fafsa4caster.ed.gov

Financial Aid Forms

FAFSA
www.fafsa.ed.gov

College Board (CSS) PROFILE
profileonline.collegeboard.com/prf/index.jsp

U.S. Department of Education PIN Registration
www.pin.ed.gov

Financial Aid Basics

Financial Aid Resource Center
www.nasfaa.org/redesign/parentsstudents.html

Funding Education Beyond High School
studentaid.ed.gov/students/publications/student_guide/index.html

Student Aid on the Web
studentaid.ed.gov

Financial Aid Blogs

CollegeScholarships.org
www.collegescholarships.org/blog

FinancialAidNews
www.financialaidnews.com

Top Scholarship Blog
topscholarshipblog.com

Financial Planning

Certified Financial Planner Board of Standards, Inc.
www.cfp.net

Financial Planner Database
www.bankrate.com/funnel/certified-financial-planner/cfp.aspx

Federal Tax Liabilities and Benefits

IRS Tax Info for Students
www.irs.gov/individuals/students

IRS Tax Benefits for Education
www.irs.gov/publications/p970

Internships

Vault Internship Database
www.vault.com/graddegree/internships/internshipsearchform.jsp

RisingStar Internships
www.rsinternships.com

Internships.Com
www.internships.com/students.cfm

Loan Forgiveness

For community service volunteers
www.americorps.org

For international service
www.peacecorps.gov

For military personnel
www.usmilitary.about.com/cs/joiningup/a/clrp.htm

For teachers
www.aft.org/tools4teachers/loan-forgiveness.htm

For lawyers
www.abanet.org/legalservices/sclaid/lrap/statelraps.html

For health care workers
nhsc.bhpr.hrsa.gov/applications/lrp

For public sector workers
studentaid.ed.gov/students/attachments/siteresources/LoanForgivenessv4.pdf

Money from the Military

Financial Aid for Veterans, Military Personnel, and Their Dependents
www.rspfunding.com/catalog/item/1414261/872354.htm

Military.Com
www.aid.military.com/scholarship/search-for-scholarships.do

Military Officers Association of America
www.moaa.org/scholarshipfinder

Private Student Loans

SLA Student Loan Ratings
www.studentlendinganalytics.com/SLA/ratings.html

FinAid Student Loan Comparisons
www.finaid.org/loans/privatestudentloans.phtml

Regional Exchange Programs:

Midwest Student Exchange Program
www.mhec.org/index.asp?pageID=329

New England Regional Student Program
www.nebhe.org/content/view/18/53

SREB's Academic Common Market
www.sreb.org/programs/acm/acmindex.aspx

WICHE's Western Undergraduate Program
www.wiche.edu/States

Scholarship Scams

State Consumer Protection Office
www.consumeraction.gov/state.shtml

Better Business Bureau
www.bbb.org/us/Find-Business-Reviews

State Attorney General Offices
www.naag.org

Federal Trade Commission
http://www.ftc.gov/scholarshipscams

National Fraud Information Center
www.fraud.org

U.S. Postal Service
postalinspectors.uspis.gov/contactUs/filecomplaint.aspx

Searching for Scholarships:

American Educational Guidance Center
www.college-scholarships.com/free_scholarship_searches.htm

College Board's Scholarship Search
www.apps.collegeboard.com/cbsearch_ss/welcome.jsp

FastWeb's Scholarship Money
www.fastweb.com

Google Alerts
www.google.com/alerts

Peterson's Scholarship Central
www.petersons.com/finaid/landing.asp?id=806&path=ug.pfs.scholarships

Reference Service Press
www.rspfunding.com/prod_prodalpha.html

SallieMae Fund's Scholarship Searches
www.thesalliemaefund.org/smfnew/sections/search.html

Scholarships.com
www.scholarships.com

Scholarship Experts
www.scholarshipexperts.com

U.S. Department of Education's Scholarship Wizard
www.studentaid2.ed.gov/getmoney/scholarship/v3browse.asp

State Aid

State Higher Education Agencies Directory
www.ed.gov/Programs/bastmp/SHEA.htm

Study Abroad Scholarships

Go Abroad.com
scholarships.goabroad.com/index.cfm

IIEPassport's Study Abroad Funding
www.studyabroadfunding.org

University Minnesota's Learning Abroad Center
www.umabroad.umn.edu/financial/scholarships/index.html

Tuition Discounting

The Council of Independent Colleges
www.cic.org/tep

The Tuition Exchange
www.tuitionexchange.org

Catholic College Cooperative Tuition Exchange
www.cccte.org

College Board
professionals.collegeboard.com/data-reports-research/trends/tuition-discounting

Council for Christian Colleges & Universities
www.cccu.org

Tuition Free Military Academies

U.S. Air Force Academy
www.academyadmissions.com

U.S. Coast Guard Academy
www.admissions.uscga.edu

U.S. Merchant Marine Academy
www.usmma.edu/admissions

U.S. Military Academy at West Point
www.admissions.usma.edu

U.S. Naval Academy
www.usna.edu/Admissions

Tuition Free Schools:

Alice Lloyd College
www.alc.edu

Berea College
www.berea.edu

College of the Ozarks
www.cofo.edu

Cooper Union
www.cooper.edu

Curtis Institute of Music
www.curtis.edu

Deep Springs College
www.deepsprings.edu

F.W. Olin College of Engineering
www.olin.edu

Ways to Save

Bargain Textbooks
www.studenthacks.org/2008/01/23/used-cheap-textbook

Best Bank Interest Rates
www.bankrate.com
www.bankaholic.com

Community College Finder
www.aacc.nche.edu
www.utexas.edu/world/comcol/state

Discount Brokers
www.fool.com/investing/brokers/index.aspx
www.tradewiser.com/brokers.html

529 Savings Plans
www.collegesavings.org
www.savingforcollege.com

Free Credit Report
www.ftc.gov/bcp/edu/pubs/consumer/credit/cre34.shtm

Frugal Living
www.creditpanda.com/blog/2007/top-50-frugality-bloggers
www.blogs.com/topten/10-popular-frugal-living-blogs

Lowest Credit Card Rates
www.cardtrak.com/cards

Savings Bonds
www.savingsbonds.gov

Student Airfare Finder
studenttravel.about.com/od/studentairfare/a/studentairfare.htm

About the Author

Dr. Gail Schlachter first became interested in the financial aid field when she was working in the library at California State University at Long Beach. With the help of her mother (who wrote out all the invoices because she didn't know how to type) and her children (who packed the books and carted them off to the post office in their Radio Flyer wagon), she issued her first financial aid title—*Directory of Financial Aid for Women*—in 1978. What started then as a casual interest has, over the years, become her career passion. Today, she is known as one of the "leading authorities on scholarships." She has written more than 25 financial aid resources and has won numerous awards in recognition of the outstanding contributions she has made to the field, including the National Education and Information Center Advisory Committee's Best of the Best award and *Library Journal's* Best Reference Book of the Year Award. Having spent many years in academic pursuits—working on her bachelor's degree at U.C. Berkeley, her master's degrees at the University of Wisconsin and the University of Southern California, and her Ph.D. at the University of Minnesota—she knows first hand the challenges involved in making college affordable. She has drawn on her extensive personal experience and professional expertise to put together this edition of *Paying for College*.

Previous edition by

Trent Anderson is the vice president for education at Cablevision, Inc., where he oversees the "Power to Learn" initiative. Before joining Cablevision, Trent was the vice president of publishing for Kaplan, Inc., where he developed book projects for the education market. During his 10 years with Kaplan, Trent was a test prep instructor, admissions advisor, financial aid expert, and author and contributing editor of several books, including *Once Upon a Campus, The Unofficial, Unbiased Guide to the 328 Most Interesting Colleges*, and Kaplan's precollege and pregrad school test prep titles. Trent spent his college years in Southern California, where he earned his bachelor's degree at UCLA and his J.D. and M.B.A. at the University of Southern California. Prior to working at Kaplan, Inc., Trent taught undergraduate business law at the University of Southern California.

Seppy Basili, Kaplan's resident "College Guru," has been analyzing college trends for more than 15 years. During his Kaplan career, Seppy has overseen Kaplan's test preparation programs and publications for the SAT, ACT, and PSAT exams as well as college admissions services. Along with Trent Anderson, he is the co-author of *Once Upon a Campus and The Unofficial, Unbiased Guide to the 328 Most Interesting Colleges*. He also founded the Kaplan-Newsweek imprint publications, which include the annual *How to Get Into College* guide. Seppy has spent many years on college campuses, receiving his B.A. from Kenyon College, M.Ed. from the University of California, Berkeley, and J.D. from Emory University.

Index